NORWICH CITY COLLEGE LIBRARY

Stock No.		190783	
Class		530	
Cat.		Proc.	OS

D1628438

Physics 2

David Sang

Series editor: David Sang

CAMBRIDGE
UNIVERSITY

190 783

PUBLISHED BY THE PRESS SYNDICATE OF THE UNIVERSITY OF CAMBRIDGE
The Pitt Building, Trumpington Street, Cambridge, United Kingdom

CAMBRIDGE UNIVERSITY PRESS
The Edinburgh Building, Cambridge CB2 2RU, UK
40 West 20th Street, New York, NY 10011-4211, USA
10 Stamford Road, Oakleigh, VIC 3166, Australia
Ruiz de Alarcón 13, 28014 Madrid, Spain
Dock House, The Waterfront, Cape Town 8001, South Africa

http://www.cambridge.org

© Cambridge University Press 2001

First published 2001
Reprinted 2001

Printed in the United Kingdom at the University Press, Cambridge

Typeface   Swift   *System*   QuarkXPress®

A catalogue record for this book is available from the British Library

ISBN 0 521 79715 2 paperback

Produced by Gecko Ltd, Bicester, Oxon

Front cover photograph: Prism with multicoloured beam,
Telegraph Colour Library

NOTICE TO TEACHERS
It is illegal to reproduce any part of this work in material form (including
photocopying and electronic storage) except under the following circumstances:
(i)   where you are abiding by a licence granted to your school or institution by
        the Copyright Licensing Agency;
(ii)   where no such licence exists, or where you wish to exceed the terms of a
        licence, and you have gained the written permission of Cambridge
        University Press;
(iii)   where you are allowed to reproduce without permission under the
        provisions of Chapter 3 of the Copyright, Designs and Patents Act 1988.

Contents

Introduction   v

Forces, Fields and Energy

1   Work and energy   1
The idea of energy   1
Kinetic energy   2
Gravitational potential energy   3
Doing work   5
Energy conservation   7

2   Collisions and explosions   11
The idea of momentum   11
Understanding collisions   14
Momentum in space   16
Explosions and crash-landings   19
Momentum and Newton's laws   21

3   Moving in a circle   24
Describing circular motion   24
Steady speed, changing velocity   26
Calculating force and acceleration   28

4   Oscillations   33
Free and forced vibrations   33
Simple harmonic motion   37
Equations of s.h.m.   41
Energy   42
Damped oscillations   43
Resonance   45

5   Gravitational fields   50
Gravitational forces and fields   50
Gravitational field strength   53

6   Electric fields   57
Attraction and repulsion   57
Electric field strength   60
Coulomb's law   63
Comparing gravitational and electric fields   65

7   Capacitors   67
Using capacitors   67
Energy stored in a capacitor   69
Capacitors in parallel   72
Capacitors in series   72
Comparing capacitors and resistors   74
Capacitor networks   74
Capacitor discharge   76

8   Electromagnetic forces   81
Magnetic fields   81
Moving particles   82
The magnetic force on a moving charge   84
Orbiting charges   85

9   Electromagnetic induction   88
Generating electricity   88
Explaining electromagnetic induction   89
Calculating magnetic flux   92
Faraday's law   93
Lenz's law   95
Using electromagnetic induction   98

10   Thermal physics   100
A particle model   100
Changes of state   102
Internal energy   104
Calculating energy changes   106
Measuring specific heat capacity   108
Measuring specific latent heat   109

11   Ideal gases   111
Gases   111
Explaining pressure   112
The gas laws and absolute zero   113
The pressure law   115
Ideal gas equation   117
Temperature and molecular energy   118

12 Atomic structure   120

Looking inside the atom   120
Rutherford scattering and the nucleus   121
The structure of the nucleus   122
Nucleons and electrons   123
Isotopes and their uses   124
The scale of things   127

13 Nuclear physics   130

Nuclear processes   130
Explaining fission and fusion   132
Mass–energy conservation   136

14 Radioactivity   139

Ionising radiation   139
Hazards of ionising radiation   143
Randomness and decay   144
Decay graphs and equations   146

Answers to questions   150

Glossary   162

Index   164

Introduction

Cambridge Advanced Sciences

The *Cambridge Advanced Sciences* series has been developed to meet the demands of all the new AS and A level science examinations. In particular, it has been endorsed by OCR as providing complete coverage of their specifications. The AS material is presented as a single text for each of biology, chemistry and physics. Material for the A2 year comprises six books in each subject: one of core material and one for each option. Some material has been drawn from the existing *Cambridge Modular Sciences* books; however, many parts are entirely new.

During the development of this series, the opportunity has been taken to improve the design, and a complete and thorough new writing and editing process has been applied. Much more material is now presented in colour. Although the existing *Cambridge Modular Sciences* texts do cover most of the new specifications, the *Cambridge Advanced Sciences* books cover every OCR learning objective in detail. They are the key to success in the new AS and A level examinations.

OCR is one of the three unitary awarding bodies offering the full range of academic and vocational qualifications in the UK. For full details of the new specifications, please contact OCR:

OCR
1 Hills Rd
Cambridge CB1 2EU
Tel: 01223 553311

Physics 2 – the A2 physics text

Physics 2 is all that is needed to cover the whole of the A2 physics material, corresponding to the module Forces, Fields and Energy. It is designed to be accessible to students with a double-award science GCSE background. This book combines entirely new text and illustrations with revised and updated material from *Foundation Physics*, *Basic Physics 1 and 2*, and *Further Physics*, formerly available in the *Cambridge Modular Sciences* series. Some particularly valuable features of this book are that SAQs and end of chapter questions are largely new. End of chapter summaries and the new glossary at the end will both be helpful to students of A2 physics preparing for new specifications.

Chapter 1 is based on chapter 5 of *Foundation Physics*, although as is the case throughout this book, material has been updated and substantially rewritten in accordance with specification changes. Chapter 2, 'Collisions and explosions', looks at the subject of dynamics, in part making use of material from chapters 3 and 5 of *Foundation Physics*.

The rest of the book makes use of a combination of *Basic Physics 1 and 2* and *Further Physics*. The opening chapters of both these existing titles are used to form the new chapter, 'Moving in a circle'. Similarly, the next two chapters, 'Oscillations' and 'Gravitational Fields', integrate material from the second and third chapters of both of these existing texts. There are some sections of brand new material in the rest of the book which should be noted. In particular, capacitance in chapter 7 and the hazards of ionising radiation in chapter 14, should be particularly useful to students.

Acknowledgements

1, Popperfoto; 2, TRH/Beoing; 3l, Prof. Harold Edgerton/Science Photo Library; 3r, 14, 50, 57, Images Colour Library; 7, 21, Science Photo Library; 11, 12, 17r, 19r, 34, 38, 39, 44, 46, 59, 61, 64, 67, 82, 85, 105, 108, 143, Andrew Lambert; 16, Space Telescope Science Institute/NASA/Science Photo Library; 17l, 31, NASA/Science Photo Library; 18, Lawrence Berkeley Laboratory/Science Photo Library; 19l, Kieran Doherty/Reuters/Popperfoto; 20, I Virga Regt. USA; 24, ©MSI/Sutton USA; 32, Roger G. Howard; 33, Kim Taylor/Bruce Coleman Collection; 37, Jonathan Watts/Science Photo Library; 45, UPI/Corbis; 47l, Robert Harding Picture Library; 47r, JC Revy/Science Photo Library; 55, PASCO Scientific; 88, Peter Menzel/Science Photo Library; 92, Bill Longchore/Science Photo Library; 100, Philippe Plailly/Science Photo Library; 101, Science Museum/Science & Society Picture Library; 120, 121, University of Cambridge, Cavendish Laboratory, Madingley Road, Cambridge, England; 125, Royal Observatory, Edinburgh/AAO/Science Photo Library; 127l, Michael Holford; 127r, Dr MB Hursthouse/Science Photo Library; 128, 144, David Parker/Science Photo Library; 130, US Navy/Science Photo Library; 132l, ©Travel Ink/JET/Life File; 132r, David Austen/ Bruce Coleman Collection; 139, BSIP/Science Photo Library; 142, N Feather/Science Photo Library

Work and energy

By the end of this chapter you should be able to:

1 recall and use the equation for kinetic energy, $E_k = \frac{1}{2}mv^2$;

2 recall and use the equation $\Delta E_p = mg\,\Delta h$ for potential energy changes near the Earth's surface;

3 give examples of energy in different forms, its conversion and conservation;

4 calculate the work done by a constant force in situations including those where the force is not in the same direction as the displacement;

5 apply the principle of the conservation of energy to simple examples.

The idea of energy

The Industrial Revolution started in England (though many of the pioneers of industrial technology came from other parts of the British Isles). Engineers developed new machines that were capable of doing the work of hundreds of craftspeople and labourers. At first, they made use of the traditional techniques of water power and wind power. Water stored behind a dam was used to turn a wheel, which turned many machines. By developing new mechanisms, the designers tried to extract as much as possible of the energy stored in the water.

Steam engines were developed, initially for pumping water out of mines. Steam engines use a fuel such as coal; there is much more energy stored in 1 kg of coal than in 1 kg of water behind a dam. Steam engines soon powered the looms of the textile mills (*figure 1.1*), and the British industry came to dominate world trade in textiles.

Nowadays, most factories and mills in the UK rely on electrical power, generated by burning coal at a power station. The fuel is burned to release its store of energy. High-pressure steam is generated, and this turns a turbine, which turns a generator. Even in the most efficient coal-fired power station, only about 40% of the energy from the fuel is transferred to the electric current that the station supplies to the grid.

● **Figure 1.1** At one time, smoking chimneys like these were prominent landmarks in the industrial regions of the UK.

Engineers strove to develop machines that made the most efficient use of the energy supplied to them. At the same time, scientists were working out the basic ideas of energy transfer and energy transformations. The idea of energy itself had to be developed; it wasn't obvious at first that heat, light, electricity and so on could all be thought of as being, in some way, forms of the same thing. (In fact, steam engines had been in use for 150 years before it was realised that their energy came from the heat supplied to them from their fuel. Previously it had been thought that the heat was necessary only as a 'fluid' through which energy was transferred.)

The earliest steam engines had very low efficiencies – many converted less than 1% of the energy supplied to them into useful work. The understanding of the relationship between work and energy developed by physicists and engineers in the nineteenth century led to many ingenious ways of making the most of the energy supplied by fuel. This improvement in energy efficiency has led to the design of modern engines, such as the jet engines that have made long-distance air travel a commercial possibility (*figure 1.2*).

In this chapter, we will recap the ideas of gravitational potential energy and kinetic energy which you studied in part 1 of *Physics 1*. We will extend the idea of the transfer of energy by doing work, and think a little more about conservation of energy.

Kinetic energy

The jet aircraft shown in *figure 1.2* is designed to carry hundreds of passengers on long journeys. Its mass on take-off is 400 tonnes, and its cruising speed is $250\,\mathrm{m\,s^{-1}}$ (900 km/hour). When it is moving at this speed, it has a great deal of **kinetic energy**. The kinetic energy E_k of an object depends on two quantities:

■ the object's speed v,
■ the object's mass m.

● **Figure 1.2** The jet engines of this jumbo jet are designed to make efficient use of their fuel. If they were less efficient, their thrust might only be sufficient to lift the empty aircraft, and the passengers would have to be left behind.

We can calculate the object's kinetic energy as follows:

$$\text{kinetic energy} = \tfrac{1}{2} \times \text{mass} \times (\text{speed})^2$$

$$E_k = \tfrac{1}{2}mv^2$$

Working in standard units gives the value in joules (J), the SI unit of energy. (Note that the correct symbol for kinetic energy is E_k, although people often write KE as an abbreviation.)

Worked example

Calculate the kinetic energy of a jumbo jet of mass 400 tonnes flying at $250\,\mathrm{m\,s^{-1}}$.

Mass $m = 400$ tonnes $= 400 \times 10^3\,\mathrm{kg}$
Speed $v = 250\,\mathrm{m\,s^{-1}}$
Kinetic energy is therefore

$$E_k = \tfrac{1}{2}mv^2 = \tfrac{1}{2} \times 400 \times 10^3\,\mathrm{kg} \times (250\,\mathrm{m\,s^{-1}})^2$$

$$= 1.25 \times 10^{10}\,\mathrm{J} = 12.5\,\mathrm{GJ}\ \text{(gigajoules)}$$

SAQ 1.1

A car of mass 1000 kg and a truck of mass 40 000 kg are travelling side-by-side along a motorway at $30\,\mathrm{m\,s^{-1}}$. Calculate the kinetic energy of the car in kJ and of the truck in MJ.

KE – where from?

When the jet aircraft is stationary, it has no kinetic energy. It has a store of energy in its fuel. As the fuel is burned with oxygen from the air, this energy is released. (Strictly speaking, the energy is stored in the fuel–oxygen mixture.) The jet engines provide a force to push the aircraft forwards. The aircraft accelerates, and so its kinetic energy increases. So the force of the engine on the aircraft is the means by which energy is transferred to it.

For any moving object, we can try to identify two things: where its kinetic energy came from, and the force that transferred the energy to it – see *figure 1.3*. For example, if you hit a tennis ball:

■ its kinetic energy comes from the kinetic energy of the racket that hit it – the racket moves more slowly after striking the ball;
■ the force of the racket on the ball transfers the energy.

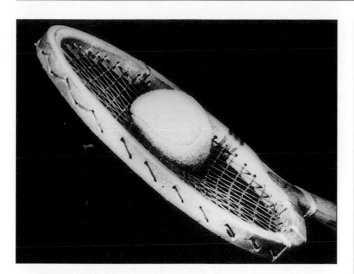

● **Figure 1.3** The force exerted by the tennis racket transfers energy to the ball. The ball gains kinetic energy; the racket loses kinetic energy.

SAQ 1.2

You throw a ball to a friend.
a Where does the ball's kinetic energy come from?
b What force transfers the energy to the ball?

KE – vector or scalar?

Although kinetic energy is the energy of movement, and movement has direction, kinetic energy is a *scalar* quantity, not a vector. Energy is always a scalar. The fuel in the jet aircraft's tank is a store of billions of joules of energy, but this is not energy in a particular direction. Similarly, if you boil a kettle of water, the water gains a lot of energy, but there is no direction associated with the energy.

This is important in the case of circular motion (chapter 3). An object moving at a steady speed around a circular path has a constantly changing *velocity*, because its direction is always changing. However, its *speed* isn't changing, so its kinetic energy remains constant.

Gravitational potential energy

A motor drags a roller-coaster car to the top of the first hill. The car runs down the other side, picking up speed as it goes (see *figure 1.4*). It is moving just fast enough to reach the top of the second hill, slightly lower than the first. It accelerates down-hill again. Everybody screams.

● **Figure 1.4** The roller-coaster car accelerates as it comes down-hill. It's even more exciting if it runs through water.

The motor provides a force to pull the roller-coaster car to the top of the hill. It transfers energy to the car. But where is this energy when the car is waiting at the top of the hill? The car now has **gravitational potential energy** (sometimes abbreviated to GPE). This is not as easy to visualise as kinetic energy, because the car is not doing anything. However, we know that it has energy because, as soon as it is given a small push to set it moving, it accelerates. It gains kinetic energy, and at the same time it loses gravitational potential energy.

Gravitational potential energy is given this name for the following reasons:
■ gravitational – because the car is pulled up-hill, against the pull of gravity;
■ potential – because the car has the potential to do something, to run down-hill.

Down, up, down – energy changes

As the car runs along the roller-coaster track (*figure 1.5*, next page), its energy changes.
1 At the start, it has gravitational potential energy.
2 As it runs down-hill, its GPE decreases and its kinetic energy increases.
3 At the bottom of the hill, all of its GPE has been changed to KE.
4 As it runs back up-hill, gravity slows it down. KE is being changed to GPE.

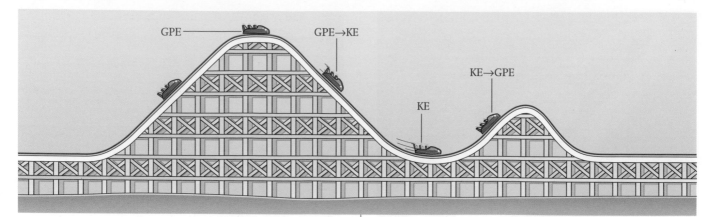

● **Figure 1.5** Energy changes along a roller-coaster.

Inevitably, some energy is lost by the car. There is friction with the track, and air resistance. So the car cannot return to its original height. That is why the second hill must be slightly lower than the first.

It's fun if the car runs through a trough of water, but that takes even more energy, and the car cannot rise so high.

There are many situations where an object's energy changes between gravitational potential energy and kinetic energy. For example:

- raindrops falling – GPE changes to KE;
- a ball is thrown upwards – KE changes to GPE;
- a child on a swing – energy changes back and forth between GPE and KE.

Calculating GPE

To lift an object (*figure 1.6*), you have to provide an upward force to overcome the downward pull of gravity. In lifting it, you increase its gravitational potential energy. The increase in its GPE depends on two factors:

- its weight mg – the heavier the object, the bigger the force needed to lift it;

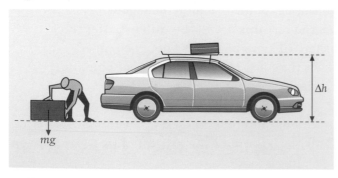

● **Figure 1.6** When you lift an object, you increase its gravitational potential energy.

- the change in its height Δh – the greater the distance through which it is lifted, the greater its increase in energy.

Combining these gives

change in gravitational potential energy
= weight × change in height
$\Delta E_p = mg\,\Delta h$

As with kinetic energy, gravitational potential energy E_p is measured in joules (J).

Note that it is the object's weight, not its mass, which is important. On the Moon, where gravity is weaker, its weight would be less and you would need to give it less energy when lifting it. The equation $\Delta E_p = mg\,\Delta h$ can only be applied near the Earth's surface, where the value of g is more-or-less constant. (Gravity is discussed in greater depth in chapter 5.)

Worked example

A stone is dropped from a height of 1.0 m – see *figure 1.7*. At what speed will it hit the floor? [$g = 9.8\,\mathrm{m\,s^{-2}}$]

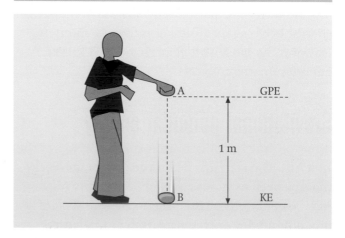

● **Figure 1.7** See the worked example.

At first sight, this may seem to have nothing to do with energy. Indeed, you could solve the problem using one of the equations of motion. However, the diagram suggests how we can use the idea of energy as an alternative approach.

At point A, the stone has gravitational potential energy. At B, some of this has been transformed to kinetic energy. So these two quantities must be equal:

decrease in GPE between A and B = KE at B

$$mg\Delta h = \tfrac{1}{2}mv^2$$

Note that m is common to both sides, and cancels out. Substituting values for g and h gives:

$$9.8\,\text{m}\,\text{s}^{-2} \times 1.0\,\text{m} = \tfrac{1}{2}v^2$$

$$v^2 = 2 \times 9.8\,\text{m}\,\text{s}^{-2} \times 1.0\,\text{m} = 19.6 \text{ m}^2\,\text{s}^{-2}$$

$$v = 4.4\,\text{m}\,\text{s}^{-1}$$

So the stone is moving at $4.4\,\text{m}\,\text{s}^{-1}$ when it reaches the floor.

(Notice that *any* stone dropped from this height will reach the same speed, provided that we can ignore air resistance. This follows from the fact that m cancels from the equation.)

SAQ 1.3

A mountaineer of mass 80 kg reaches the summit of Mt Everest, 8900 m above sea level. Calculate her gravitational potential energy at this point (relative to sea level). [$g = 9.8\,\text{m}\,\text{s}^{-2}$]

SAQ 1.4

If you fell from the top of a 50 m tall building, how fast would you be moving when you reached the ground below? [$g = 9.8\,\text{m}\,\text{s}^{-2}$] Try this calculation two ways – each should give the same answer:
a using the idea of gravitational potential energy changing to kinetic energy;
b using one of the equations of motion.

Doing work

A force can increase the kinetic energy or gravitational potential energy of an object. The force moves through a distance, and we say that it does work. The amount of **work done** tells us the amount of energy transferred by the force:

work done (J) = energy transferred (J)

To calculate the amount of work done W, we need to know two quantities:
■ the magnitude of the force F;
■ the distance d moved by the force, in the direction of the force.
Then

work done = force × distance moved in the direction of the force

$$W = F \times d$$

Calculating work done

Calculations are relatively simple when the distance moved is along the line of the force. Examples of this are shown in *figure 1.8a,b.*
a The motive force of the car's engine pushes the car forward.
b The upward push of the child's hand raises the book.
In each of these cases, we simply calculate work done as $W = F \times d$. The example shown in *figure 1.8c* is more complex. A rope is being used to pull a heavy box up a slope. Four forces act on the box, and we will consider each separately.

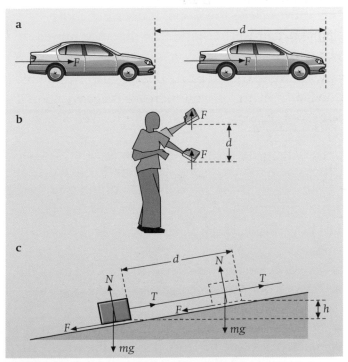

● **Figure 1.8** Three situations in which work is done by forces.

The pulling force is the tension T in the rope. This pulls the box a distance d up the slope. T and d are in the same direction, so we have the simple result:

work done by tension = $T \times d$

The frictional force F acts down the slope. The box moves distance d up the slope. F and d are in opposite directions (but in the same straight line), so we have:

work done against friction = $-F \times d$

The minus sign shows that this is energy transferred *from* the box, not to it. (The tension in the rope is transferring energy *to* the box.)

The weight mg of the box acts vertically downwards. The box moves distance d up the slope, but it moves a smaller distance h vertically. So we have:

work done by gravity = $-mg \times h$

Again, this is negative because the force and the distance moved are in opposite directions. An alternative way to express this would be to say that the work done *against* gravity is mgh. (See the next worked example for another way to calculate the work done by gravity in a situation like this.)

Finally, the contact force (normal reaction) N acts at right-angles to the surface of the slope. The box moves *along* the slope; it does not move *perpendicular* to the slope. The distance moved in the direction of N is zero, and so we have:

work done by contact force = $N \times 0 = 0$

Worked example

Figure 1.9 is essentially the same as figure 1.8c, with numerical values for the quantities involved. Calculate the work done by each of the four forces shown when the box moves 0.5 m up the slope.

We will consider each force in turn, as discussed above.

- T: work done by tension = $100\,\text{N} \times 0.5\,\text{m} = 50\,\text{J}$
- F: work done against friction = $-30\,\text{N} \times 0.5\,\text{m}$
$$= -15\,\text{J}$$
- N: work done by contact force = $70\,\text{N} \times 0\,\text{m} = 0\,\text{J}$
- mg: to calculate the work done by the weight, we could calculate the vertical height risen by the box; we will arrive at the same result using an alternative

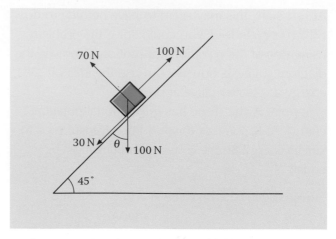

● **Figure 1.9** For the worked example.

method, involving calculating the component of the box's weight which acts down the slope:

component of weight acting down the slope
$= mg \sin \theta = 100\,\text{N} \times \sin 45° = 71\,\text{N}$

work done against this component of the box's weight $= 71\,\text{N} \times 0.5\,\text{m} = 35\,\text{J}$

This example should serve to remind you about the components of a force. We can replace mg by its two components:

- $mg \sin \theta$ down the slope,
- $mg \cos \theta$ perpendicular to the slope.
    (The work done by this second component is zero, because the box does not move in the direction of this component.)

A final point to note: the work done by the tension is equal to the sum of the work done against the other three forces:

$$50\,\text{J} = 35\,\text{J} + 15\,\text{J} + 0\,\text{J}$$

This tells us that the box does not gain kinetic energy as it is pulled up the slope.

SAQ 1.5

In each of the following examples, explain whether or not any work is done by the force mentioned.

a You pull a heavy sack along level ground.

b Gravity pulls you downwards when you fall off a wall.

c The contact force of the bedroom floor stops you from falling into the room below.

d The tension in a string pulls on a conker when you whirl it around in a circle at a steady speed.

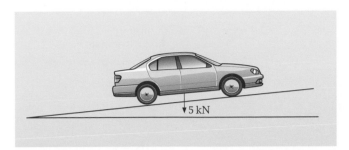

● **Figure 1.10** See SAQ 1.7.

SAQ 1.6

You push a car of mass 500 kg for a distance of 10 m with a force of 100 N.
a How much work have you done?
b If the car is initially at rest and half of the energy that you transfer to the car is transferred as kinetic energy, how fast will the car be moving?

SAQ 1.7

A car of weight 5 kN travels 1 km along a long sloping road – see *figure 1.10*. The gradient of the road is 1 in 10; for every 10 m it travels along the slope, the car rises 1 m vertically. Calculate the work done against gravity by the car.

Energy conservation

Figure 1.11 shows James Joule, the English scientist after whom the unit of energy is named. Joule is

● **Figure 1.11** James Prescott Joule (1818–1889); he helped to develop our idea of energy.

famous for having taken a thermometer on his honeymoon in the Alps. He knew that water at the top of a waterfall had gravitational potential energy; it lost this energy as it fell. Joule was able to show that the water was warmer at the foot of the waterfall than at the top, and so he was able to explain where the water's energy went to when it fell.

The idea of energy can be difficult to grasp. When Newton was working on his theories of mechanics, more than three centuries ago, the idea did not exist. It took several generations of physicists to develop the concept fully. So far, we have considered two forms of energy (kinetic and gravitational potential), and one way of transferring energy (by doing work). Later, in chapter 10, we will look at another form of energy (internal energy), and another transfer mechanism (heating). But now, we will look at the idea of energy conservation.

Climbing bars

If you are going to climb a mountain, you will need a supply of energy. This is because your gravitational potential energy is greater at the top of the mountain than at the base. A good supply of energy would be some bars of chocolate. Each bar supplies about 1200 kJ.

Suppose your weight is 600 N and you climb a 2000 m mountain. The work done by your muscles is then 600 N × 2000 m = 1200 kJ. So one bar of chocolate will do the trick. Of course, it won't. Your body is inefficient. It cannot convert 100% of the energy from food into gravitational potential energy. A lot of energy is wasted as your muscles warm up, you perspire, you bounce up and down along the path. Your body is perhaps only 5% efficient as far as climbing is concerned, and you will need to eat 20 chocolate bars to get you to the top of the mountain. And you will need to eat more to get you back down again.

Many energy transfers are inefficient; that is, only part of the energy is transferred to where it is wanted. The rest is wasted, and appears in some form that is not wanted (such as waste heat), or in the wrong place.

A car engine is more efficient than a human body, but not much more. *Figure 1.12* shows one

● **Figure 1.12** We want a car engine to supply kinetic energy. This Sankey diagram shows that only 20% of the energy supplied to the engine ends up as kinetic energy – it is 20% efficient.

way of representing this, by a Sankey diagram. The width of the arrow represents the fraction of the energy that is transformed to each new form. In the case of a car engine, we want it to provide kinetic energy to turn the wheels. In practice, 80% of the energy ends up as heat energy: the engine gets hot, and heat escapes into the surroundings. So the engine is only 20% efficient.

We have previously considered situations where an object is falling, and all of its gravitational potential energy changes to kinetic energy. In the next worked example, we will look at a similar situation, but in this case the energy change is not 100% efficient.

Worked example

Figure 1.13 shows a dam that stores water. The outlet of the dam is 20 m below the surface of the water in the reservoir. Water leaving the dam is moving at 16 m s⁻¹. How much of the water's GPE is converted to KE?

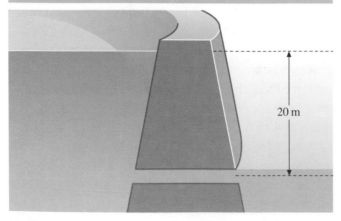

● **Figure 1.13** Water stored behind the dam has gravitational potential energy; the fast-flowing water leaving the foot of the dam has kinetic energy.

We will picture 1 kg of water, starting at the surface of the lake (where it has GPE, but no KE) and flowing downwards and out at the foot (where it has KE, but less GPE):

change in GPE of water between surface and outflow

$$= mg\Delta h = 1\,\text{kg} \times 9.8\,\text{m s}^{-2} \times 20\,\text{m} = 196\,\text{J}$$

$$\text{KE of water leaving dam} = \tfrac{1}{2}mv^2$$
$$= \tfrac{1}{2} \times 1\,\text{kg} \times (16\,\text{m s}^{-1})^2$$
$$= 128\,\text{J}$$

So each kilogram of water loses $196\,\text{J} - 128\,\text{J} = 68\,\text{J}$ of energy as it flows out of the dam. If you wanted to use this moving water to generate electricity, you would have already lost more than a third of the energy that it stores when it is behind the dam.

Conservation

Where does the lost energy from the water in the reservoir go? Most of it ends up warming the water, or warming the pipes that the water flows through. The outflow of water is probably noisy, so some sound energy is produced.

Here, we are assuming that all of the energy ends up somewhere. None of it disappears. We assume the same thing when we draw a Sankey diagram. The total thickness of the arrow remains constant. We could not have an arrow that got thinner (energy disappearing) or thicker (energy appearing out of nowhere).

We are assuming that **energy is conserved**. This is a principle that we expect to apply in all situations. We should always be able to add up the total amount of energy at the beginning, and be able to account for it all at the end. We cannot be sure that this is always the case, but we expect it to hold true. The principle of conservation of energy states that:

> While energy may be converted from one form to another, the total amount of energy in a closed system is constant.

We have to think about energy changes *within a closed system*; that is, we have to draw an imaginary boundary around all of the interacting objects that are involved in an energy transfer.

Sometimes, applying the principle of conservation of energy can seem like a scientific fiddle. When physicists were investigating radioactive decay involving beta particles, they found that the particles after the decay had less energy in total than the particles before. They guessed that there was another, invisible particle that was carrying away the missing energy. This particle, named the neutrino, was proposed by Wolfgang Pauli in 1931; it wasn't detected by experimenters until 25 years later.

Although we cannot prove that energy is always conserved, this example shows that the principle of conservation can be a powerful tool in helping us to understand what is going on in Nature, and that it can help us to make fruitful predictions about future experiments.

SAQ 1.8

A stone falls from the top of a cliff, 80 m high. When it reaches the foot of the cliff, its speed is $38\,\mathrm{m\,s^{-1}}$.

a What fraction of the stone's initial GPE is converted to KE? [$g = 9.8\,\mathrm{m\,s^{-2}}$]

b What happens to the rest of the stone's initial energy?

SUMMARY

◆ The kinetic energy of a body is given by $E_k = \frac{1}{2}mv^2$.

◆ The change in gravitational potential energy of a body is given by $E_p = mg\,\Delta h$.

◆ When a force moves through a distance, energy is transferred.

◆ Work done = energy transferred.

◆ Work done = force × distance moved in the direction of the force.

◆ The principle of conservation of energy states that, while energy may be converted from one form to another, the total amount of energy in a closed system is constant.

Questions

1 A lift is operated by an electric motor. When it is raising an empty car, it is supplied with 10 000 J of electrical energy each second. The lift car's gravitational potential energy increases by 3000 J each second. The remainder of the energy is wasted as heat energy in the motor and as a result of friction in the mechanism.

a What fraction of the energy supplied to the lift car is wasted?

b Describe the energy conversions involved when the lift car is raised.

2 A pulley system is used to lift 10 kg blocks of stone to the top of a building 30 m high.

a How much work is done by the pulley system in lifting each block? [$g = 9.8\,\mathrm{m\,s^{-2}}$]

b During the lifting of a single block, 8700 J of energy is supplied to the pulley system. How much of this energy is wasted? Where does it go?

3 Comets orbit the Sun in elliptical orbits. An example is shown in *figure 1.14*. Periodically, a comet will 'fall' towards the Sun, pass around it, and then disappear out beyond the furthest planets.

a At which point will the comet be moving fastest? At which point will it be moving most slowly?

b Describe how the comet's gravitational potential energy and its kinetic energy change as it travels round its orbit.

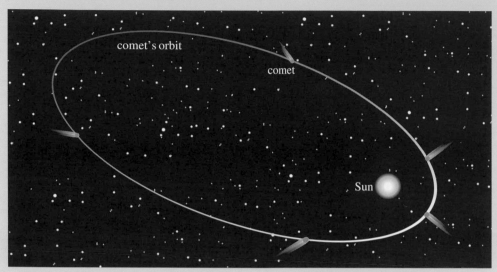

● **Figure 1.14** For question 3.

CHAPTER 2

Collisions and explosions

By the end of this chapter you should be able to:

1 define linear momentum as the product of mass and velocity;

2 recall and use $p = mv$;

3 state the principle of conservation of momentum;

4 use the principle of conservation of momentum in simple applications including elastic and inelastic interactions between two bodies in one dimension, and the separation of an initially stationary object into two parts;

5 understand that, whilst momentum of an isolated system is always conserved in interactions between bodies, kinetic energy is conserved only in elastic collisions;

6 define force as rate of change of momentum, and use this definition in situations where mass is constant;

7 state each of Newton's laws of motion.

The idea of momentum

Snooker players can perform some amazing moves on the table, without necessarily knowing Newton's laws of motion – see *figure 2.1*. However, the laws of physics can help us to understand what happens when one moving, spinning ball collides with another ball, or bounces off the cushion at the edge of the snooker table.

● **Figure 2.1** If you play snooker often enough, you will be able to predict how the balls will move. Alternatively, you can use the laws of physics to calculate where they will go.

In this chapter, we will look at collisions and explosions, and find out how we can predict how objects will move as a result. You will already have some intuitive ideas about what happens when things collide. Here are some examples of situations involving collisions:

■ two vehicles collide head-on;

■ a fast-moving vehicle runs in to the back of a slower vehicle in front;

■ a rugby player performs a tackle on the legs of an opponent;

■ a hockey stick strikes a ball;

■ a comet collides with a planet as it orbits the Sun;

■ two distant galaxies collide over millions of years;

■ the atoms of the air collide constantly with each other, and with the walls of their surroundings;

■ electrons that form an electric current collide with the atoms that make up a metal wire.

From these examples, we can see that collisions are happening all around us, all the time. They happen on the microscopic scale of atoms and electrons, they happen in our everyday world, and they happen on the cosmic scale of space.

Model collisions

Figure 2.2a shows what happens when one snooker ball collides head-on with a second, stationary ball. The result can seem surprising. The moving ball stops dead, and the stationary ball moves off. Its velocity is the same as that of the original ball. To achieve this, a snooker player must observe two conditions:

■ The collision must be head-on; if one ball strikes a glancing blow on the side of the other, they will both move off at different angles.

■ The moving ball must not be given any spin; spin is an added complication, which we will ignore in our present study, although it plays a vital part in the game of snooker.

You can mimic the collision of the snooker balls in the laboratory, using two trolleys as shown in *figure 2.2b*. The moving trolley has its spring-load

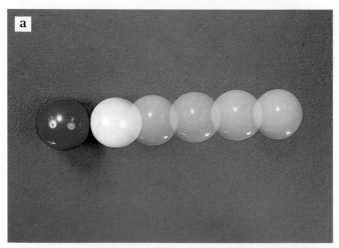

● **Figure 2.2 a** One snooker ball hits another head-on. **b** You can do the same thing with two trolleys in the lab.

released, so that the collision is springy. As one trolley runs in to the other, the spring is at first compressed, and then it pushes out again to set the second trolley moving. The first trolley comes to a complete halt. The 'motion' of one trolley has been passed on to the other.

You can see another interesting result if two moving trolleys collide head-on. If the collision is springy, both trolleys bounce backwards. If a fast-moving trolley collides with a slower one, the fast trolley bounces back at the speed of the slow one, and the slow one bounces back at the speed of the fast one. Again, it is as if the 'motion' of each trolley has been transferred to the other.

Sticky collisions

Figure 2.3 shows another type of collision. In this case, the trolleys have Velcro pads so that they stick together when they collide. A sticky collision like this is the opposite of a springy collision like the ones described above.

If a single moving trolley collides with a single stationary one, they both move off together. Their combined speed is half that of the original trolley. It is as if the 'motion' of the original trolley has been shared between the two. If a single trolley collides with a double one (twice the mass), they move off with one-third of the original velocity.

From these examples of sticky collisions, you can see that, when the mass of the trolley increases as a result of a collision, its velocity decreases. Doubling the mass halves the velocity, and so on.

● **Figure 2.3** If a moving trolley sticks to a stationary trolley, they both move off together.

SAQ 2.1

Here are two collisions to picture in your mind. Answer the question for each.

a Ball A, moving towards the right, collides with stationary ball B. Ball A bounces back; B moves off slowly to the right. Which has a greater mass, A or B?

b Trolley A, moving towards the right, collides with stationary trolley B. They stick together, and move off slightly slower than A's original speed. Which has the greater mass, A or B?

Defining momentum

From the examples discussed above, we can see that two quantities are important in understanding collisions:

■ mass m,
■ velocity v.

These are combined to give a single quantity, called the **momentum** p of an object:

momentum = mass × velocity

$$p = mv$$

The units of momentum are $kg\,m\,s^{-1}$. (There is no special name for this unit in the SI system.) Because velocity is a vector quantity (and mass is a scalar), momentum is also a vector, in the same direction as the object's velocity.

In the earlier examples, we described how the 'motion' of one trolley appeared to be transferred to a second trolley, or shared with it. It is more correct to say that it is the trolley's momentum that is transferred or shared. (Strictly speaking, we should refer to *linear momentum*, because there is another quantity called *angular momentum*, which is possessed by rotating objects.)

Like energy, we find that **momentum is conserved**. We have to consider bodies which form a closed system – that is, no external force acts on them. The principle of the conservation of momentum states that:

> Within a closed system, the total momentum in any specified direction remains constant.

A group of colliding objects always has as much momentum after the collision as it had before the

collision. This is illustrated in the worked example that follows.

Worked example

In *figure 2.4*, trolley B has twice the mass of trolley A. Trolley A, moving at $3\,m\,s^{-1}$, collides with stationary trolley B. They move off together at $1\,m\,s^{-1}$. Show that momentum is conserved in this collision.

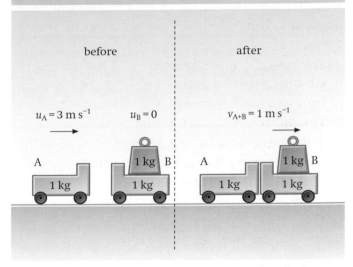

● **Figure 2.4** Trolleys A and B before and after the collision.

Notice that we need two diagrams, to show the situations *before* and *after* the collision. Similarly, we need two calculations:

momentum of trolleys before collision
$$= m_A \times u_A + m_B \times u_B$$
$$= 1\,kg \times 3\,m\,s^{-1} + 0 = 3\,kg\,m\,s^{-1}$$

(trolley B has no momentum before the collision, because it is not moving) and

momentum of trolleys after collision
$$= (m_A + m_B) \times v_{A+B}$$
$$= 3\,kg \times 1\,m\,s^{-1} = 3\,kg\,m\,s^{-1}$$

So, both before and after the collision, the trolleys have a combined momentum of $3\,kg\,m\,s^{-1}$. Momentum has been conserved.

SAQ 2.2

Calculate the momentum of each of the following:

a a stone, mass 0.5 kg, moving at $20\,m\,s^{-1}$;

b a bus, mass 25 tonnes, moving at $20\,m\,s^{-1}$;

c an electron, mass 9.1×10^{-31} kg, moving at $2 \times 10^7\,m\,s^{-1}$.

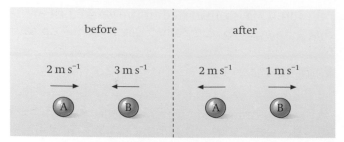

- **Figure 2.5** For SAQ 2.3.

SAQ 2.3 _____

Two balls, each of mass 0.5 kg, collide as shown in *figure 2.5*. Show that their total momentum before the collision is equal to their total momentum after the collision.

Understanding collisions

The car in *figure 2.6* has been badly damaged by a collision with another car. The front of the car is designed to absorb the impact of the crash. It has a 'crumple zone', which collapses on impact. This absorbs most of the kinetic energy that the car had before the collision. It's better that the car's energy should be transferred to the crumple zone than to the driver and passengers.

Motor manufacturers make use of test labs to investigate how their cars respond to impacts. When a car is designed, the manufacturers combine soft, compressible materials that absorb energy with rigid structures that protect the car's occupants. Old-fashioned cars had much more rigid structures. In a collision, they were more likely to bounce back, and the violent forces involved were much more likely to prove fatal.

- **Figure 2.6** The front of this car has crumpled in, as a result of a head-on collision.

Two types of collision

When two objects collide, they may crumple and deform. Their kinetic energy may disappear completely, and they come to a halt. This is an example of an **inelastic collision**. Alternatively, they may spring apart, retaining all of their kinetic energy. This is an **elastic collision** (sometimes referred to as a *perfectly* elastic collision). In practice, in most collisions, some kinetic energy disappears, and the collision is inelastic.

We will look at examples of these two types of collision, and consider what happens to momentum and kinetic energy in each.

An elastic collision

Two identical objects, moving at the same speed but in opposite directions, have a head-on collision, as shown in *figure 2.7*. This is a springy collision, and each bounces back with its velocity reversed.

You should be able to see that, in this collision, both momentum and kinetic energy are conserved. Before the collision, we have 1 kg moving to the right at $10\,\mathrm{m\,s^{-1}}$, and 1 kg moving to the left at $10\,\mathrm{m\,s^{-1}}$. Afterwards, we have the same, but now mass A is moving to the left, and B is moving to the right. Mathematically, we can express this as follows.

- **Before the collision**

  Mass A has velocity v, momentum mv and kinetic energy $\frac{1}{2}mv^2$; and mass B has velocity $-v$, momentum $-mv$ and kinetic energy $\frac{1}{2}mv^2$. Therefore we have

  total momentum before collision
  = momentum of A + momentum of B
  = $mv + (-mv) = 0$

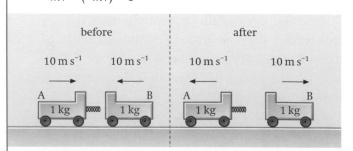

- **Figure 2.7** Two objects may collide in different ways: this is an elastic collision. An inelastic collision of the same two objects is shown in *figure 2.8*.

total kinetic energy before collision
= KE of A + KE of B
$= \frac{1}{2}mv^2 + \frac{1}{2}mv^2 = mv^2$

Note that, although both objects are moving, their combined momentum is zero, because they are moving in opposite directions. (Momentum is a vector quantity.)

■ **After the collision**
Both objects have their velocities reversed, and we have

total momentum after collision = $(-mv) + mv = 0$
total kinetic energy after collision
$= \frac{1}{2}mv^2 + \frac{1}{2}mv^2 = mv^2$

So the total momentum and the total kinetic energy are unchanged (they are conserved) in a perfectly elastic collision such as this.

An inelastic collision

In *figure 2.8*, the same two objects collide, this time in a squashy, inelastic way. They come to a complete halt. Clearly, total momentum and total kinetic energy are both zero after the collision, since neither mass is moving. We have:

	Before collision	After collision
momentum	0	0
kinetic energy	mv^2	0

Again we see that momentum is conserved here. However, kinetic energy is not conserved. It is lost because work is done in deforming the two masses.

In fact, **momentum is *always* conserved**. There is nothing else into which momentum can be converted. Kinetic energy is usually not conserved in a collision, because it can be transformed into other forms of energy – sound energy if the

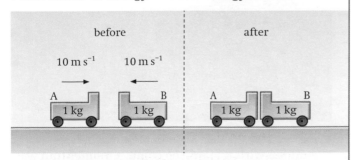

● **Figure 2.8** An inelastic collision between two identical objects.

collision is noisy, and the energy involved in deforming the objects (which usually ends up as heat – they get warmer). Of course, the *total* amount of energy remains constant.

SAQ 2.4
Copy the table below, choosing the correct words from each pair.

Type of collision	Momentum	Kinetic energy
elastic	conserved / not conserved	conserved / not conserved
inelastic	conserved / not conserved	conserved / not conserved

Solving numerical problems
We can use the idea of conservation of momentum to solve numerical problems, as illustrated by the example that follows.

Worked example

In the game of bowls, a player rolls a large ball towards a smaller, stationary ball. If the large ball rolls too fast, it may knock the smaller ball flying. A large ball of mass 5.0 kg moving at $10\,m\,s^{-1}$ strikes a stationary ball of mass 1.0 kg. The smaller ball flies off at $10\,m\,s^{-1}$.

a How fast does the large ball move after the impact?

b How much kinetic energy is lost in the impact?

It is helpful to draw two diagrams, showing the situations before and after the collision. *Figure 2.9* shows the values of masses and velocities; since we don't know the velocity of the large ball after the collision, this is shown as v.

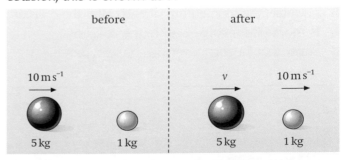

● **Figure 2.9** When tackling problems involving collisions, it is useful to draw diagrams showing the situations before and after the collision. Include the values of all the quantities that you know, including momentum and kinetic energy.

The diagrams also show the calculated values of momentum and kinetic energy for both balls, before and after the collision.

a Now we can use the idea of conservation of momentum:

total momentum before = total momentum after
collision collision

$50\,\text{kg}\,\text{m}\,\text{s}^{-1} + 0\,\text{kg}\,\text{m}\,\text{s}^{-1} = 10\,\text{kg}\,\text{m}\,\text{s}^{-1} + 5\,\text{kg} \times v$

$40\,\text{kg}\,\text{m}\,\text{s}^{-1} = 5\,\text{kg} \times v$

$v = (40\,\text{kg}\,\text{m}\,\text{s}^{-1})/(5\,\text{kg}) = 8\,\text{m}\,\text{s}^{-1}$

So the speed of the large ball decreases to $8\,\text{m}\,\text{s}^{-1}$ after the collision. Its direction of motion is unchanged.

b Now that we know the large ball's final velocity, we can calculate the change in kinetic energy during the collision:

total KE before collision $= \frac{1}{2} \times 5\,\text{kg} \times (10\,\text{m}\,\text{s}^{-1})^2$
$= 250\,\text{J}$

total KE after collision $= \frac{1}{2} \times 5\,\text{kg} \times (8\,\text{m}\,\text{s}^{-1})^2$
$+ \frac{1}{2} \times 1\,\text{kg} \times (10\,\text{m}\,\text{s}^{-1})^2$
$= 160\,\text{J} + 50\,\text{J} = 210\,\text{J}$

KE lost in the collision $= 250\,\text{J} - 210\,\text{J} = 40\,\text{J}$

This energy will appear as heat energy (the two balls get warmer) and as sound energy (we hear the collision between the balls).

SAQ 2.5

Two moving balls, A and B, have a head–on collision, as shown in *figure 2.10*. Ball A bounces back at $1.5\,\text{m}\,\text{s}^{-1}$; ball B bounces back at $2.5\,\text{m}\,\text{s}^{-1}$. The mass of each ball is 4 kg.

a Calculate the momentum of each ball before the collision.

b Calculate the momentum of each after the collision.

c Is momentum conserved in the collision?

d Show that kinetic energy is conserved in the collision.

2.5 m s⁻¹   1.5 m s⁻¹

A   B

● **Figure 2.10** For SAQ 2.5. Velocities before collision.

SAQ 2.6

A trolley of mass 1 kg is moving at $2\,\text{m}\,\text{s}^{-1}$. It collides with a stationary trolley of mass 2 kg. This second trolley moves off at $1.2\,\text{m}\,\text{s}^{-1}$.

a Draw *before* and *after* diagrams to show the situation.

b Use the idea of conservation of momentum to calculate how fast the first trolley moves after the collision. In what direction does it move?

Momentum in space

We can learn a lot about momentum by looking at how things move in space. When Comet Shoemaker-Levy collided with the planet Jupiter (*figure 2.11*), it transferred momentum to the planet (and much of its kinetic energy). The course of Jupiter in its orbit was slightly altered as a result. Some scientists are concerned that a similar fate could befall the Earth, and they have suggested that a series of telescopes should be set up to monitor the skies for any signs of danger. Nuclear missiles would be used to deflect any threatening comets.

The Space Shuttle is used to transport astronauts up to orbiting space stations. The Shuttle docks with the space station, and this is a form of collision. The Shuttle must dock very gently, or it will push the space station out of its orbit. Docking is like a collision; if the Shuttle is travelling fast when it docks, it will transfer a lot of

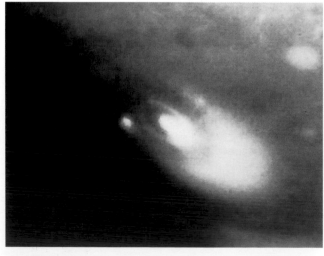

● **Figure 2.11** In 1994, Comet Shoemaker-Levy collided with Jupiter. The comet's momentum was transferred to the planet, causing a change in Jupiter's movement around the Sun.

momentum to the space station. A change in momentum means a change in velocity, so the space station will change speed and move off in a different direction.

Creating momentum

The astronaut shown in *figure 2.12* is on a 'space walk'. A cable tethers him to the Shuttle. To return to the craft, he pulls on the tether. This gives him some momentum towards the craft, and he moves gently back to it.

Where does this momentum come from? Has it been created out of nothing? The astronaut gives himself momentum towards the space-craft by tugging on the tether. At the same time, his tug pulls on the space-craft, and causes it to accelerate towards him. The craft gains momentum towards the astronaut. These two momenta must be equal and opposite, so that their sum is zero; otherwise the astronaut really will have created momentum out of nothing. The astronaut has a small mass, and moves relatively quickly towards the space-craft. The craft's mass is much greater, and so its velocity must be much smaller.

Here is another momentum problem for an astronaut. Suppose he is working with tools on the outside of the craft, and then realises that his tether has snapped. How can he get back to the craft?

He wants to have some momentum towards the space-craft, so he must create some momentum away from it as well. The solution is to throw one of his tools out into space. It has momentum away from the craft, so he has momentum towards the craft.

Fortunately, astronauts now usually wear backpacks with 'Manned Manoeuvring Units' attached. These are rocket-powered units which allow the astronaut to move around. The rocket blasts a jet of gas into space; this gives the astronaut momentum in the opposite direction.

Left and right

Figure 2.13 shows a collision between two snooker balls. This is different from the collisions we have discussed before because it takes place in two dimensions, not simply in a straight line. From the multiple images, we can see how the velocities of the two balls change:

- At first, the white ball is moving straight forwards. When it hits the red ball, it moves off to the right. Its speed decreases; we can see this because the images get closer together.
- The red ball moves off to the left. It moves off at a bigger angle than the white ball, but more slowly – the images are even closer together.

How can we understand what happens in this collision, using the ideas of momentum and kinetic energy?

At first, only the white ball has momentum, and this is in the forwards direction. During the collision, this momentum is shared between the two balls. We can see this because each has a component of velocity in the forward direction.

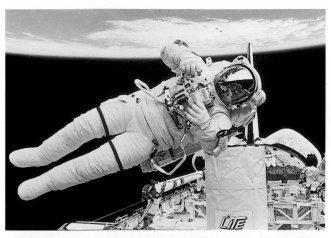

● **Figure 2.12** Astronauts often carry out 'space walks', when they leave the shuttle to work outside. They have a tether so that they don't drift off into space.

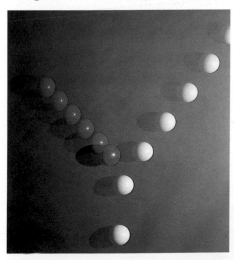

● **Figure 2.13** The white ball strikes the red a glancing blow. The two balls move off in different directions.

At the same time, each ball gains momentum in the sideways direction, because each has a sideways component of velocity – the white ball to the right, and the red ball to the left. These must be equal in magnitude and opposite in direction, otherwise we would conclude that momentum had been created out of nothing. The red ball moves at a greater angle, but its velocity is less than that of the white ball, so that the component of its velocity at right-angles to the original track is the same as the white ball's.

We can draw a vector triangle to represent these results (*figure 2.14*). The two velocities after the collision add up to equal the velocity of the white ball before the collision.

Measurements would show that these conclusions are indeed true. Momentum is conserved in this two-dimensional collision. We can also think about how the white ball's initial kinetic energy is shared between the two balls. After the collision, each has less energy than the original ball; their combined kinetic energy is probably somewhat less than that of the original ball, i.e. it is not an elastic collision.

Spot the ball

We would all have been surprised if both balls had moved off to the same side during the collision. We would have intuitively realised that momentum had not been conserved.

Strange effects are sometimes observed by physicists studying the tracks of sub-atomic

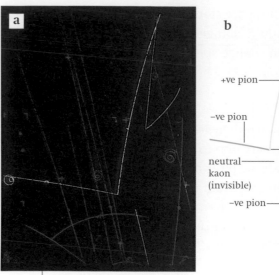

● **Figure 2.15 a** These tracks were produced in a bubble chamber. They show the paths of charged particles when a pion interacts with a proton. **b** An interpretation of the bubble chamber tracks. Uncharged particles (such as kaons) do not leave tracks, but we can work out their paths using the idea of conservation of momentum.

particles. By understanding how momentum is conserved, they can deduce what is going on.

Figure 2.15a shows an example. A particle enters from the left and collides with a second, stationary particle. The first particle appears to stop dead – giving the impression that momentum has not been conserved. In fact, two invisible particles have been produced, one moving to the left, the other up to the right. Particle physicists have to 'join up the dots' to deduce where this particle went. *Figure 2.15b* shows a reconstruction of the event.

SAQ 2.7
Draw diagrams to show elastic collisions between two identical billiard balls, one of which is initially stationary:
a when they collide head-on;
b when one strikes the other a glancing blow.

SAQ 2.8
An astronaut of mass 100 kg is adrift in space. He is 10 m from his space-craft. To get back, he throws a spanner of mass 1 kg directly away from the craft at $5\,\mathrm{m\,s^{-1}}$.
a Explain why he moves back towards the craft.
b How long will it take him to reach the craft?

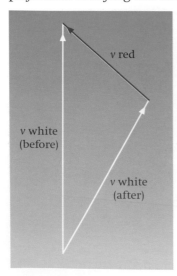

● **Figure 2.14** This velocity triangle corresponds to the motion shown in *figure 2.13*. Each arrow represents a velocity in both magnitude and direction. The sum of the two velocities after the collision equals the white ball's velocity before the collision.

● **Figure 2.16** These rockets produce a spectacular display of exploding stars in the night sky.

Explosions and crash-landings

The rockets shown in *figure 2.16* rise high into the sky. As they start to fall, they send out showers of chemical packages, each of which explodes to produce a brilliant sphere of burning chemicals. Material flies out in all directions to create a spectacular effect.

Does an explosion create momentum out of nothing? The important point to note here is that the burning material spreads out equally in all directions. Each tiny spark has momentum, but for every spark, there is another moving in the opposite direction, i.e. with opposite momentum. So, because momentum is a vector quantity, the total amount of momentum created is zero.

At the same time, the exploding stars continue to fall towards the ground. The chemical package from which they formed was falling before it exploded. It had momentum towards the ground. So the exploding stars must continue to fall, because they have this momentum. Momentum is conserved.

At the same time, kinetic energy is created in an explosion. Burning material flies outwards; its kinetic energy has come from the chemical potential energy stored in the chemical materials before they burn.

An explosion in the lab

You can investigate momentum in explosions using trolleys, as shown in *figure 2.17*. When the

● **Figure 2.17** These two trolleys move apart when the spring-load is released.

spring-load of trolley A is released, the two trolleys are pushed apart in a one-dimensional explosion (1-D because they move in a straight line). The spring-load stores elastic potential energy when it is compressed; this gives the trolleys kinetic energy when it is released, like the chemical potential energy stored in explosives.

Worked example

Consider the 1–D explosion between two trolleys, A and B. Trolley A has half the mass of trolley B, and moves at $1\,\mathrm{m\,s^{-1}}$. How fast will trolley B move?

You can probably guess the answer: its mass is twice that of A, so it will move at half the speed. Here is how to show this mathematically.

In an explosion, momentum is conserved, so

momentum before = momentum after
explosion   explosion

Before the explosion, the trolleys were not moving:

momentum before explosion = 0

After the explosion, both trolleys are moving:

momentum after explosion = $m_A \times v_A + m_B \times v_B$

So we must have

$$m_A \times v_A + m_B \times v_B = 0$$

and substituting in values gives

$$1\,\mathrm{kg} \times 1\,\mathrm{m\,s^{-1}} + 2\,\mathrm{kg} \times v_B = 0$$

Rearranging gives

$$2\,\mathrm{kg} \times v_B = -1\,\mathrm{kg} \times 1\,\mathrm{m\,s^{-1}}$$
$$v_B = (-1\,\mathrm{kg\,m\,s^{-1}})/(2\,\mathrm{kg}) = -0.5\,\mathrm{m\,s^{-1}}$$

Notice how the minus sign appears when we rearrange the equation. This shows that trolley B has a negative velocity; it is moving in the opposite direction to trolley A. Its speed is, as we guessed, half that of trolley A.

More fireworks

A roman candle fires a jet of burning material up into the sky. This is another type of explosion, but it doesn't send material in all directions. The firework tube directs all of the material upwards. Has momentum been created out of nothing here?

Again, the answer is no. The chemicals have momentum upwards, but at the same time, the roman candle pushes downwards on the Earth. An equal amount of downwards momentum is given to the Earth. Of course, the Earth is massive, and we don't notice the tiny change in its velocity which results.

In a similar way, when a gun is fired, a relatively small mass (the bullet) moves rapidly away in one direction; the gun is pushed back into the shoulder of the person who fired it. This is known as the recoil of the gun. *Figure 2.18* shows a cannon recoiling as it is fired.

(We have already considered some examples of 'explosions' like this on page 17: the astronaut throwing a tool to get back to the space-craft is relying on recoil, as does a rocket-powered back-pack for moving about in space.)

Down to Earth

If you fall over a cliff, you speed up as you fall; where does your momentum come from? And when you land, where does your momentum disappear to?

● **Figure 2.18** When a cannon like this was fired, the gun-crew had to keep clear as the cannon recoiled.

You fall because of the pull of the Earth's gravity on you. The force makes you accelerate: it does work, transferring kinetic energy to you. You gain momentum downwards; something must be gaining an equal amount of momentum in the opposite direction, upwards. It is the Earth, which starts to move upwards as you fall downwards. As before, the mass of the Earth is so great that its change in velocity is small, far too small to be noticeable.

When you hit the ground, your momentum becomes zero. At the same instant, the Earth also stops moving upwards. Your momentum cancels out the Earth's momentum. At all times during your fall and crash-landing, momentum has been conserved.

If you fall towards the Earth at $20 \, \text{m s}^{-1}$, how fast does the Earth move towards you? From *figure 2.19*, we can see that:

downward momentum = upward momentum
of falling person   of Earth

$$60 \, \text{kg} \times 20 \, \text{m s}^{-1} = 6 \times 10^{24} \, \text{kg} \times v$$
$$v = 2 \times 10^{-22} \, \text{m s}^{-1}$$

The Earth moves very slowly indeed; in the time of your fall, it will move much less than the diameter of the nucleus of an atom.

SAQ 2.9

Discuss whether momentum is conserved in each of the following situations:

a A star explodes in all directions – a supernova.

b You jump up from a trampoline. As you go up, your speed decreases; as you come down again, your speed increases.

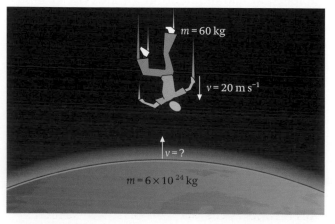

● **Figure 2.19** One way to make the Earth move.

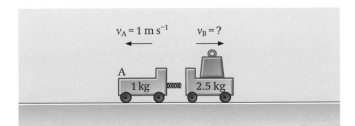

● **Figure 2.20** For SAQ 2.10.

SAQ 2.10

The two trolleys shown in *figure 2.20* are used to demonstrate that momentum is conserved in an explosion. When the spring-load is released, trolley A moves back at $1\,\mathrm{m\,s^{-1}}$. What is trolley B's speed?

SAQ 2.11

A gun of mass 2.5 kg fires a bullet of mass 20 g with an initial speed of $200\,\mathrm{m\,s^{-1}}$. Calculate the speed of recoil of the gun.

Momentum and Newton's laws

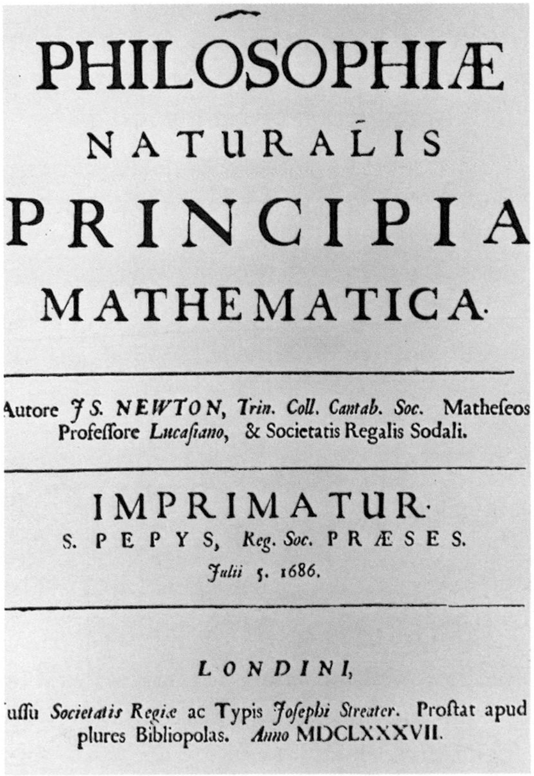

PHILOSOPHIÆ

NATURALIS

PRINCIPIA

MATHEMATICA·

Autore *JS. NEWTON, Trin. Coll. Cantab. Soc.* Matheseos Professore *Lucasiano,* & Societatis Regalis Sodali.

IMPRIMATUR·

S. P E P Y S, *Reg. Soc.* P R Æ S E S.

Julii 5. 1686.

LONDINI,

ussu *Societatis Regiæ* ac Typis *Josephi Streater.* Prostat apud plures Bibliopolas. *Anno* MDCLXXXVII.

● **Figure 2.21** This is a page from Newton's book called *Principia* (Principles) in which he outlined his theories of the laws that governed the motion of objects.

In *Physics 1*, we looked at Newton's three laws of motion. We can get further insight into these laws by thinking about them in terms of momentum.

Newton's first law of motion

In everyday speech, we sometimes say that something has *momentum* when we mean that it has a tendency to keep on moving of its own free will. An oil tanker is difficult to stop at sea, because of its momentum. We use the same word in a figurative sense: 'The election campaign is gaining momentum.' This idea of *keeping on moving* is just what we discussed in connection with Newton's first law:

> An object will remain at rest or in a state of uniform motion (at constant speed in a straight line) unless it is acted on by an external force.

Newton's second law of motion

We can think of Newton's second law as being summed up by the equation $F = ma$. In a sense, this tells us what we mean by a force: it is something that causes an object to accelerate; it changes an object's motion.

If we examine the equation a little more, we can restate this in terms of momentum. We can think of acceleration a as the rate of change of velocity: $a = (v - u)/t$. Substituting this in $F = ma$ gives:

$$F = m(v - u)/t = (mv - mu)/t$$

In words, this is:

force = (change in momentum)/time
$$F = \Delta p/t$$

This says that a force changes the momentum of an object; the greater the force, the greater the rate of change of momentum. We must bear in mind that both force and momentum are vector quantities; if the force pushes something upwards, it will gain momentum in the upwards direction. In *Physics 1*, we stated Newton's second law as follows:

> For an object with constant mass, its acceleration is proportional to the force producing the acceleration, and is in the direction of the force.

Now we can give a new version of Newton's second law, which is more generally true:

> The rate of change of momentum of an object is proportional to the force that produces it, and takes place in the direction of the force.

Defining force

This version of Newton's second law helps us to see more clearly just what we mean by a 'force'. It is something which, when it acts on a body, causes that body's momentum to change. The bigger the force, the greater the rate of change of momentum that it produces.

Worked example

If you squirt water out of a hose, the water is gaining momentum. You feel a force pushing back on you – a kind of recoil. If you let go of the hose, it will move backwards. (Fire-fighters have to be strong to hold their hoses, because they are squirting large masses of water at high speed, and this gives a strong recoil force.)

Figure 2.22 shows a hose squirting 0.5 kg of water per second. The water moves through the pipe at $1 \, \text{m s}^{-1}$, and leaves the nozzle at $5 \, \text{m s}^{-1}$. Calculate the force F needed to push the water forwards.

We will consider a time interval t of 1 s. In this time, 0.5 kg of water leaves the hose. We have:

$$t = 1 \, \text{s}$$
$$m = 0.5 \, \text{kg}$$
$$u = 1 \, \text{m s}^{-1}$$
$$v = 5 \, \text{m s}^{-1}$$

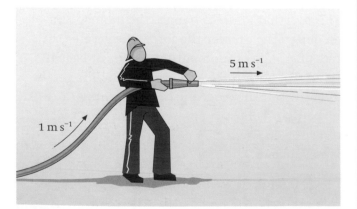

● **Figure 2.22** Water accelerates as it emerges from the hosepipe – see the worked example.

Substituting in $F = m(v - u)/t$ gives

$$F = 0.5 \, \text{kg} \times (5 \, \text{m s}^{-1} - 1 \, \text{m s}^{-1})/(1 \, \text{s})$$
$$= 0.5 \, \text{kg s}^{-1} \times 4 \, \text{m s}^{-1} = 2 \, \text{N}$$

Note that the final units are kg m s^{-2}, which is the same as N. The water is pushed forwards by a force of 2 N, and you would feel a force of 2 N pushing back on you.

Newton's third law of motion

This is the 'equal and opposite reaction' law:

> When two bodies interact, the forces they exert on each other are equal and opposite.

It can help us to understand why momentum is always conserved. Think again about the two trolleys pushing each other apart – the one-dimensional explosion discussed above. Each pushes on the other, and Newton's third law tells us that the forces which they exert on each other are equal and opposite. They also act for the same time – the time during which the trolleys remain in contact. So the trolleys have equal increases in momentum, in opposite directions. These changes in momentum cancel each other out, so the total amount of momentum remains constant.

SAQ 2.12

A golf ball has a mass of 0.046 kg. What average force does a golf club exert on the ball during a contact time of 1.3 ms (milliseconds) if the ball's velocity immediately after being struck is $50 \, \text{m s}^{-1}$?

SAQ 2.13

Water pouring from a broken pipe lands on a flat roof. The water is moving at $5 \, \text{m s}^{-1}$ when it strikes the roof. Every second, 10 kg of water hits the roof. Calculate the force of the water on the roof.

(Assume that the water does not bounce as it hits the roof. If it did bounce, would your answer be greater or smaller?)

SUMMARY

◆ The linear momentum of an object is defined as the product of its mass and velocity: $p = mv$.

◆ Within a closed system, the total momentum in any specified direction remains constant. This is the principle of conservation of momentum.

◆ In an elastic collision, kinetic energy is conserved; other collisions are described as inelastic.

◆ Force can be defined as the rate of change of momentum that it produces.

◆ Newton's first law of motion states that:

> An object will remain at rest or in a state of uniform motion (at constant speed in a straight line) unless it is acted on by an external force.

◆ Newton's second law of motion states that:

> The rate of change of momentum of an object is proportional to the force that produces it, and takes place in the direction of the force.

◆ Newton's third law of motion states that:

> When two bodies interact, the forces they exert on each other are equal and opposite.

Questions

1 a Write down the equation that defines linear momentum.
   b What are the SI units of momentum?
   c Is momentum a vector or a scalar quantity?

2 What is the momentum of a sprinter of mass 50 kg when, at the end of a 60 m race, she is travelling with a speed of $9.4 \, \text{m s}^{-1}$?

3 A trolley of mass 2.0 kg is moving with a velocity of $0.6 \, \text{m s}^{-1}$. It collides with a second, stationary trolley of mass 4.0 kg. They stick together and move off at $0.2 \, \text{m s}^{-1}$.
   a Show that momentum is conserved in this collision.
   b Explain whether the collision is elastic or inelastic.

4 A snooker ball of mass 0.350 kg hits the side of a snooker table at right-angles, and bounces off also at right-angles. If its speed before collision is $2.8 \, \text{m s}^{-1}$ and its speed after is $2.5 \, \text{m s}^{-1}$, calculate the change in its momentum. [The answer to this question is *not* $0.105 \, \text{kg m s}^{-1}$.]

5 A stationary radioactive atom of mass 238 atomic mass units undergoes radioactive decay. It emits an alpha particle of mass 4 atomic units.
   a If the alpha particle's speed is $2 \times 10^7 \, \text{m s}^{-1}$, with what speed does the atom recoil?
   b All of the energy released in the decay is in the form of the kinetic energies of the two particles. Calculate the alpha particle's kinetic energy as a fraction of the total energy released.

6 A rocket of mass 2×10^5 kg is initially stationary. It lifts off the ground and, after 10 s, it is moving at $50 \, \text{m s}^{-1}$. [Assume that the mass of the rocket remains constant during this time.]
   a By how much has the rocket's momentum increased in the first 10 s?
   b Use your answer to **a** to calculate the resultant force acting on the rocket.
   c Explain why the rocket's mass *must* decrease as it accelerates upwards.

CHAPTER 3

Moving in a circle

By the end of this chapter you should be able to:

1 express angular displacement in radians;

2 describe qualitatively motion in a curved path due to a perpendicular force;

3 understand the centripetal acceleration in the case of uniform motion in a circle;

4 recall and use centripetal acceleration $a = v^2/r$;

5 apply the equation $F = ma$ to uniform motion in a circle to derive $F = mv^2/r$.

Describing circular motion

Many things move in circles. Here are some examples:

- the wheels of a car or bicycle;
- the Earth in its (approximately circular) orbit round the Sun;
- the hands of a clock;
- a spinning hard disk in a computer;
- the drum of a washing machine.

Sometimes, things move along a path that is part of a circle. For example, a car may travel around a bend in the road which is an arc of a circle – see *figure 3.1*.

Circular motion is different from the straight-line motion that we have discussed previously in our study of dynamics. However, we can use the ideas of dynamics, and extend them, to build up a picture of circular motion.

Around the clock

The second hand of a clock moves steadily round the clock-face. It takes one minute to travel all the way round the circle. There are 360° in a complete circle, and 60 s in a minute, so the hand moves 6° every second. If we know the angle θ through which the hand has moved from the vertical (12 o'clock) position, we know the position of the hand.

In the same way, we can describe the position of any object as it moves around a circle simply by stating the angle θ of the arc through which it has

● **Figure 3.1** Two examples of circular motion: the racing car's wheels spin around the axles, and the car follows a curved path as it speeds round the bend.

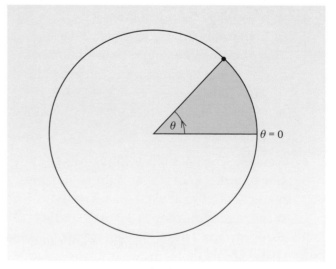

● **Figure 3.2** To know how far an object has moved round the circle, we need to know the angle θ.

moved from its starting position. This is shown in *figure 3.2*. There are two conventions to note:

- the starting position is horizontal, on the right;
- the object moves anticlockwise around the circle.

So, in this convention, we think of an object moving around in the opposite sense to the hands of a clock, and with a different starting position.

The angle θ through which the object has moved is known as its **angular displacement**. For an object moving in a straight line, its position was defined by its displacement x, the *distance* it has travelled from its starting position. The corresponding quantity for circular motion is angular displacement θ, the *angle* of the arc through which the object has moved from its starting position.

SAQ 3.1

a By how many degrees does the angular displacement of the hour hand of a clock change each hour?

b Think about a clock that is showing 3.30. What are the angular displacements (in degrees) from the 12 at the top to the minute hand, and to the hour hand?

Radians

In practice, it is usual to measure angles and angular displacements in units called radians rather than in degrees. One **radian** is the angle subtended at the centre of a circle by an arc equal in length to the radius of the circle. This means that there are 2π radians (rad) in a complete circle (*figure 3.3*). In other words:

$$2\pi \text{ rad} = 360° \quad \text{and} \quad \pi \text{ rad} = 180°$$

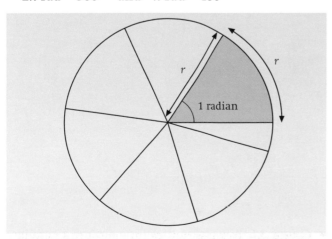

● **Figure 3.3** There are 2π radians in a complete circle.

From this it follows that 1 rad is equal to $360°/2\pi$, so that:

$$1 \text{ rad} \simeq 57.3°$$

If you can remember that there are 2π rad in a full circle, you will be able to convert between radians and degrees:

- to convert from degrees to radians, multiply by $2\pi/360°$;
- to convert from radians to degrees, multiply by $360°/2\pi$.

Worked example

If $\theta = 60°$, what is the value of θ in radians?

$$\theta = 60°$$
$$= 60° \times \frac{2\pi}{360°} \text{ rad}$$
$$= \frac{\pi}{3} \text{ rad} = 1.05 \text{ rad}$$

(Note that it is often useful to express an angle as a multiple of π radians.)

SAQ 3.2

a Convert the following angles from degrees into radians: 30°, 90°, 105°.

b Convert these angles from radians to degrees: 0.5 rad, 0.75 rad, π rad, $\pi/2$ rad.

c Express the following angles as multiples of π radians: 60°, 90°, 180°, 360°.

Defining an angle

If an object moves a distance s around a circular path of radius r (*figure 3.4a*), its angular displacement θ is given by

$$\text{angle} = \frac{\text{length of arc}}{\text{radius}} \quad \text{or} \quad \theta = \frac{s}{r}$$

Since both s and r are distances measured in metres, it follows that the angle θ is simply a ratio. It is a dimensionless quantity. We give it units of radians. If the object moves twice as far around a circle of twice the radius (*figure 3.4b*), its angular displacement is the same:

$$\theta = \frac{2s}{2r} = \frac{s}{r}$$

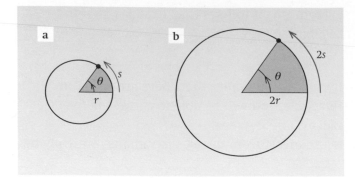

● **Figure 3.4** The size of an angle depends on the radius and the length of the arc. Doubling both leaves the angle unchanged.

If the object moves all the way round the circumference of the circle, it moves a distance $2\pi r$. Its angular displacement is then $2\pi r/r = 2\pi$ rad. Hence a complete circle contains 2π rad.

Steady speed, changing velocity

If we are to use Newton's laws of motion to explain circular motion, we must consider the *velocity* of an object going round in a circle, rather than its *speed*.

There is an important distinction between speed and velocity: **speed** is a scalar quantity, but **velocity** is a vector quantity, with both magnitude and direction. We need to think about the direction of motion of an orbiting object.

Figure 3.5a shows how we can represent the velocity of an object at various points around its orbit. The arrows are straight (to show the direction of motion at a particular instant). They are drawn as tangents to the circular path. As the object orbits through points A, B, C, etc., its speed remains constant but its direction changes. The arrows representing velocity at these points are collected together in *figure 3.5b*, to show how the direction changes.

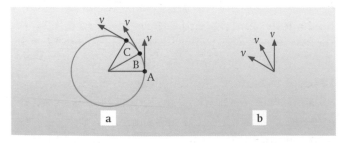

● **Figure 3.5** The velocity *v* of an object changes direction as it moves along a circular path.

Since the direction of velocity *v* is changing, it follows that *v* itself (a vector quantity) is changing as the body orbits. Remember, though, that the body's speed is constant.

SAQ 3.3
Why are all the arrows in *figure 3.5a* (or *figure 3.5b*) drawn the same length?

SAQ 3.4
A toy train travels at a steady speed of $0.2\,\text{m\,s}^{-1}$ around a circular track. A and B are two points diametrically opposite to one another on the track (*figure 3.6*).

a   By how much does the train's speed change as it travels from A to B?

b   By how much does the train's velocity change as it travels from A to B?

Centripetal forces

When an object's velocity is changing, we say that it is accelerating. In the case of uniform circular motion, the acceleration is rather unusual because, as we have seen, the object's speed does not change but its velocity does. How can an object accelerate, and at the same time have a steady speed?

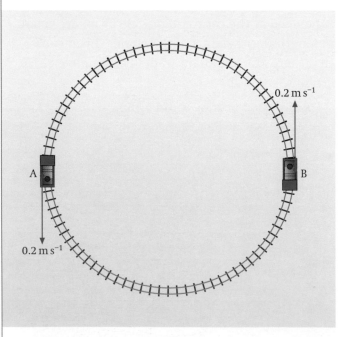

● **Figure 3.6** A toy train travelling around a circular track.

One way to understand this is to think about what Newton's laws of motion can tell us about this situation.

Newton's first law

> An object will remain at rest or in a state of uniform motion (at constant speed in a straight line) unless it is acted on by an external force.

In the case of an object moving at steady speed in a circle, we have a body whose velocity is not constant; therefore, there must be a resultant or unbalanced force acting on it.

Now we can think about various situations where objects are going round in a circle, and try to find the force that is acting on them.

Consider a conker on the end of a string. Imagine whirling it in a horizontal circle above your head (*figure 3.7*). To make it go round in a circle, you have to pull on the string. The pull of the string on the conker is the unbalanced force, which is constantly acting to change its velocity as it orbits your head. If you let go of the string, suddenly there is no tension in the string, and the conker will fly off at a tangent to the circle.

Similarly, the Earth as it orbits the Sun has a constantly changing velocity. Newton's first law says that there must be an unbalanced force acting on it. That force is the gravitational pull of the Sun. If the force disappeared, we would travel off in a straight line towards some terrible fate beyond the Solar System.

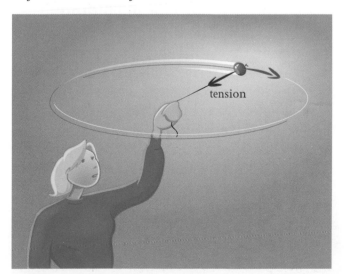

● **Figure 3.7** Whirling a conker.

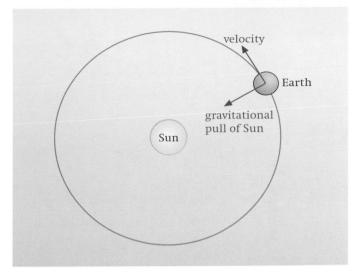

● **Figure 3.8** Gravity pulls the Earth towards the Sun.

Similarly, an electron is held in its orbit of the nucleus of an atom by the force of electrostatic attraction. Electrons are negatively charged, while nuclei are positive, and this results in a force that keeps the electrons orbiting.

In each of these cases, you should be able to see why the direction of the force is as shown in *figure 3.8*. The force on the object is directed towards the centre of the circle. We describe each of these forces as **centripetal** – that is, directed towards the centre.

It is important to note that the word *centripetal* is an adjective. We use it to describe a force that is making something travel along a circular path. It does not tell us what causes this force, which might be gravitational, electrostatic, magnetic, frictional or whatever.

SAQ 3.5

In each of the following cases, say what provides the centripetal force:
a the Moon orbiting the Earth;
b a car going round a bend on a flat, rough road;
c the weight on the end of a swinging pendulum.

SAQ 3.6

A car is travelling along a flat road. Explain why it cannot go around a bend if the road surface is perfectly smooth. What will happen if the driver tries turning the steering wheel?

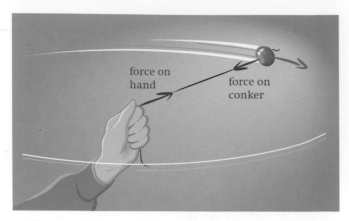

- **Figure 3.9** A centrifugal force and a centripetal force.

Centripetal or centrifugal?

The force needed to make an object follow a circular path must be directed towards the centre of the circle. (Think of the tension in the string as you whirl the conker round.) The word *centrifugal* means directed away from the centre of the circle. A force can be centrifugal; for example, the force that you feel the string exerting on your hand is outwards, towards the conker (*figure 3.9*). We could therefore describe this force as centrifugal. However, we are usually concerned with the resultant force acting on the orbiting object, and this is a centripetal force.

Vector diagrams

Figure 3.10a shows an object travelling along a circular path, at two positions in its orbit. It reaches position B a short time after A. How has its velocity changed between these two positions?

Figure 3.10b shows the two velocity vectors corresponding to A and B. You can see that the object has been pushed so that its velocity has been changed by a small amount, represented by the small arrow that closes the triangle. The direction of this arrow tells us about the direction

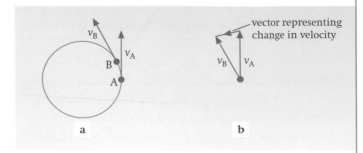

- **Figure 3.10** Changes in the velocity vector.

of the object's acceleration. Notice that it is (more or less) at right-angles to the velocity arrow at A.

You need to know that the velocity is always at a tangent to the circle, while the acceleration is always at right-angles, directed along a radius towards the centre of the circle. Because the acceleration (like the force that causes it) is directed towards the centre of the circle, we can describe it as a centripetal acceleration.

Acceleration at steady speed

Now that we know that the centripetal force and acceleration are always at right-angles to the object's velocity, we can explain why it does not speed up or slow down. If the force is to make the object speed up, it must have a component in the direction of the object's velocity; it must provide a push in the direction in which the object is already travelling. However, here we have a force at 90° to the velocity, so it has no component in the required direction. It acts to pull the object around the circle, without ever making it speed up or slow down.

SAQ 3.7

In uniform circular motion, an object follows a circular path at a steady speed. Describe how each of the following quantities changes as it follows this path: speed, velocity, kinetic energy, momentum, centripetal force, centripetal acceleration. (Refer to both magnitude and direction, as appropriate.)

Calculating force and acceleration

Isaac Newton devised an ingenious 'thought experiment' that allows us to think about circular motion, particularly in connection with objects orbiting the Earth. Consider a large gun on some high point on the Earth's surface, capable of firing objects horizontally. *Figure 3.11* shows what will happen if we fire them at different speeds.

If the object is fired too slowly, gravity will pull it down towards the ground and it will land at some distance from the gun. A faster initial speed results in the object landing further from the gun.

Now, if we try a bit faster than this, the object will travel all the way round the Earth. We have to get just the right speed to do this. As the object is

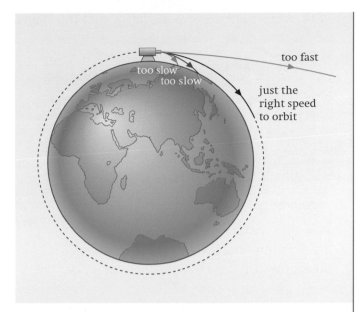

● **Figure 3.11** Newton's 'thought experiment'.

pulled down towards the Earth, the curved surface of the Earth falls away beneath it. The object follows a circular path, constantly falling under gravity but never getting any closer to the surface.

If the object is fired too fast, it travels off into space, and fails to get into a circular orbit. So we can see that there is just one correct speed to achieve a circular orbit under gravity.

An equation for centripetal force

We can think of this another way round. If an object having a particular mass m is to travel in an orbit of radius r and at speed v, there is a particular value of centripetal force F needed to keep it in orbit. The force F must depend on m, v and r. You can investigate the relationship between these quantities in the 'whirling conker' experiment.

Here is the equation for F:

$$\text{centripetal force, } F = \frac{mv^2}{r}$$

If you think about whirling a conker on a string, you should be able to see that the relationships between force, mass and speed are reasonable. A conker of greater mass will require a greater force. When it is moving faster you will also require a greater force. However, you may not find it obvious that to make it go at the same speed in a bigger circle will require a smaller force, but that is how it behaves.

Newton's second law

Now that we have an equation for centripetal force, we can use Newton's second law of motion to deduce an equation for centripetal acceleration. If we write this law as $a = F/m$, we find

$$\text{centripetal acceleration, } a = \frac{v^2}{r}$$

Remembering that an object accelerates in the direction of the resultant force on it, it follows that both F and a are in the same direction, towards the centre of the circle.

Strictly speaking, it is more correct to think of the relationship between centripetal force and acceleration the other way round: we should say that the acceleration is given by $a = v^2/r$, and then use $F = ma$ to deduce that $F = mv^2/r$.

The right speed

We can use the equation for a to calculate the speed that an object must have to orbit the Earth under gravity, as in Newton's thought experiment. The necessary centripetal force mv^2/r is provided by the Earth's gravitational pull mg. Hence $mg = mv^2/r$, or $g = v^2/r$, where g is the acceleration due to the Earth's gravity, i.e. 9.8 m s^{-2} close to the Earth's surface. The radius of its orbit is equal to the Earth's radius, approximately 6400 km. Hence, we have

$$9.8 \text{ m s}^{-2} = v^2/(6.4 \times 10^6 \text{ m})$$

$$v = \sqrt{9.8 \times 6.4 \times 10^6} \text{ m s}^{-1} = 7920 \text{ m s}^{-1}$$

Thus if you were to throw or hit a ball horizontally at almost 8 km s^{-1}, it would go into orbit around the Earth.

SAQ 3.8
How long would it take to orbit the Earth once at this speed of 7920 m s^{-1}?

SAQ 3.9
A stone of mass 0.2 kg is whirled round on the end of a string of length 30 cm. If the string will break when the tension in it exceeds 8 N, what is the greatest speed at which the stone can be whirled without the string breaking?

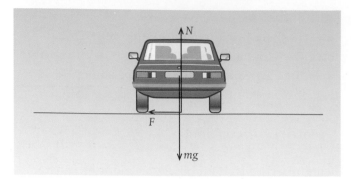

● **Figure 3.12** This car is moving away from us and turning to the left; friction provides the centripetal force. *N* and *F* are the *total* normal reaction and friction forces (respectively) provided by the contact of all four wheels with the ground.

The origins of centripetal forces

It is useful to look at one or two situations where the physical origin of the centripetal force may not be immediately obvious. In each case, you will notice that the forces acting on the moving object are not balanced. An object moving along a circular path is not in equilibrium, and the resultant force acting on it is the centripetal force.

1 A car cornering on a level road (*figure 3.12*). Here, the road provides two forces. The normal reaction *N* is a contact force which balances the weight *mg* of the car. The second force is the force of friction *F* between the tyres and the road surface. This is the unbalanced, centripetal force. If the road or tyres do not provide enough friction, the car will not go round the bend along the desired path.

2 A car cornering on a banked road (*figure 3.13a*). Here, the normal reaction has a horizontal component which can provide the centripetal force. The vertical component of *N* balances the car's weight.

   If a car travels around the bend too slowly, it will tend to slide down the slope and friction

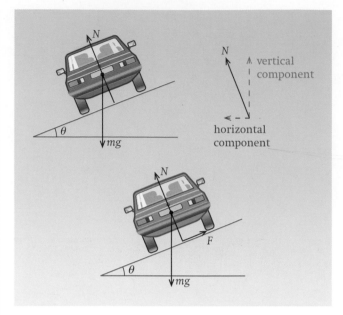

● **Figure 3.13** **a** On a banked road, the normal reaction of the road can provide the centripetal force needed for cornering. **b** For a slow car, friction acts up the slope to stop it from sliding down.

will act up the slope to keep it on course (*figure 3.13b*). If it travels too fast, it will tend to slide up the slope. If friction is insufficient, it will move up the slope and come off the road.

3 An aircraft banking (*figure 3.14a*). To change direction, the pilot tips the aircraft's wings. The vertical component of the lift force *L* on the wings balances the weight. The horizontal component of *L* provides the centripetal force.

4 A stone being whirled in a horizontal circle on the end of a string (*figure 3.14b*). The vertical and horizontal components of the tension *T* balance the weight and provide the centripetal force respectively.

5 At the fairground (*figure 3.14c*). As the cylinder spins, the floor drops away. Friction balances your weight. The normal reaction of the wall provides the centripetal force. You feel as

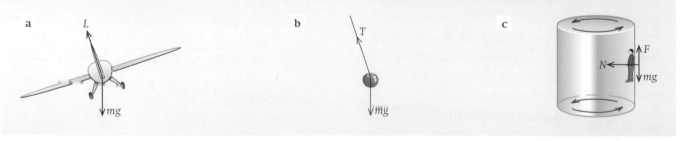

● **Figure 3.14** Three more ways of providing a centripetal force.

though you are being pushed back against the wall; what you are feeling is the push of the wall on your back.

Note that the three situations shown in *figures 3.13a, 3.14a* and *3.14b* are all equivalent. The moving object's weight acts downwards, and the second force has a vertical component, which balances the weight, and a horizontal component, which provides the centripetal force.

SAQ 3.10

Explain why it is impossible to whirl a conker around on the end of a string in such a way that the string remains perfectly horizontal.

SAQ 3.11

Explain why an aircraft will tend to lose height when banking, unless the pilot increases its speed to provide more lift.

SUMMARY

◆ Angular displacement is measured in radians.

◆ An object moving at a steady speed along a circular path has uniform circular motion.

◆ Its angular displacement θ is a measure of the angle through which the object has moved around its orbit.

◆ It is not in equilibrium; there must be an unbalanced force acting on it.

◆ Such a force is called a centripetal force, and acts at right-angles to the object's velocity, towards the centre of the circle.

◆ The object has a centripetal acceleration that is related to its speed and the radius of the orbit: $a = v^2/r$.

◆ Since $F = ma$, the centripetal force is given by $F = mv^2/r$.

Questions

1   Helen Sharman, the first Briton in space, worked in the Mir space station (*figure 3.15*). This had a mass of 20 900 kg, and orbited the Earth at an average height of 350 km, where the gravitational acceleration is $8.8\,\mathrm{m\,s^{-2}}$. Calculate:
   a   the centripetal force on the space station;
   b   the speed at which it orbited;
   c   the time taken for each orbit;
   d   the number of times it orbited the Earth each day.
   [radius of Earth = 6400 km]

● **Figure 3.15** The Mir space station orbiting Earth over Australia.

2   A stone of mass 0.5 kg is whirled round on the end of a string 0.5 m long. It makes three complete revolutions each second. Calculate:
   a   its speed;
   b   its centripetal acceleration;
   c   the tension in the string.

Questions

3   Mars orbits the Sun once every 687 days at a distance of 2.3×10^{11} m. The mass of Mars is 6.4×10^{23} kg. Calculate:

   a   its orbital speed;
   b   its centripetal acceleration;
   c   the force exerted on Mars by the Sun.

4   If you have ever been down a water-slide (a flume) (*figure 3.16*) you will know that you tend to slide up the side as you go around a bend. Explain how this provides the centripetal force needed to push you around the bend. Why do you slide higher if you are going faster?

● **Figure 3.16** A water-slide is a good place to experience centripetal forces.

CHAPTER 4

Oscillations

By the end of this chapter you should be able to:

1 describe experimental investigations of free oscillations;

2 understand and use the terms displacement, amplitude, period, frequency, angular frequency (ω) and phase difference;

3 express period in terms of frequency: period = 1/frequency;

4 define simple harmonic motion;

5 describe graphically the changes in displacement, velocity and acceleration during oscillations;

6 understand velocity as the gradient of the displacement–time graph;

7 recall and use $a = -(2\pi f)^2 x$, and the solutions $x = A\sin(2\pi ft)$ and $x = A\cos(2\pi ft)$ for simple harmonic motion;

8 describe the interchange between kinetic energy and potential energy during simple harmonic motion;

9 describe practical examples of damped oscillations with particular reference to the effects of the degree of damping in such cases as a car suspension system;

10 define critical damping as the degree of damping required for the displacement of a system to reach a constant value in the minimum time without oscillation;

11 describe practical examples of forced oscillations and resonance;

12 describe graphically how the amplitude of a forced oscillation changes with frequency near to the natural frequency of the system;

13 understand qualitatively the factors that determine the frequency response and sharpness of resonance.

Free and forced vibrations

A bird in flight flaps its wings up and down (*figure 4.1*). An aircraft's wings also vibrate up and down; but this is not how it flies. The wings are long and thin, and they vibrate slightly because they are not perfectly rigid. Many other structures vibrate – bridges when traffic flows across, buildings in high winds.

A more specific term than vibration is oscillation. An object **oscillates** when it moves back and forth repeatedly, on either side of some fixed position. If we stop it from oscillating, it returns to the fixed position.

● **Figure 4.1** The wings of a bird oscillate as it flies.

We make use of oscillations in many different ways – for pleasure (a child on a swing), for music (the vibrations of a guitar string), for timing (the movement of a pendulum or the vibrations of a quartz crystal). Whenever we make a sound, the molecules of the air oscillate back and forth, passing the sound energy along. The atoms of a solid vibrate more and more as the temperature rises.

These examples of oscillations and vibrations may seem very different from one another. In this chapter, we will look at the characteristics that are shared by all oscillations.

Free or forced?

The easiest oscillations to understand are free oscillations. If you pluck a guitar string, it continues to vibrate for some time after you have released it. It vibrates at a particular **frequency** (the number of vibrations per second). This is called its natural frequency of vibration, and it gives rise to the particular note that you hear. Change the length of the string, and you change the natural frequency. In a similar way, the prongs of a tuning fork have a natural frequency of vibration, which you can observe when you strike it on a cork. Every oscillator has a natural frequency of vibration, the frequency with which it vibrates freely after an initial disturbance.

On the other hand, many objects can be forced to vibrate. If you sit on a bus, you may notice that the vibrations from the engine are transmitted to your body, causing you to vibrate with the same frequency. These are not free vibrations of your body; they are forced vibrations. Their frequency is not the natural frequency of vibration of your body, but the forcing frequency of the bus.

In the same way, you can force a metre ruler to oscillate by waving it up and down; however, its natural frequency of vibration will be much greater than this, as you will discover if you hold one end down on the bench and twang the other end (*figure 4.2*).

SAQ 4.1

Which of the following are free oscillations, and which are forced: the wing beat of a mosquito; the movement of the pendulum in a grandfather clock; the vibrations of a cymbal after it has been struck; the shaking of a building during an earthquake?

Observing oscillations

Many oscillations are too rapid or too small for us to observe. Our eyes cannot respond rapidly enough if the frequency of oscillation is more than about 5 Hz (five oscillations per second); anything faster than this appears as a blur. In order to see the general characteristics of oscillating systems, we need to find suitable systems that oscillate slowly. Here are three suitable situations to look at.

■ **A mass–spring system**
   A trolley, loaded with extra masses, is tethered by identical springs in between two clamps (*figure 4.3*). Displace the trolley to one side and it will oscillate back and forth along the bench. Listen to the sound of the trolley moving. Where is it moving fastest? What happens to its speed as it reaches the ends of its oscillation? What is happening to the springs as the trolley oscillates?

● **Figure 4.2** A ruler with one end free can be stimulated to vibrate.

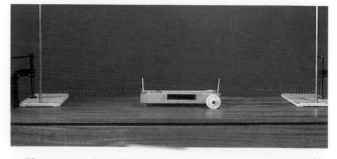

● **Figure 4.3** A trolley tethered between springs will oscillate from side to side.

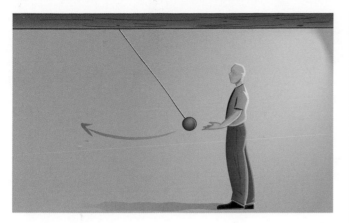

● **Figure 4.4** A long pendulum oscillates back and forth.

■ **A long pendulum**

A string, at least 2 m long, hangs from the ceiling with a large mass fixed at the end (*figure 4.4*). Pull the mass some distance to one side, and let go. The pendulum will swing back and forth at its natural frequency of oscillation. Try to note the characteristics of its motion. In what ways is it similar to the motion of the oscillating trolley? In what ways is it different?

■ **A loudspeaker cone**

A signal generator, set to a low frequency (say, 1 Hz), drives a loudspeaker (*figure 4.5*). You need to be able to see the cone of the loudspeaker. How does this motion compare with that of the pendulum and the mass–spring system? Try using a higher frequency (say, 100 Hz). Use an electronic stroboscope flashing at a similar frequency to show up the movement of the cone. (It may help to paint a white spot on the centre of the cone.) Do you observe the same pattern of movement?

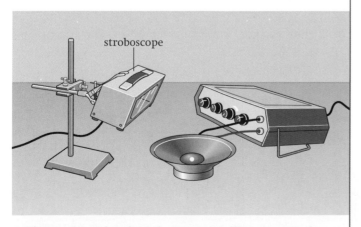

● **Figure 4.5** A loudspeaker cone oscillates up and down.

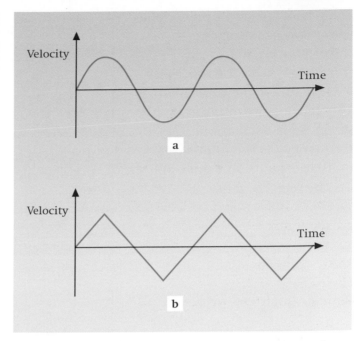

● **Figure 4.6** Two possible velocity–time graphs for vibrating objects.

SAQ 4.2

If you could draw a graph to show how the velocity of any of these oscillators changes, what would it look like? Would it be curved like *figure 4.6a*, or saw-toothed like *figure 4.6b*?

Describing oscillations

All of these examples show the same pattern of movement. The trolley speeds up (accelerates) as it moves towards the centre of the oscillation. It is moving fastest at the centre; it slows down again (decelerates) as it moves towards the end of the oscillation. At the extreme position, it stops momentarily, reverses its direction, and accelerates back towards the centre again.

Many oscillating systems can be represented by a displacement–time graph like that shown in *figure 4.7*, next page. The displacement varies in a smooth way on either side of the midpoint; the shape of this graph is a sine curve, and the motion is sometimes described as sinusoidal.

Notice that the displacement changes between positive and negative values, as the mass moves through the midpoint. The greatest displacement is called the **amplitude** of the oscillation.

The displacement–time graph can also be used to find the period and frequency of the oscillation.

The **period** T is the time for one complete oscillation; note that the oscillating mass must go from one side to the other and back again (or the equivalent). This tells us the number of seconds per oscillation. The **frequency** f is the number of oscillations per unit time, and so f is the reciprocal of T:

$$\text{frequency} = \frac{1}{\text{period}} \quad \text{or}$$

$$f = \frac{1}{T}$$

which can also be written as

$$\text{period} = \frac{1}{\text{frequency}}$$

SAQ 4.3

From the displacement–time graph shown in *figure 4.8*, deduce the amplitude, period and frequency of the oscillations represented.

Phase

The term **phase** describes the point that an oscillating mass has reached within the complete cycle of an oscillation. It is often important to describe the **phase difference** between two oscillations. The graph of *figure 4.9a* shows two oscillations, which are identical except for their phase. They are out of step with one another; in this example, they have a phase difference of one-quarter of a cycle.

SAQ 4.4

a By what fraction of a cycle are the two oscillations represented in *figure 4.9b* out of phase?

b Why would it not make sense to ask the same question about *figure 4.9c*?

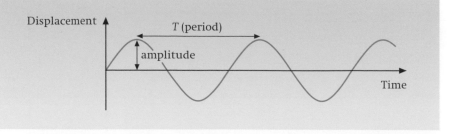

● **Figure 4.7** A displacement–time graph to show the meanings of amplitude and period.

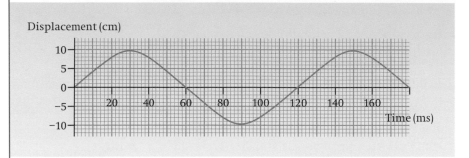

● **Figure 4.8** A displacement–time graph for an oscillating body.

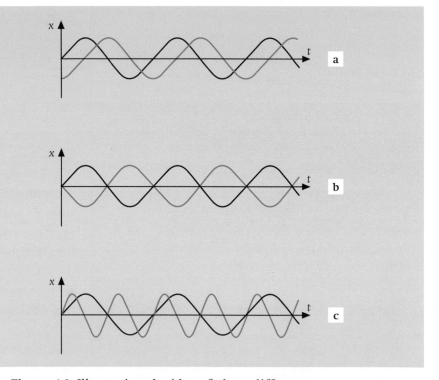

● **Figure 4.9** Illustrating the idea of phase difference.

Worked example

Figure 4.10 shows two identical waves with a phase difference between them. Calculate this phase difference; give your answer in degrees and in radians.

Step 1. Measure the *horizontal* separation of two corresponding points on the two waves. The diagram shows the separation of two peaks,

● **Figure 4.10** Two identical but out of phase waves, for use with the worked example.

but crossing-points on the *x*-axis would do instead.
Separation of peaks = 17 divisions
(The answer is given in scale divisions. There is no need to convert to units of time.)

Step 2. Measure the width of one complete oscillation.
Width of oscillation = 58 divisions

Step 3. Now you can calculate the phase difference as a fraction of an oscillation.
Phase difference = 17 div/58 div = 0.29 cycle

Step 4. Convert to degrees and radians. Recall that there are 360° and 2π rad in one oscillation.
Phase difference = $0.29 \times 360° = 104°$
Phase difference = $0.29 \times 2\pi$ rad = 1.82 rad
(You can calculate the phase of a particular point on a wave in the same way. Phase = 0 where the graph crosses the *x*-axis with a positive slope; measure the horizontal distance from this point to the point of interest, and calculate the phase difference as above.)

Simple harmonic motion

There are many situations where we can observe the special kind of oscillations called simple harmonic motion (s.h.m.). Some are more obvious than others. For example, the vibrating strings of a musical instrument show s.h.m. When plucked or bowed, the strings move back and forth about the midpoint of their oscillation.

Here are some other, less obvious, situations where simple harmonic motion can be found.
■ When a sound wave travels through air, the molecules of the air vibrate back and forth with s.h.m.
■ When an alternating current flows in a wire, the electrons in the wire move with s.h.m.

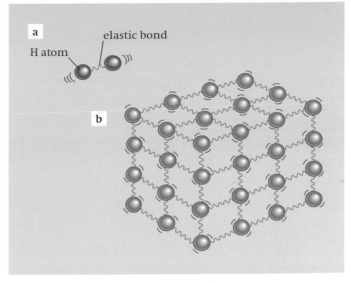

● **Figure 4.11** We can think of the bonds between atoms as being springy; this leads to vibrations in **a** a molecule of hydrogen and **b** a solid crystal.

■ There is a small alternating electric current in a radio or television aerial when it is tuned to a signal, in the form of electrons moving with s.h.m.
■ Any electromagnetic waves such as light or radio waves consist of simple harmonic vibrations of both electric and magnetic fields.
■ The atoms that make up a molecule vibrate with s.h.m. (see for example the hydrogen molecule in *figure 4.11a*).

Oscillations can be very complex, with many different frequencies of oscillation occurring at the same time. Examples include the vibrations of machinery, the motion of waves on the sea, and the vibration of a solid crystal formed when atoms, ions or molecules bond together (*figure 4.11b*). It is possible to break down a complex oscillation into a sum of simple oscillations, and so we will focus our attention in this chapter on s.h.m. with only one frequency. We will also concentrate on large-scale mechanical oscillations, but you should bear in mind that this analysis can be extended to the situations mentioned above, and many more besides.

The requirements for s.h.m.

If a simple pendulum is undisturbed, it is in equilibrium. To start it swinging (*figure 4.12*), it must be pulled to one side. Gravity pulls on the mass, and this force moves the mass back to its central equilibrium position. The mass swings past the

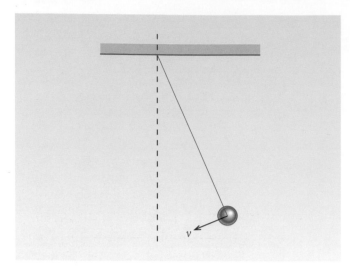

● **Figure 4.12** This pendulum has positive displacement and negative velocity.

midpoint until it comes to rest momentarily at the other side; the process is then repeated in the opposite direction. Note that a complete oscillation is from right to left and back again. The three requirements for s.h.m. of a mechanical system are:

1 a mass that oscillates;
2 a central position where the mass is in equilibrium (conventionally, displacements to the right of this position are taken as positive, to the left they are negative);
3 a restoring force that acts to return the mass to the central position (the restoring force is proportional to the distance of the mass from the equilibrium position).

SAQ 4.5

Identify the features of the motion of the simple pendulum that satisfy the three requirements for s.h.m.

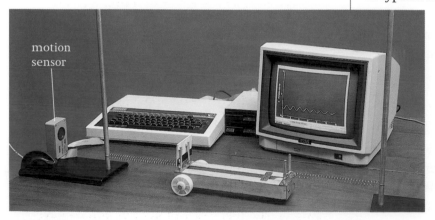

● **Figure 4.13** Using a motion sensor to measure s.h.m. of a spring–trolley system.

The changes of velocity in s.h.m.

As the pendulum swings back and forth, its velocity is constantly changing. As it swings from right to left (as shown in *figure 4.12*) its velocity is negative. It speeds up towards the central position, and then slows down as it approaches the other end of the oscillation. It has positive velocity as it swings back from left to right. Again, it is travelling fastest at the midpoint, and slows down as it swings up to its starting position.

This pattern of speeding up – slowing down – reversing – speeding up again is characteristic of simple harmonic motion. There are no sudden changes of velocity. Note also that, because its velocity is always changing, the mass must be accelerating and decelerating all the time. In the next section we will see how we can observe these changes, and how we can represent them graphically.

Graphical representations

If you set up a trolley tethered between springs (*figure 4.13*) you can hear the characteristic rhythm of s.h.m. as the trolley oscillates back and forth. By adjusting the load carried by the trolley, you can achieve oscillations with a period of about two seconds.

The motion sensor allows you to record how the displacement of the trolley varies with time. Ultrasonic pulses from the sensor are reflected by the card on the trolley, and the reflected pulses are detected. This 'sonar' technique allows the sensor to determine the displacement of the trolley. A typical screen display is shown in *figure 4.14*.

The computer can then determine the velocity of the trolley by calculating the rate of change of displacement. Similarly, it can calculate the rate of change of velocity to determine the acceleration.

Idealised graphs of displacement, velocity and acceleration against time are shown in *figure 4.15*; we will examine these graphs in sequence to see what they tell us about s.h.m. and how the three graphs are related to one another.

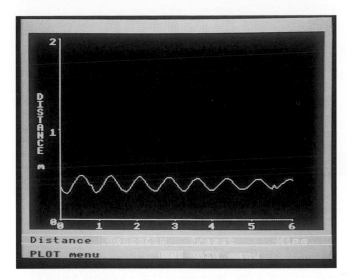

● **Figure 4.14** The screen display for a motion sensor detecting s.h.m.

■ **Displacement–time (x–t) graph**

The displacement of the oscillating mass varies according to the smooth curve shown in *figure 4.15a*. (Mathematically, this is a sine curve; its variation is described as sinusoidal.) Note that this graph allows us to determine the amplitude and the period of the oscillations.

In this graph, the displacement x of the oscillation is shown as zero at the start (when t is zero). We have chosen to consider the motion to start when the mass is at the midpoint of its oscillation and is moving to the right. We could have chosen any other point in the cycle as the starting point, but it is conventional to start as shown here.

■ **Velocity–time (v–t) graph**

Again, we have a smooth curve (*figure 4.15b*), which shows how the velocity v depends on time t. The shape of the curve is the same as for the displacement–time graph, but it starts at a different point in the cycle. When t is zero, the mass is at the midpoint of its oscillation, and this is where it is moving fastest. Hence the velocity has its maximum value at this point. Its value is positive, since it is moving towards the right.

■ **Acceleration–time (a–t) graph**

Finally, we have a third curve of the same general form (*figure 4.15c*), which shows how the acceleration a depends on time t. At the start of the oscillation, the mass is at the midpoint, where it is in equilibrium. Since there is no

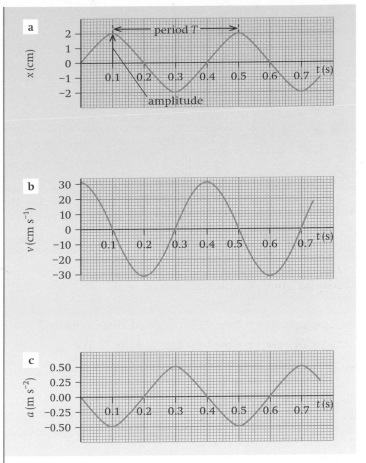

● **Figure 4.15** Displacement, velocity and acceleration graphs for s.h.m.

resultant force acting on it, its acceleration is zero. As it moves to the right, the restoring force acts towards the left, giving it a negative acceleration. The acceleration has its greatest value when the mass is displaced furthest from the equilibrium position. Notice that, whenever the mass has a positive displacement (to the right), its acceleration is to the left, and vice versa. Hence the acceleration graph is an upside-down version of the displacement graph.

SAQ 4.6

Use the graphs shown in *figure 4.15* to determine the values of the following quantities: **a** amplitude, **b** period, **c** maximum velocity and **d** maximum acceleration.

SAQ 4.7

At what point in an oscillation does a mass have zero velocity but positive acceleration?

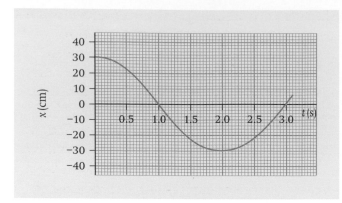

● **Figure 4.16** A displacement–time graph.

Relating the graphs

Displacement, velocity and acceleration are related as follows:

velocity = rate of change of displacement
acceleration = rate of change of velocity

So we can deduce the velocity from the gradient of the *x*–*t* graph, and the acceleration from the gradient of the *v*–*t* graph. We can see these relationships at work if we compare the three graphs shown in *figure 4.15*.

Consider the *x*–*t* graph and the *v*–*t* graph. You should be able to see that, wherever the gradient of the *x*–*t* graph is positive, the velocity is positive. Wherever the gradient of the *x*–*t* graph is negative, the velocity is negative.

The *v*–*t* and *a*–*t* graphs are related similarly. Wherever the gradient of the *v*–*t* graph is positive, the acceleration is positive. Wherever the gradient of the *v*–*t* graph is negative, the acceleration is negative.

SAQ 4.8 _____

Look at the *x*–*t* graph (*figure 4.15a*). When *t* = 0.1 s, what is the gradient of the graph? What does this tell you about the velocity at this instant?

_____

SAQ 4.9 _____

Figure 4.16 shows how the displacement of an oscillating mass changes with time. Use the graph to deduce the following quantities:
a the velocity when *t* = 0 s;
b the maximum velocity;
c the acceleration when *t* = 1 s.

_____

Frequency and angular frequency

The frequency *f* of s.h.m. tells us how many cycles of the oscillations take place per unit time. As we saw earlier, *f* is related to the period *T* by

$$f = \frac{1}{T}$$

We can think of a complete cycle of s.h.m. as being represented by 2π radians. (Recall that, in a complete cycle of circular motion, an object moves round through 2π rad.) We say that the phase of the oscillation changes by 2π rad during one cycle. Hence, if there are *f* cycles in unit time, we can say that there are $2\pi f$ rad in unit time. This quantity is the angular frequency of the s.h.m. and it is represented by the symbol ω.

Angular frequency is thus related to frequency and period as follows:

$$\omega = 2\pi f = \frac{2\pi}{T} \qquad \text{or} \qquad T = \frac{2\pi}{\omega}$$

In *figure 4.17*, a single cycle of s.h.m. is shown, but with the *x*-axis marked with the phase of the motion in radians.

Circular motion and s.h.m.

There is a close relationship between circular motion and s.h.m. One way to see this is to picture a turntable, turning at a steady speed (*figure 4.18a*). When viewed from above, the marker X moves round at a steady speed. However, if viewed from the side as in *figure 4.18b*, the marker moves with apparent s.h.m. It shows the speeding up – slowing down behaviour characteristic of s.h.m., and its angular frequency is ω.

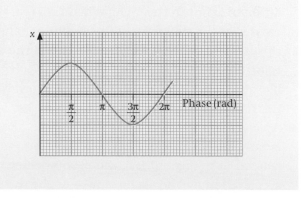

● **Figure 4.17** The phase of an oscillation varies from 0 to 2π during one cycle.

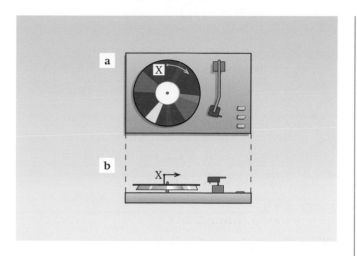

● **Figure 4.18** A marker on a turntable viewed from above, **a**, shows circular motion, but from the side, **b**, it shows apparent s.h.m.

SAQ 4.10

An object moving with s.h.m. goes through two complete cycles in 1 s. Calculate the values of:
a T, **b** f, **c** ω.

Equations of s.h.m.

The graph of *figure 4.15a* shown earlier represents how the displacement of an object varies during s.h.m. We have already said that this is a sine curve. We can present the same information in the form of an equation. The displacement x depends on time t according to

$$x = A \sin (2\pi f t)$$

In this equation, A is the amplitude of the motion and f is its frequency. Sometimes the same motion is represented using a cosine function, rather than a sine function:

$$x = A \cos (2\pi f t)$$

The difference between these two equations is illustrated in *figure 4.19*. The sine version starts at $x = 0$; i.e. the oscillating mass is at the midpoint of its oscillation when $t = 0$. The cosine version starts at $x = A$, so that the mass is at its maximum displacement when $t = 0$.

Note that, in calculations using these equations, the quantity $(2\pi f t)$ is in radians. Make sure that your calculator is working in radians for any calculation – see the worked example below. The presence of the π in the equation should remind you of this.

Worked example

A pendulum oscillates with frequency 1.5 Hz and amplitude 0.1 m. If it is passing through the midpoint of its oscillation when $t = 0$, write an equation to represent its displacement in terms of amplitude, frequency and time. Deduce its displacement when $t = 0.5$ s.

Step 1: Select the correct equation. In this case, the displacement is zero when $t = 0$, so we use the sine form:

$$x = A \sin (2\pi f t)$$

Step 2: Substitute values using the information given in the question: $A = 0.1$ m, $f = 1.5$ Hz:

$$x = (0.1 \text{ m}) \times \sin (2\pi \times 1.5 \text{ Hz} \times t)$$

It is easier to see what this means if we omit the units:

$$x = 0.1 \sin (2\pi \times 1.5 t)$$

Step 3: To find x when $t = 0.5$ s, substitute for t and calculate the answer:

$$x = 0.1 \sin (2\pi \times 1.5 \times 0.5) = 0.1 \sin (4.71) = -0.1 \text{ m}$$

This means that the pendulum is at the extreme end of its oscillation; the minus sign means that it is at the

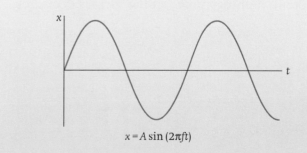

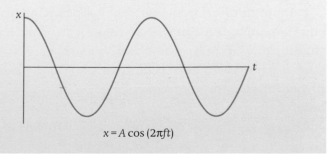

● **Figure 4.19** These two graphs represent the same simple harmonic motion. The difference in starting points is related to the sine and cosine forms of the equation for x as a function of t.

negative or left-hand end, assuming you have chosen to consider displacements to the right as positive.

[If your calculation above went like this:

$x = 0.1 \sin (2\pi \times 1.5 \times 0.5) = 0.1 \sin (4.71)$
$= -8.2 \times 10^{-3}$ m, then your calculator was set to work in degrees, not radians.]

SAQ 4.11

The vibration of a component in a machine is represented by the equation

$x = 0.3$ mm $\times \sin (2\pi \times 120\,\text{Hz} \times t)$

What are the values of **a** the amplitude, and **b** the frequency of its vibration?

SAQ 4.12

A trolley is at rest, tethered between two springs. It is pulled 20 cm to one side and, when $t = 0$, it is released so that it oscillates back and forth. The period of its motion is 2.0 s. Assuming that its motion is s.h.m., write down an equation to represent this motion. Sketch a graph to show two cycles of the motion, giving values where appropriate.

Acceleration and displacement

In s.h.m., an object's acceleration depends on how far it is displaced from the midpoint of the oscillation. The greater the displacement x, the greater the acceleration a. In fact, a is proportional to x. We can write an equation to represent this:

$$a = -(2\pi f)^2 x$$

This equation says that a is proportional to x; the constant of proportionality is $(2\pi f)^2$. The minus sign shows that, when the object is displaced to the *right*, its acceleration is to the *left*.

It shouldn't be surprising that f appears in this equation. Imagine a mass hanging on a spring, so that it can vibrate up and down. If the spring is stiff, the mass will be accelerated more for a given displacement, and its frequency of oscillation will be higher.

The equation $a = -(2\pi f)^2 x$ tells us how to define simple harmonic motion. Acceleration a is proportional to displacement x; and the minus sign tells us that it is in the opposite direction.

A body executes simple harmonic motion if its acceleration is proportional to its displacement from a fixed point, and is directed towards that point.

If a and x were in the same direction (no minus sign), the body's acceleration would increase as it moved away from the fixed point and it would move away faster and faster, never to return.

SAQ 4.13

A mass on a spring moves with s.h.m. The frequency of its motion is 1.4 Hz.

a Write an equation of the form $a = -(2\pi f)^2 x$ to show how the mass's acceleration depends on its displacement.

b Calculate the acceleration of the mass when it is displaced 5 cm from the midpoint of its oscillation.

SAQ 4.14

A short pendulum oscillates with s.h.m. such that its acceleration a (in m s^{-2}) is related to its displacement x (in m) by $a = -300x$. What is the frequency of the pendulum's oscillation?

Energy

During simple harmonic motion, there is a constant interchange of energy between two forms: potential and kinetic. We can see this by considering the mass–spring system shown in *figure 4.20*. When the mass is pulled to one side (to start the oscillations), one spring is compressed and the other is stretched. The springs store elastic potential energy. When the mass is released, it moves back towards the central position, accelerating as it goes. It has increasing kinetic energy. The potential energy stored in the springs decreases,

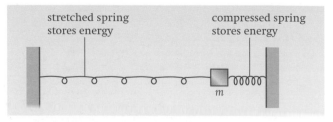

stretched spring stores energy   compressed spring stores energy

m

● **Figure 4.20** The elastic potential energy stored in the springs is converted to kinetic energy when the mass is released.

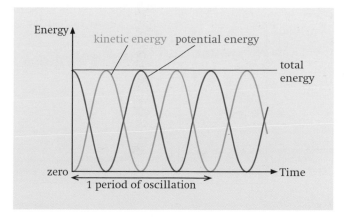

● **Figure 4.21** The kinetic energy and potential energy of an oscillator vary periodically, but the total energy remains constant if the system is undamped.

and the kinetic energy of the mass increases by a corresponding amount. Once the mass has passed the midpoint of its oscillation, its kinetic energy decreases and the energy is transferred back to the springs. Provided the oscillations are undamped, the total energy in the system remains constant.

Energy graphs

We can represent these energy changes in two ways. *Figure 4.21* shows how the two forms of energy change with time. Potential energy is maximum when displacement is maximum (positive or negative); kinetic energy is maximum when displacement is zero. Total energy remains constant throughout. Note that both kinetic energy and potential energy go through *two* complete cycles during *one* period of the oscillation. This is because kinetic energy is maximum when the mass is passing through the midpoint to the left and to the right; potential energy is maximum at both ends of the oscillation. A second way to show this is to draw a graph of how potential energy and kinetic energy vary with displacement (*figure 4.22*).

SAQ 4.15

To start a pendulum swinging, you pull it slightly to one side.
a What kind of energy does this transfer to the mass?
b Describe the energy changes that occur when the mass is released.

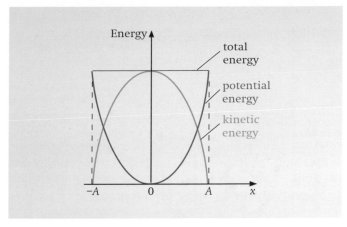

● **Figure 4.22** The kinetic energy is maximum at zero displacement; the potential energy is maximum at maximum displacement (A and $-A$).

SAQ 4.16

Figure 4.22 shows how the different forms of energy change with displacement during s.h.m. Copy the graph, and show how the graph would differ if the oscillating mass were given only half the initial input of energy.

Damped oscillations

In principle, oscillations can go on for ever. In practice, however, the oscillations we observe around us do not. They die out, either rapidly or gradually. A child on a swing knows that the amplitude of her swinging will decline until eventually she will come to rest, unless she can put some more energy into the swinging to keep it going.

This happens because of friction. On a swing, there is friction where the swing is attached to the frame, and there is friction with the air. The amplitude of the child's oscillations decreases as the friction transfers energy away from her to the surroundings.

We say that these oscillations are **damped**. Their amplitude decreases according to a particular pattern. This is shown in *figure 4.23*, next page.

The amplitude of damped oscillations does not decrease linearly. It follows an exponential pattern – this is a particular mathematical pattern that arises as follows. At first, the swing moves rapidly. There is a lot of air resistance to overcome, so the swing loses energy quickly, and its amplitude decreases at a high rate. Later, it is

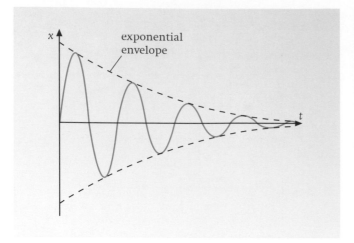

● **Figure 4.23** Damped oscillations.

moving more slowly. There is less air resistance, and so energy is lost more slowly, and the amplitude decreases at a slower rate. Hence we get the characteristic curved shape, which is the 'envelope' of the graph in *figure 4.23*.

Notice that the frequency of the oscillations does not change as the amplitude decreases. This is a characteristic of simple harmonic motion. The child may swing back and forth once every two seconds, and this stays the same whether the amplitude is large or small.

Investigating damping

You can investigate the exponential decrease in the amplitude of oscillations using a simple laboratory arrangement (*figure 4.24*). A hacksaw blade or other springy metal strip is clamped (vertically or horizontally) to the bench. A mass is attached to the free end. This will oscillate freely if you displace it to one side.

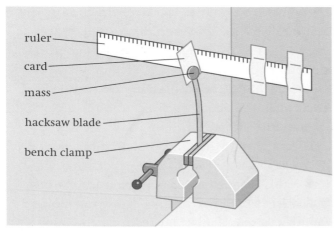

● **Figure 4.24** Damped oscillations with a hacksaw blade.

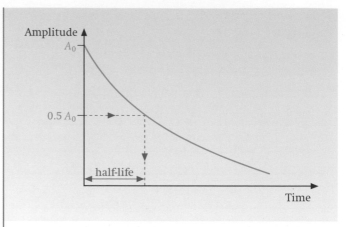

● **Figure 4.25** A typical amplitude–time graph for damped oscillations.

A card is attached to the mass so that there is a lot of air resistance as the mass oscillates. The amplitude of the oscillations decreases, and can be measured every five oscillations by judging the position of the blade against a ruler fixed alongside.

A graph of amplitude against time will show the characteristic exponential decrease. You can find the 'half-life' of this graph by determining the time it takes to decrease to half its initial amplitude (*figure 4.25*).

By changing the size of the card, it is possible to change the degree of damping, and hence alter the half-life of the motion.

High, low and critical damping

Damping can be very useful if we want to get rid of vibrations. For example, a car has springs

● **Figure 4.26** The springs and shock absorbers in a car suspension system form a damped system.

(*figure 4.26*), which make the ride much more comfortable for us when the car goes over a bump. However, we wouldn't want to spend every car journey vibrating up and down as a reminder of the last bump we went over. So the springs are damped by the shock absorbers, and we return rapidly to a smooth ride after every bump.

Figure 4.27 illustrates how oscillations change when the degree of damping is increased. With light damping, the amplitude of the oscillations decreases exponentially over a period of several oscillations. With heavy damping, there is no oscillation at all. There is an intermediate level of damping, called **critical damping**, when the oscillating mass returns to rest in the shortest possible time without any oscillation. A car's suspension system is usually adjusted so that the damping is slightly less than critical.

Energy and damping

Damping is achieved by introducing the force of friction into a mechanical system. In an undamped oscillation, the total energy of the oscillation remains constant. There is a regular interchange between potential and kinetic energy. By introducing friction, damping has the effect of removing energy from the oscillating system, and the amplitude and maximum speed of the oscillation decrease.

SAQ 4.17

a Sketch graphs to show how each of the following quantities changes during the course of a single complete oscillation of an undamped pendulum: kinetic energy; potential energy; total energy.

b How would your graphs be different for a critically damped pendulum?

Resonance

Resonance is an important physical phenomenon that can appear in a great many different situations. A tragic example is the Tacoma Narrows bridge disaster (*figure 4.28*). This suspension bridge in Washington State, USA, collapsed in a mild gale on 1 July 1940. The wind set up oscillating vortices of air around the bridge, which vibrated more and more violently until it broke up under the stress.

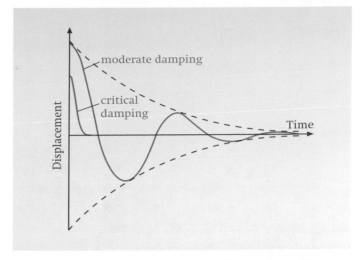

● **Figure 4.27** Different degrees of damping affect the time for which an object oscillates.

The bridge had been in use for just four months; engineers learnt a lot about how oscillations can build up when a mechanical structure is subjected to repeated forces.

You will have observed a much more familiar example of resonance when pushing a small child on a swing; the swing plus child has a natural frequency of oscillation; a small push on each swing results in the amplitude increasing until the child is swinging high in the air.

Observing resonance

Resonance can be observed with almost any oscillating system. The system is forced to oscillate at a particular frequency; if the forcing frequency happens to match the system's natural frequency of oscillation, the amplitude of the resulting oscillations can build up to become very large.

● **Figure 4.28** The Tacoma Narrows bridge collapsed in 1940, a victim of resonant failure.

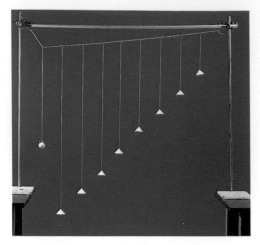

● **Figure 4.29** Barton's pendulums.

Barton's pendulums is a demonstration of this (*figure 4.29*). Several pendulums of different lengths hang from a horizontal string. Each has its own natural frequency of oscillation. The 'driver' pendulum at the end is different; it has a large mass at the end, and its length is equal to that of one of the others. When the driver is set swinging, the others gradually start to move. However, only the pendulum whose length matches that of the driver pendulum builds up a large amplitude.

What is going on here? All the pendulums are coupled together by the suspension. As the driver swings, it moves the suspension, which in turn moves the other pendulums. The frequency of the matching pendulum is the same as that of the driver, and so it gains energy and its amplitude gradually builds up. The other pendulums have different natural frequencies, so the driver has little effect.

In a similar way, if you were to push the child on the swing once every three-quarters of an oscillation, you would soon find that the swing was moving backwards as you tried to push it forwards, so that your push would slow it down.

You can observe resonance for yourself with a simple mass–spring system. You need a mass on the end of a spring (*figure 4.30*), chosen so that the mass oscillates up and down with a natural frequency of about 1 Hz. Now hold the top end of the spring and move your hand up and down rapidly, with an amplitude of a centimetre or two. Very little happens. Now move your hand up and down more slowly, close to 1 Hz. You should see the

● **Figure 4.30** Resonance with a mass on a spring.

mass oscillating with gradually increasing amplitude. Adjust your movements to the exact frequency of the natural vibrations of the mass and you will see the greatest effect.

Defining resonance

For resonance to occur, we must have a system that is capable of oscillating freely. We must also have some way in which the system is forced to oscillate. When the forcing frequency matches the natural frequency of the system, the amplitude of the oscillations grows dramatically.

If the driving frequency does not quite match the natural frequency, the amplitude of the oscillations will increase, but not to the same extent as when resonance is achieved. *Figure 4.31* shows how

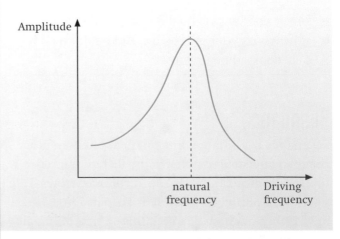

● **Figure 4.31** Maximum amplitude is achieved when the driving frequency matches the natural frequency of oscillation.

● **Figure 4.32** Resonance during the Peru earthquake in 1970 caused the collapse of these buildings.

the amplitude of oscillations depends on the driving frequency in the region close to resonance.

In resonance, energy is transferred from the driver to the resonating system more efficiently than when resonance does not occur. For example, in the case of the Tacoma Narrows bridge, energy was transferred from the wind to the bridge, causing very large-amplitude oscillations.

Resonance and damping

During earthquakes, buildings are forced to oscillate by the vibrations of the Earth. Resonance can occur, resulting in serious damage (*figure 4.32*). In regions of the world where earthquakes happen regularly, buildings may be built on foundations that absorb the energy of the shock waves. In this way, the vibrations are 'damped' so that the

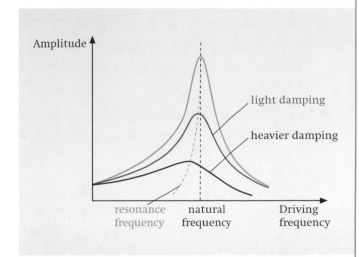

● **Figure 4.33** Damping reduces the amplitude of resonant vibrations.

amplitude of the oscillations cannot reach dangerous levels. This is an expensive business, and so far is restricted to the wealthier parts of the world.

Damping is thus useful if we want to reduce the damaging effects of resonance. *Figure 4.33* shows how damping alters the resonance response curve of *figure 4.31*. Notice that, as the degree of damping is increased, the amplitude of the resonant vibrations decreases. The resonance peak becomes broader. There is also an effect on the frequency at which resonance occurs, which becomes lower.

Using resonance

As we have seen, resonance can be a problem in mechanical systems. However, it can also be useful. For example, many musical instruments rely on resonance.

Resonance is not confined to mechanical systems. It is made use of in, for example,

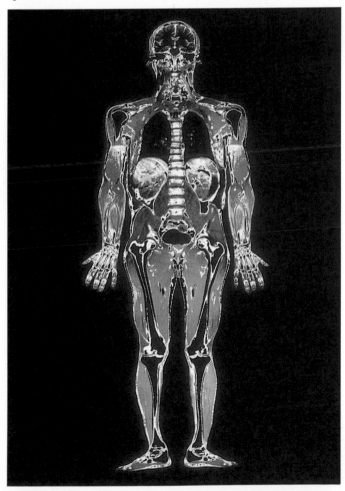

● **Figure 4.34** This magnetic resonance imaging (MRI) picture shows a whole human body. The bones show up with particular clarity.

microwave cooking. The microwaves used have a frequency that matches a natural frequency of vibration of water molecules. The water molecules in the food are forced to vibrate, and they absorb the energy of the radiation. The water gets hotter, and the absorbed energy spreads through the food and cooks or heats it.

Magnetic resonance imaging (MRI) is increasingly used in medicine to produce images such as *figure 4.34*, showing aspects of a patient's internal organs. Radio waves having a range of frequencies are used, and particular frequencies are absorbed by particular atomic nuclei. The frequency absorbed depends on the type of nucleus and on its surroundings. By analysing the absorption of the radio waves, a computer-generated image can be produced.

A radio or television also depends on resonance for its tuning circuitry. The aerial picks up signals of many different frequencies from many transmitters. The tuner can be adjusted to resonate at the frequency of the station you are interested in, and the circuit produces a large-amplitude signal for this frequency only.

SAQ 4.18

List three examples of situations where resonance is a problem, and three others where resonance is useful. In each case, say what the oscillating system is, and what forces it to resonate.

SUMMARY

◆ Many systems, mechanical and otherwise, will oscillate freely when stimulated.

◆ Some display a particular form of movement called *simple harmonic motion* (s.h.m.). For these systems, graphs of displacement, velocity and acceleration against time are sinusoidal curves – see *figure 4.35*.

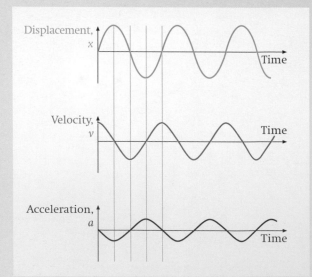

● **Figure 4.35** Graphs for s.h.m.

◆ During a single cycle of s.h.m., the phase changes by 2π radians. The angular frequency ω of the motion is related to its period T by $T = 2\pi/\omega$.

◆ In s.h.m., displacement can be represented as a function of time by equations of the form:

$$x = A \sin (2\pi f t) \quad \text{and} \quad x = A \cos (2\pi f t)$$

◆ A body executes simple harmonic motion if its acceleration is proportional to its displacement from a fixed point, and is directed towards that point. Acceleration is then related to displacement by $a = -(2\pi f)^2 x$.

◆ In s.h.m., there is a regular interchange between kinetic energy and potential energy.

◆ Resistive forces remove energy from an oscillating system. This is known as damping. Damping reduces the amplitude of oscillations.

◆ When an oscillating system is forced to vibrate close to its natural frequency, the amplitude of vibration increases rapidly. The amplitude is maximum when the forcing frequency matches the natural frequency; this is resonance.

◆ Resonance can be a problem, but it can also be very useful.

Questions

1   Explain why the motion of someone jumping up and down on a trampoline is not simple harmonic motion. (Their feet lose contact with the trampoline during each bounce.)

2   *Figure 4.36* shows the displacement–time graph for an oscillating mass. Use the graph to deduce the following quantities:
    a amplitude,   **b** period,   **c** frequency,
    d displacement at A,   **e** velocity at B, and
    f velocity at C.

3   An atom in a crystal vibrates back and forth with a frequency of 10^{14} Hz. The amplitude of its motion is 2×10^{-12} m.
    a Sketch a graph to show how the displacement of the atom varies during one cycle, assuming the motion is simple harmonic.
    b Use your graph to estimate the atom's greatest speed.

4   The pendulum of a grandfather clock swings from one side to the other in 1 s. Calculate:
    a the period of its motion,
    b the frequency, and
    c the angular frequency.
    d Write an equation of the form $a = -(2\pi f)^2 x$ to show how the pendulum weight's acceleration depends on its displacement.

5   *Figure 4.37* shows how the velocity of a 2 kg mass was found to vary during an investigation of the simple harmonic motion of a pendulum. Using information from the graph, estimate:
    a the mass's greatest velocity;
    b its greatest kinetic energy;
    c its greatest potential energy;
    d its greatest acceleration;
    e the greatest restoring force that acted on it.

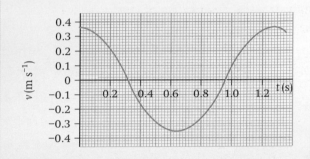

● **Figure 4.37** A velocity–time graph – see question 5.

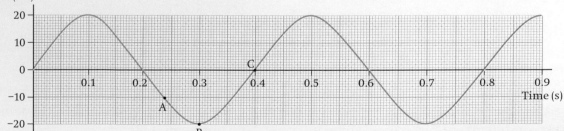

● **Figure 4.36** A displacement–time graph – see question 2.

CHAPTER 5

Gravitational fields

By the end of this chapter you should be able to:

1 understand a gravitational field as a field of force;

2 use field lines to represent a gravitational field;

3 recall and use Newton's law of gravitation for point masses in the form $F = Gm_1m_2/r^2$;

4 appreciate that, for a uniform spherical mass, the external field is equivalent to that of an equal point mass at the centre of the sphere;

5 define gravitational field strength as force per unit mass;

6 recall and use $g = F/m$;

7 recall and use $g = -GM/r^2$ for the gravitational field strength of a point mass M;

8 appreciate that, on the surface of the Earth, the magnitude of g is approximately constant and is equal to the acceleration of free fall.

Gravitational forces and fields

In chapter 3, we considered the motion of objects moving in circular paths, including objects orbiting under the influence of gravity. But what is gravity? How can we describe it, and how can we explain it?

We live our lives with the constant experience of gravity. We know that things fall when we let go of them. We know that we will return to the ground if we jump up in the air. We can live quite happily without thinking about why this is so. Once we start thinking about the force of gravity, which makes things fall, we may come up with some odd ideas.

Young children take it for granted that things fall. They are mystified if you ask them to explain it. They also take it for granted that things stay where they are on the ground; they don't think it necessary to talk about two balanced forces. Surely gravity disappears as soon as something stops falling?

You have probably learnt to show a stationary object with two forces acting on it: the force of

● **Figure 5.1** Skydivers balance the forces of gravity and air resistance.

gravity (its weight) and the normal force exerted by the ground (*figure 5.2*). A child does not have this mental picture, but these forces really do exist, as you would discover if you put your fingers underneath a large weight!

Children learn at school that there is a force called *gravity*, which holds us on to the Earth's

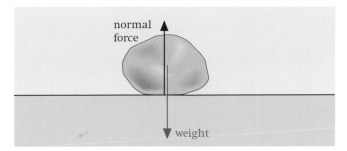

● **Figure 5.2** Two balanced forces on a stationary object.

surface. So, what causes this gravitational pull of the Earth? Try asking some children. Here are some of the ideas that they may come up with – many adults have similar ideas.

> 'Gravity is made by the Earth spinning. If it stopped spinning, we would all fall off.'
> 'If the Earth spun faster and faster, we would all fall off' (*figure 5.3*).
> 'Gravity is caused by the Earth's atmosphere pressing down on us.'
> 'If you dropped something on the Moon, it would just float about, because there is no air.'
> 'There is a giant magnet inside the Earth. It attracts us to the Earth.'

Gravity is not caused by the Earth's rotation, but it is true that, if the Earth spun a lot faster, gravity might not be strong enough to hold us on. Nor is gravity caused by the atmosphere. Perhaps

● **Figure 5.3** Hold on to the pole if you don't want to fall off!

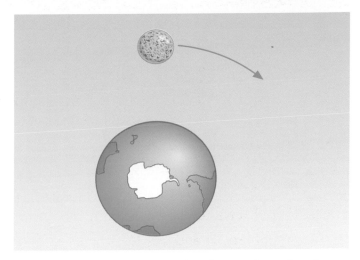

● **Figure 5.4** The Moon orbits the Earth under the influence of the Earth's gravity. In reality, the Moon is much further from Earth.

this idea comes from seeing astronauts in orbit above the Earth's atmosphere ('in space'), where they appear to be weightless. On the Moon, gravity is weaker than on the Earth, so objects fall more slowly and astronauts can jump higher.

Isaac Newton investigated the question of the Earth's gravity. In particular, he wondered whether the Earth's gravitational pull was confined to the Earth's surface, or whether it extended into space – as far as the Moon. Previously, it had been suggested that the Moon was held in its orbit around the Earth by magnetic attraction. After all, it was known that the Earth is magnetic, and that magnetic forces act at a distance.

Newton rejected this theory, partly on the grounds that the Sun is very hot, and magnets lose their magnetism when they are heated. Instead, he suggested that it is the mass of a body that causes it to attract other bodies. Objects fall towards the ground because their mass is attracted by the mass of the Earth. The Moon continues in its orbit round the Earth because their two masses attract each other (*figure 5.4*).

Newton's great achievement was to relate the falling of an apple to the ground to the 'falling' of the Moon as it orbits the Earth.

A field of force

The influence of the Earth's gravity extends well beyond its surface. The Moon stays in its orbit, 400 000 km away, because of the Earth's pull. The

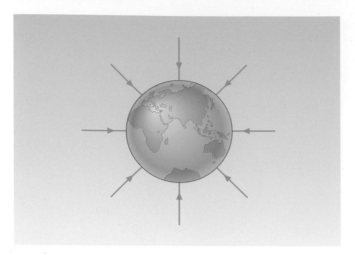

● **Figure 5.5** Lines of force represent the Earth's gravitational field.

Earth orbits the Sun at a distance of 150 000 000 km because of their attraction for each other. We can picture the Earth's influence by representing it as a field of force. Anywhere in this field, an object that has mass will feel a force attracting it towards the Earth.

To make the idea of a field of force seem rather more concrete, we can represent it by drawing lines of force, as shown in *figure 5.5*. (You will be familiar with this from drawings of magnetic fields between bar magnets.) The lines of force tell us two things:

■ The arrows on the lines show us the direction of the force on a mass placed in the field.
■ The spacing of the lines tells us about the strength of the field – the farther apart they are, the weaker the field.

The drawing of the Earth's field shows that all objects are attracted towards the *centre* of the Earth – even if they are below the surface of the Earth – and that the force gets weaker as you get farther away from the Earth's surface.

Roughly speaking, the Earth is a uniform spherical mass. The field outside the Earth (the external field) is the same as the field we would have if all of its mass was concentrated at its centre.

The drawing (*figure 5.6*) of the gravitational field inside a building on the Earth's surface shows that the force is directed downwards everywhere in the room, and (because the lines are parallel and evenly spaced) the force is the same at all points in the building. Your weight does not get significantly less when you go upstairs.

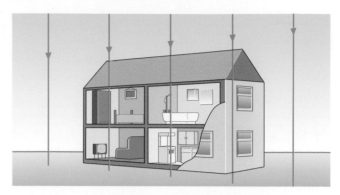

● **Figure 5.6** The Earth's gravitational field is uniform on the scale of a building.

We describe the Earth's field as **radial**, since the lines of force *diverge* (spread out) radially from its surface. However, on the scale of a building, the field is **uniform**, since it is equally strong at all points in the building.

Jupiter is a more massive planet than the Earth, and so we would represent its field by showing more closely spaced lines of force.

Newton's law of gravitation

Newton used his ideas about mass and gravity, and his knowledge of magnetic fields, to suggest a **law of gravitation** for two point masses (*figure 5.7*):

> Any two point masses attract each other with a force that is proportional to each of their masses and inversely proportional to the square of the distance between them.

Note that we have to talk about 'point masses' (or, alternatively, 'particles'). Things are more complicated if we think about solid bodies which occupy a volume of space. Each particle of one body attracts every particle of the other body, and we would have to add all these forces together to work out the force each body has on the other. Newton was able to show that two uniform

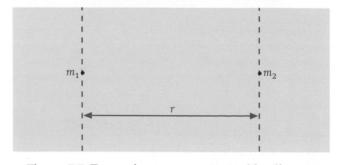

● **Figure 5.7** Two point masses separated by distance r.

spheres attract one another with a force which is the same as if their masses were concentrated at their centres (provided their radii are much smaller than their separation).

We can write Newton's law of gravitation in a mathematical form (where ∝ means 'proportional to'):

$$F \propto \frac{m_1 m_2}{r^2}$$

To make this into an equation, we introduce the gravitational constant G. We also need a minus sign (explained later):

$$F = -G \frac{m_1 m_2}{r^2}$$

In this equation, the symbols have the following meanings: F is the force of attraction of each body on the other, m_1 and m_2 are their masses, r is the distance between them (in fact, distance between their centres of mass – see below), and G is the gravitational constant, with the value $G = 6.67 \times 10^{-11} \, \text{N} \, \text{m}^2 \, \text{kg}^{-2}$.

Let us examine this equation to see why it seems reasonable.

First, each of the two masses is important. Your weight depends on your mass, and on the mass of the planet you happen to be standing on.

Secondly, the further away you are from the planet, the weaker its pull. Twice as far away gives one-quarter of the force. (This can be seen from the diagram of the lines of force in *figure 5.8*.) If the distance is doubled, the lines are spread out over four times the area, so their concentration is reduced to one-quarter. This is called an inverse square law – you may have come across a similar law for radiation such as light or γ-rays (gamma-rays) spreading out from a point source.

The minus sign represents the fact that this is an attractive force. The radial distance r is measured outwards from the attracting body; the force F acts in the opposite direction, and so our sign convention requires that F is negative.

Note that we measure distances from the centre of mass of one body to the centre of mass of the other (*figure 5.9*). We treat each body as if its mass was concentrated at one point. Note also that the two bodies attract each other with equal and opposite forces. (This is an example of a pair of equal and opposite forces, as required by Newton's third law of motion.) The Earth pulls on you with a force (your weight) directed towards the centre of the Earth; you attract the Earth with an equal force, directed away from its centre and towards you. Your pull on an object as massive as the Earth has little effect on it. The Sun's pull on the Earth, however, has a very significant effect.

SAQ 5.1
Calculate the gravitational force of attraction between two objects each of mass 0.1 kg, separated by 1 cm.

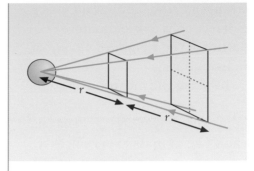

● **Figure 5.8** Lines of force are spread out over a greater area at greater distances.

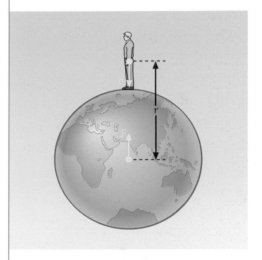

● **Figure 5.9** A person and the Earth exert equal and opposite attractions on each other.

SAQ 5.2
Estimate the gravitational force of attraction between two people sitting side-by-side on a park bench. How does this force compare with the gravitational force exerted on each of them by the Earth, i.e. their weight?

Gravitational field strength

We can describe how strong a gravitational field is by stating its field strength. We are used to this idea for objects on or near the Earth's surface – the field strength is the familiar quantity g. Its value is approximately $9.8 \, \text{m} \, \text{s}^{-2}$. The weight of a body of mass m is mg.

To make the meaning of g clearer, we should say that it is approximately $9.8 \, \text{N} \, \text{kg}^{-1}$. That is, each 1 kg of mass experiences a force of 9.8 N. Gravitational field strength is thus defined as:

> The gravitational field strength at a point is the force per unit mass exerted on a mass placed at that point.

This can be written in equation form as:

$$g = F/m \qquad \text{or} \qquad F = mg$$

The second arrangement of this equation should be very familiar to you.

Thus gravitational field strength is the answer to the question: 'What force would a 1 kg mass placed at a point in the field experience?' Since force is a vector quantity (having both size and direction), it follows that field strength is also a vector. We need to give its direction as well as its magnitude in order to specify it completely.

Now we have two ways of saying what force is exerted on a body of mass m by a second body of mass M:

$$F = mg \qquad \text{and} \qquad F = -G\frac{Mm}{r^2}$$

(Here we are using M and m as the masses of the large and small bodies respectively.) If we compare these two equations, we can see that

$$mg = -G\frac{Mm}{r^2} \quad \text{or} \quad g = -G\frac{M}{r^2}$$

Measuring G – weighing the Earth

The gravitational constant G has a very small value. We only notice the gravitational pull of very massive objects such as the Earth. We don't feel a noticeable gravitational attraction when another person walks past. This means that measuring G is rather difficult – Newton didn't manage it.

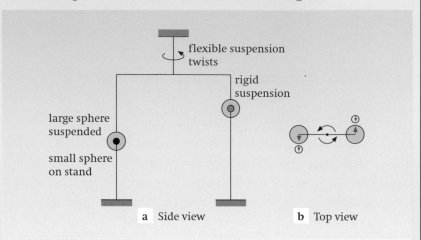

● **Figure 5.10** Cavendish's method for measuring G, using four lead spheres.

Henry Cavendish devised a method for measuring G some decades after Newton's death. The diagrams (*figure 5.10*) show how he did this. Details of Cavendish's lead spheres are as shown below:

Sphere	Mass (kg)	Radius (mm)
large	168	152
small	6.22	51

A Calculate the force of attraction between two masses, each of 1 kg, and separated by 10 cm.
B Why does this suggest that Cavendish chose to use lead spheres?
C Calculate the greatest gravitational force that Cavendish's spheres could have exerted on each other.
D Cavendish might have chosen an alternative arrangement, with a single large sphere hanging by a string, and attracted sideways by a single smaller sphere (*figure 5.11*). Calculate the largest angle θ that he might have tried to measure.
E Why was Cavendish's method using four spheres better than this alternative arrangement?
F Why did Cavendish have one large sphere hanging lower than the other?
G At the time of Cavendish's experiment, the radius of the Earth was known, but not its mass. Why do you think his experiment was described as 'weighing the Earth'?

● **Figure 5.11** An alternative method for measuring G.

So the gravitational field strength at a point depends on the mass M of the body causing the field, and the distance r of the point from the centre of gravity of the body.

Measuring g

Gravitational field strength g has units $m\,s^{-2}$; it is an acceleration. Another name for g is 'acceleration of free fall'. Any object that falls freely in a gravitational field has this acceleration, approximately $9.8\,m\,s^{-2}$ near the Earth's surface.

Figure 5.12 shows one method for determining g. When the switch is opened, the ball is released and the timer started. When the ball hits the pad, the timer is stopped. The time of fall t is related to the distance d by

$$d = \tfrac{1}{2}gt^2$$

The distance d is varied, and a graph of t^2 against d is plotted; g can be found from the gradient:

$$g = \frac{2}{\text{gradient}}$$

An alternative, less satisfactory, method is shown in *figure 5.13*. A weight with an attached card falls through a light gate. The light beam is broken by

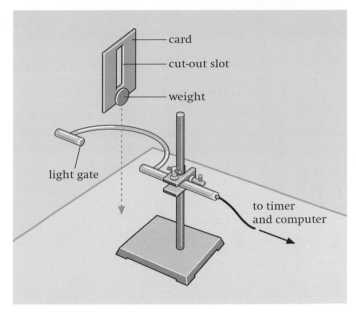

● **Figure 5.13** A less accurate method for measuring g using a light gate and timer.

the two sections of the card. The computer calculates the speed at which the card is moving as each section passes through; knowing the time interval between these speed measurements, it can then calculate the acceleration. It is worth carrying out both of these experiments, and trying to compare their accuracies. Why do you think the first method will give a more accurate value of g?

Remember that, if you are asked to describe an experiment in an examination, the theory of the experiment must be included. Although the computer gives you the answer, you must explain what measurements are needed and how the result is derived.

SAQ 5.3

A stone is dropped from rest from the top of a building. It takes 1.56 s to reach the ground, 12.0 m below. Use these values to determine g.

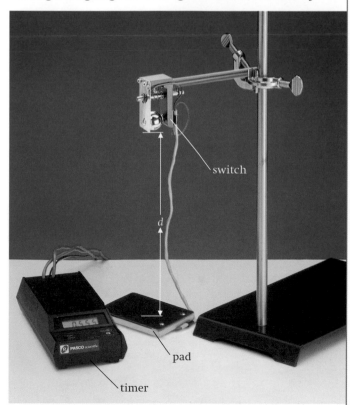

● **Figure 5.12** Measuring g by free fall.

SUMMARY

◆ The force of gravity is an attractive force between any two objects due to their masses.

◆ We can describe the gravitational effect of an object in terms of a gravitational field around it. The strength of the field at a point is the force exerted on unit mass placed in the field.

◆ The external field of a uniform spherical mass is the same as that of an equal point mass at the centre of the sphere.

◆ Newton's law gives the force between two point masses:

$$F = -G\frac{m_1 m_2}{r^2}$$

◆ Field strength at distance r from point mass M is given by:

$$g = -G\frac{M}{r^2}$$

This describes a radial field.

◆ On or near the surface of the Earth, the field is uniform: g is approximately constant; its value is equal to the acceleration of free fall.

Questions

You will need the following data to answer these questions:

	Mass (kg)	Radius (km)	Distance from Earth (km)
Earth	6.0×10^{24}	6400	
Moon	7.4×10^{22}	1740	3.8×10^5
Sun	2.0×10^{30}	700 000	1.5×10^8

1 Mount Everest is approximately 10 km high. How much less would a mountaineer of mass 100 kg (including backpack) weigh at its summit, compared to her weight at sea level? Would this difference be measurable with bathroom scales?

2 Calculate the gravitational field strength close to the surface of the Moon and close to the surface of the Sun. How does this help to explain why the Moon has only a thin atmosphere, while the Sun has a dense atmosphere?

3 Calculate the Earth's field strength at the Moon. What force does the Earth exert on the Moon? What is the Moon's acceleration towards the Earth?

4 Jupiter's mass is 320 times that of the Earth, and its radius is 11.2 times the Earth's. Calculate the acceleration of free fall close to the surface of Jupiter. (Take $g = 9.8\,\text{N}\,\text{kg}^{-1}$ on the Earth's surface.)

5 The Moon and the Sun both contribute to the tides on the Earth's oceans. Which has a bigger pull on each kilogram of sea-water, the Sun or the Moon?

6 Astrologers believe that the planets exert an influence on us, particularly at the moment of birth. (They don't necessarily believe that this is an effect of gravity!) Calculate the gravitational force on a 4 kg baby caused by Mars (mass of Mars $= 6.4 \times 10^{-3}$ kg) when the planet is at its closest to the Earth (100 000 000 km), and the force on the same baby due to its 50 kg mother at a distance of 0.5 m.

7 There is a point on the line joining the centres of the Earth and the Moon where the gravitational field strength is zero. Is this point closer to the Earth or to the Moon? How far is it from the centre of the Earth?

CHAPTER 6

Electric fields

By the end of this chapter you should be able to:

1 understand an electric field as a field of force;

2 use field lines to represent an electric field;

3 define electric field strength as force per unit charge;

4 recall and use $E = F/Q$;

5 recall and use $E = V/d$ for the magnitude of the uniform electric field strength between charged parallel plates;

6 recall and use Coulomb's law for point charges in a vacuum in the form $F = kQ_1Q_2/r^2$ where $k = 1/(4\pi\varepsilon_0)$;

7 recall and use $E = kQ/r^2$ for the electric field strength of a point charge;

8 appreciate that, for a charged and isolated conducting sphere, the external field is equivalent to that of a point charge at the centre of the sphere;

9 recognise the similarities and differences between electric fields and gravitational fields.

Attraction and repulsion

You will already know a bit about electric (or electrostatic) fields, from your experience of static electricity in everyday life, and from your studies in science. In this chapter, you will learn how we can make these ideas more formal.

This chapter follows a parallel course to our exploration of ideas about gravity in chapter 5. We will look at how electric forces are caused, and how we can represent their effects in terms of electric fields. Then we will find mathematical ways of calculating electric forces and field strengths.

Static electricity can be useful – it is important in the process of photocopying, in dust precipitation to clean up industrial emissions, and in crop-spraying, among many other applications. It can also be a nuisance. Who hasn't experienced a shock, perhaps when getting out of a car or when touching a door handle? Static electric charge has built up and gives us a shock when it discharges.

● **Figure 6.1** Lightning flashes, dramatic evidence of natural electric fields.

We explain these effects in terms of electric charge. Simple observations in the laboratory give us the following picture:

■ Objects are usually electrically neutral (uncharged), but they may become electrically charged, for example when one material is rubbed against another.

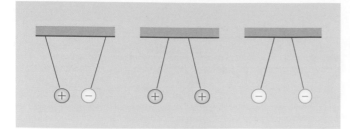

● **Figure 6.2** Attraction and repulsion between electric charges.

■ There are two types of charge, which we call positive and negative.
■ Opposite types of charge attract one another; like charges repel (*figure 6.2*).
■ A charged object may also be able to attract an uncharged one; this is as a result of electro-static induction.

These observations are macroscopic; that is, they are descriptions of phenomena that we can observe in the laboratory, without having to consider what is happening on the microscopic scale, at the level of particles such as atoms and electrons. However, we can give a more subtle explanation if we consider the microscopic picture of static electricity.

Matter may be thought to be made up of three types of particles: electrons (which have negative charge), protons (positive) and neutrons (neutral). An uncharged object has equal numbers of protons and electrons, whose charges therefore cancel out.

When one material is rubbed against another, there is friction between them, and electrons may be rubbed off one material on to the other (*figure 6.3*). The material that has gained electrons is now negatively charged, and the other material is positively charged.

If a positively charged object is brought close to an uncharged one, the electrons in the second

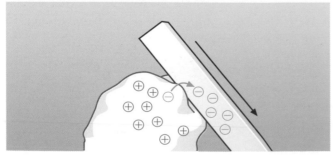

● **Figure 6.3** Friction can transfer electrons from one material to another.

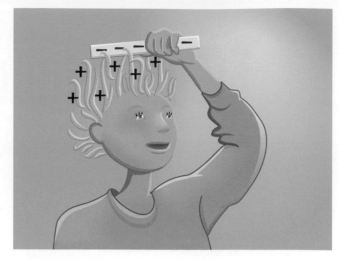

● **Figure 6.4** A hair-raising experience.

object may be attracted; we observe this as a force of attraction between the two objects. (This is electrostatic induction.)

Note that it is usually electrons that are involved in moving within a material, or from one material to another. This is because electrons, which are on the outside of atoms, are less strongly held within a material than are protons; they may be free to move about within a material (like the conduction electrons in a metal), or they may be relatively weakly bound within atoms.

Investigating electric fields

If you rub a strip of plastic so that it becomes charged, and then hold it close to your hair, you feel your hair being pulled upwards (*figure 6.4*). The influence of the charged plastic spreads into the space around it; we say that there is an

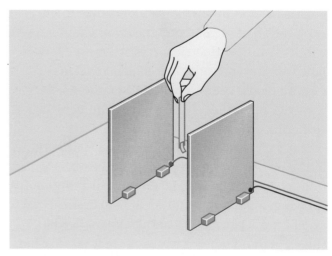

● **Figure 6.5** Investigating the electric field between two charged metal plates.

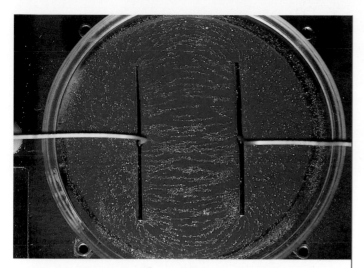

● **Figure 6.6** Apparatus showing uniform electric field.

electric field around the charge. In order to produce an electric field, we need unbalanced charges (as with the charged plastic). In order to observe the field, we need to put something in it that will respond to the field (as your hair responded). There are two simple ways in which you can do this in the laboratory.

The first uses a charged strip of gold foil, attached to an insulating handle (*figure 6.5*). The second uses grains of a material such as semolina; these line up in an electric field, rather like the way in which iron filings line up in a magnetic field (*figure 6.6*).

Representing electric fields

We can draw electric fields in much the same way that we can draw gravitational and magnetic fields, by showing lines of force. The three most important shapes are shown in *figure 6.7*.

As with gravitational fields, this representation tells us two things about the field: its direction (from the direction of the lines), and how strong it

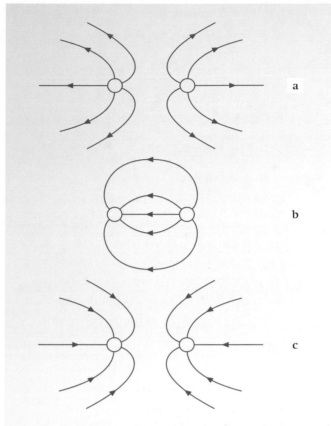

● **Figure 6.8** Electric fields between charges.

is (from their separation). The arrows go from positive to negative; they tell us the direction of the force on a positive charge in the field.

A uniform field has the same strength at all points. This is like the field found, for example, between the parallel plates of a charged capacitor.

A radial field spreads outwards in all directions, for example from a point charge or from a charged sphere.

We can draw electric fields for other arrangements. Note the symbol for an earth, which is assumed to be uncharged (i.e. at zero volts).

SAQ 6.1

Which of the three diagrams in *figure 6.8* represents two positive charges repelling each other? Which represents two negative charges? Which represents two opposite charges?

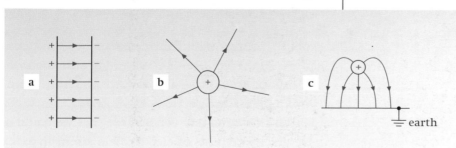

● **Figure 6.7** Lines of force representing **a** a uniform field, **b** a radial field, and **c** the field of a positive charge close to earth.

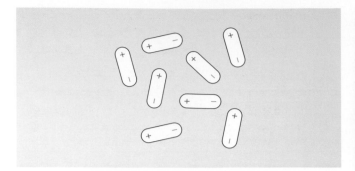

● **Figure 6.9** Polar molecules.

SAQ 6.2

Many molecules are described as polar; that is, they have regions that are positively or negatively charged, though they are neutral overall. Draw a diagram to show how sausage–shaped polar molecules like those shown in *figure 6.9* might realign themselves in a solid.

Electric field strength

For a gravitational field, we defined its strength at a point as being the force exerted on a kilogram mass placed at that point. Similarly, for electric fields, we can define electric field strength E as follows:

> The **electric field strength** at a point is the force per unit charge exerted on a positive charge placed at that point.

So to define electric field strength, we imagine putting a positive test charge in the field and measuring the electric force that it feels (*figure 6.10*). (If you have used a charged gold leaf to

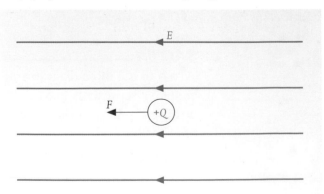

● **Figure 6.10** A field of strength E exerts force F on charge $+Q$.

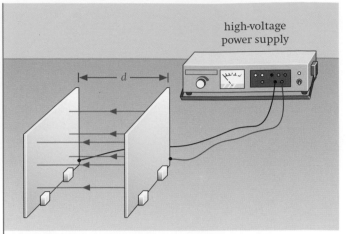

● **Figure 6.11** A uniform field exists between two parallel charged plates.

investigate a field, this illustrates the principle of testing the field with a charge.)

From this definition, we can write an equation for E:

$$E = \frac{F}{Q}$$

You should be able to see that the unit of electric field strength is the newton per coulomb ($N\,C^{-1}$).

The strength of a uniform field

You can set up a uniform field between two parallel metal plates by connecting them to the terminals of a high-voltage power supply (*figure 6.11*). The strength of the field between them depends on two factors:

■ The higher the voltage V between them, the stronger the field.
■ The greater their separation d, the weaker the field.

These factors can be combined to give an equation for E:

$$E = -\frac{V}{d}$$

(Note the minus sign. This is necessary because, in *figure 6.11*, the voltage V increases towards the right while the force F acts towards the left. V and F are in opposite directions.)

From this equation, you can see that we could have given the units of electric field strength as volts per metre ($V\,m^{-1}$).

$$1\,V\,m^{-1} = 1\,N\,C^{-1}$$

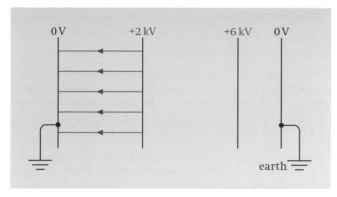

● **Figure 6.12** An arrangement of parallel plates.

SAQ 6.3

Figure 6.12 shows an arrangement of parallel plates, each at a different voltage. The electric field lines are shown between the first pair. Copy and complete the diagram.

SAQ 6.4

Air is usually a good insulator. However, a spark can jump through dry air when the electric field strength is greater than about $40\,000\,V\,cm^{-1}$. This is called electrical breakdown. The spark shows that electrical charge is passing through the air – a current is flowing. (Do not confuse this with a chemical spark such as you might see when watching fireworks; in that case, small particles of a chemical substance are burning quickly.)

a A van de Graaff generator (*figure 6.13*) is found to be able to make sparks jump across a 4 cm gap. What is the voltage produced by the generator?

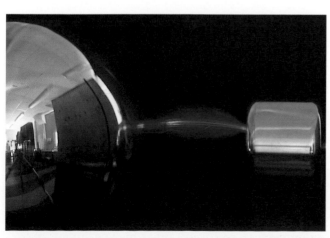

● **Figure 6.13** A Van de Graaff generator produces voltages sufficient to cause sparks in air.

b The highest voltage reached by the live wire of a conventional mains supply is 325 V. In theory (but DO NOT try this) how close would you have to get to a live wire to get a shock from it?

c Estimate the voltage of a thunder–cloud from which lightning strikes the ground 100 m below.

Force on a charge

Now we can calculate the force F on a charge Q in the uniform field between two parallel plates. We have to combine the general equation for field strength $E = F/Q$ with the equation for the strength of a uniform field $E = -V/d$. This gives

$$F = QE = -\frac{QV}{d}$$

For an electron with charge $-e$, this becomes

$$F = \frac{eV}{d}$$

Figure 6.14 shows a situation where this force is important. A beam of electrons is entering the space between two charged parallel plates. How will the beam move?

We have to think about the force on a single electron. In the diagram, the upper plate is negative relative to the lower plate, and so the electron is pushed downwards. (You can think of this simply as the negatively charged electron being attracted by the positive plate, and repelled by the negative plate.)

If the electron was stationary, it would accelerate directly downwards. However, in this example, the electron is moving to the right. Its horizontal velocity will be unaffected by the force; however, as it moves sideways, it will also accelerate

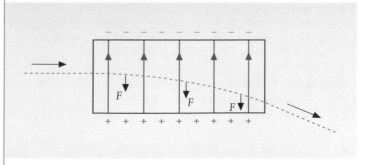

● **Figure 6.14** The parabolic path of a moving electron in a uniform electric field.

downwards. It will follow a curved path, as shown. This curve is a parabola.

Note that the force on the electron is the same at all points between the plates, and it is always in the same direction (downwards, in this example).

[This situation is equivalent to a ball being thrown horizontally in the Earth's uniform gravitational field, (figure 6.15). It continues to move at a steady speed horizontally, but at the same time it accelerates downwards. The result is the familiar curved trajectory shown. For the electron described above, the force of gravity is tiny, negligible compared to the electric force on it.]

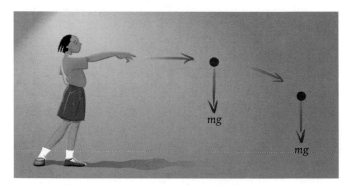

● **Figure 6.15** A ball, thrown in the uniform gravitational field of the Earth, follows a parabolic path.

SAQ 6.5

A particle of charge $+2\,\mu\text{C}$ is placed between two parallel plates, $10\,\text{cm}$ apart, and with a potential difference of $5\,\text{kV}$ between them. Calculate the field strength between the plates, and the force exerted on the charge.

SAQ 6.6

We are used to experiencing accelerations that are usually less than $10\,\text{m s}^{-2}$. For example, when we fall, our acceleration is about $9.8\,\text{m s}^{-2}$. When a car turns a corner sharply at speed, its acceleration is unlikely to be more than $5\,\text{m s}^{-2}$. However, if you were an electron, you would be used to experiencing much greater accelerations than this.

Calculate the acceleration of an electron (charge $-e = -1.6 \times 10^{-19}\,\text{C}$, mass $m_e = 9.11 \times 10^{-31}\,\text{kg}$) in a television tube where the electric field strength is $50\,000\,\text{V cm}^{-1}$.

Measuring e

The charge e of an electron is very small ($-1.6 \times 10^{-19}\,\text{C}$) and difficult to measure. The American physicist Robert Millikan devised an ingenious way to do it. He used tiny droplets of oil, charged by friction, and suspended in a uniform electric field (figure 6.16).

If a particular droplet was stationary, he knew that the electric force acting on it upwards was equal to the force of gravity acting downwards on it. (He managed to find the weight of these tiny droplets by measuring their terminal velocity as they fell through the air, another ingenious part of his technique.)

Study the diagram, and use the information it contains to help you answer the questions that follow.

A The upper plate in the diagram is connected to the positive terminal of the supply. What does this tell you about the sign of the charge on the droplet?

B What is the electric field strength between the two plates?

C What is the weight of the droplet?

D What is the electric force acting on it when it is stationary?

E What is the charge on the droplet? What is the significance of this value?

F In Millikan's experiment, he included a source of β-radiation (β is Greek beta). (This kind of radiation is simply electrons.) When an oil droplet was irradiated, it was suddenly observed to start moving upwards. What explanation can you give for this?

G Assuming that the charge on the oil droplet had increased because it had captured a single electron, what new value of voltage between the plates would you now expect to hold it stationary?

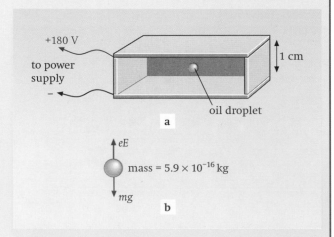

● **Figure 6.16** Millikan's oil-drop experiment to determine the charge of an electron.

SAQ 6.7

a Explain how the electric force on a charged particle could be used to separate a beam of electrons and positrons into two separate beams. (Positrons are positively charged electrons, produced in radioactive decay.)

b Explain how this effect could be used to identify different ions that have different masses and charges.

Coulomb's law

Charles Coulomb was a French physicist. In 1785 he proposed a law that describes the force that one charged particle exerts on another. This law, as you might expect, is remarkably similar to Newton's law of gravitation. **Coulomb's law** says that:

> Any two point charges exert a force on each other that is proportional to the product of their charges and inversely proportional to the square of the distance between them.

We can write this in a mathematical form:

$$F = \frac{kQ_1Q_2}{r^2}$$

In this equation, the symbols have the following meanings (see *figure 6.17*): F is the force of each charge on the other, Q_1 and Q_2 are the charges and r is the distance between them. The constant of proportionality is

$$k = 1/(4\pi\varepsilon_0)$$

where ε_0 is known as the **permittivity of free space** – a measure of how easy it is for an electric field to pass through space (ε is the Greek letter epsilon).

Since the value of ε_0 is approximately $8.85 \times 10^{-12}\,\text{F}\,\text{m}^{-1}$, it follows that, numerically,

$1/(4\pi\varepsilon_0) = 9 \times 10^9$ (approximately), and we can write Coulomb's law as

$$F = \frac{9 \times 10^9 \times Q_1Q_2}{r^2}$$

(This approximation can be useful for making rough calculations, but more precise calculations require the value of ε_0 given above to be used.)

Following your earlier study of Newton's law of gravitation, you should not be surprised by this relationship. The force depends on each of the properties producing it (in this case, the charges), and it is an inverse square law – if the particles are twice as far apart, the force is a quarter of its previous value (*figure 6.18*).

So far we have considered point charges. If we are considering charged spheres we measure the distance from the centre of one to the centre of the other – they behave as if their charge was all concentrated at the centre, even though it is probably uniformly spread over the surface.

Note also that, if we have a positive and a negative charge, then the force F is negative. We interpret this as an attraction. Positive forces, as between two like charges, are repulsive. In gravity, we only have attraction.

Investigating Coulomb's law

It is quite tricky to investigate the force between charged particles, because charge tends to leak away into the air during the course of any experiment. Also, the amount of charge we can investigate is difficult to measure, and usually small, giving rise to small forces.

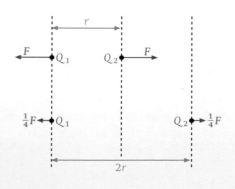

● **Figure 6.18** Double the separation results in one-quarter of the force.

● **Figure 6.17** The variables involved in Coulomb's law.

Figure 6.19 shows one way of doing this. As one charged sphere is lowered down towards the other, their separation decreases and so the force increases, giving an increased reading on the balance.

Field strength in a radial field

Field strength E is defined by the equation $E = F/Q$. So to find the field strength near a point charge (or outside a charged sphere), we have to picture a positive test charge placed in the field, and work out the force per unit charge on it. We can find this from Coulomb's law, with the second charge = 1. We get

$$E = \frac{Q}{4\pi\varepsilon_0 r^2} = \frac{kQ}{r^2}$$

This tells us the field strength E at distance r from a point charge Q.

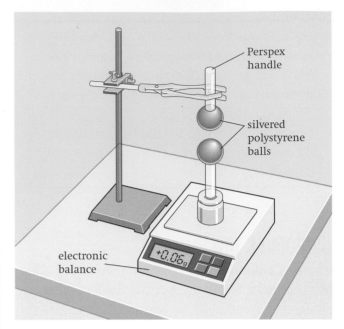

● **Figure 6.19** Investigating Coulomb's law.

Comprehension

The drawing in *figure 6.20* shows a thunder-cloud above the Earth. The electric field it creates is shown by the lines of force.

Many tall buildings have lightning conductors. These help to conduct away any lightning that strikes the building. They also help to discharge thunder-clouds without light-ning striking.

If you have a Van de Graaff generator running so that sparks ('lightning') are jumping to a nearby earthed sphere, you can simulate the effect of a lightning conductor. Bring up the sharp point of an earthed pin towards the dome of

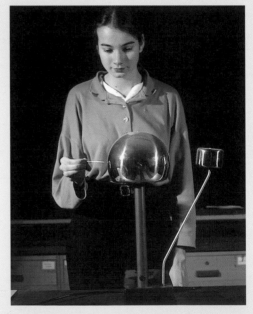

● **Figure 6.21** The effect of a sharp point in an electric field.

the generator (*figure 6.21*); the sparks will stop. A very small current is flowing through the air to the pin and through the earthing connection. Remove the pin and the sparks start again.

A Study the diagram of the thunder-cloud. Where is the electric field strongest? Explain your answer by referring to the field lines.

B Where is lightning more likely to strike?

C Draw a diagram to show why the sharp pin prevents the generator from sparking.

● **Figure 6.20** The electric field below a thunder-cloud.

Note that, for a charged metal sphere, the external field is the same as if all of the charge was concentrated at its centre.

You will need the data below to answer the self-assessment questions.

	Charge	Mass
proton	$+1.6 \times 10^{-19}$ C	1.67×10^{-27} kg

$\varepsilon_0 = 8.85 \times 10^{-12}$ F m^{-1}

$G = 6.67 \times 10^{-11}$ N m^2 kg^{-2}

Gravitational fields	Electric fields
All gravitational fields field strength $g = F/m$ i.e. field strength is force per unit *mass*	All electric fields field strength $E = F/Q$ i.e. field strength is force per unit *charge*
Units F in N, g in N kg^{-1} or m s^{-2}	Units F in N, E in N C^{-1} or V m^{-1}
Uniform gravitational fields parallel field lines g = constant	Uniform electric fields parallel field lines $E = V/d$ = constant
Spherical gravitational fields radial field lines force given by Newton's law: $F = Gm_1m_2/r^2$ field strength is therefore: $E = Gm/r^2$	Spherical electric fields radial field lines force given by Coulomb's law: $F = kQ_1Q_2/r^2$, where $k = 1/(4\pi\varepsilon_0)$ field strength is therefore: $E = kQ/r^2$
Vector forces only gravitational attraction, no repulsion	Vector forces both electrical attraction and repulsion are possible (because of positive and negative charges)

● **Table 6.1** Gravitational and electric fields compared.

SAQ 6.8
Two protons in the nucleus of an atom are separated by 10^{-15} m. Calculate the force of electro-static repulsion between them, and the force of gravitational attraction between them, assuming they behave as point charges and masses. Is gravity enough to balance the electric repulsion tending to separate them? What does this suggest to you about the forces between protons in a nucleus?

SAQ 6.9
A van de Graaff generator produces sparks when the field strength at its surface is 40 000 V cm^{-1}. If the diameter of the sphere is 40 cm, what is the charge on it?

Comparing gravitational and electric fields

There are obvious similarities between the ideas we have used in this chapter to describe electric fields and those we used in chapter 5 for gravitational fields. This can be helpful, or it can be confusing! The summary given in *table 6.1* is intended to help you to sort them out.

SUMMARY

◆ An electric field is a field of force, and can be represented by field lines.

◆ The strength of the field is the force acting per unit charge placed at a point in the field.

◆ In a uniform field (e.g. between two parallel charged plates), the force on a charge is the same at all points; the strength of the field is given by $E = -V/d$.

◆ A point charge Q gives rise to a radial field, of field strength $E = Q/(4\pi\varepsilon_0 r^2)$.

◆ These relationships are derived from Coulomb's law for the force between two point charges: $F = Q_1Q_2/(4\pi\varepsilon_0 r^2)$.

Questions

1 An electron is situated in a uniform electric field. The electric force that acts on it is 8×10^{-16} N. What is the strength of the electric field?
[Electronic charge $e = 1.6 \times 10^{-19}$ C]

2 In *figure 6.22*, two parallel plates are shown, separated by 25 cm.
   a Copy the diagram and draw field lines to represent the field between the plates.
   b What is the potential difference between points A and B?
   c What is the electric field strength at C, and at D?
   d Calculate the electric force on a charge of +5 µC placed at C. In which direction does the force act?

3 A metal sphere of radius 20 cm carries a positive electric charge of 20 µC.
   a What is the electric field strength at a distance of 25 cm from the centre of the sphere?
   b An identical metal sphere carrying a negative charge of 10 µC is placed next to the first sphere. There is a gap of 10 cm between them. Calculate the electric force that each sphere exerts on the other.

   [Permittivity of free space $\varepsilon_0 = 8.85 \times 10^{-12}$ F m^{-1}]

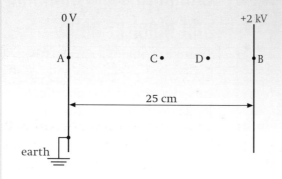

● **Figure 6.22** Two parallel, charged plates.

CHAPTER 7

Capacitors

By the end of this chapter you should be able to:

1 define capacitance and the farad;

2 recall and use $C = Q/V$;

3 use the area under a graph of potential difference against charge to derive $W = \frac{1}{2}QV$ and hence $W = \frac{1}{2}CV^2$ for the energy stored in a charged capacitor;

4 recall and use $W = \frac{1}{2}QV$, $W = \frac{1}{2}CV^2$ and $W = \frac{1}{2}Q^2/C$;

5 use formulae for the capacitance of capacitors in parallel and in series;

6 describe the discharge of a capacitor through a resistor;

7 sketch graphs showing the variation with time of the potential difference, charge stored and current during this discharge;

8 use equations of the form $x = x_0\, e^{-t/CR}$ for the discharge of a capacitor;

9 appreciate the practical importance of time constant τ for the discharge of a capacitor through a resistor;

10 recall $\tau = CR$ for the time constant of a capacitor–resistor circuit.

Using capacitors

Capacitors are components used in many electrical and electronic circuits. They store electrical charge (and energy), and this means that they have many valuable applications. For example, capacitors are used in computers; they are charged up in normal use, and then they gradually discharge if there is a power failure, so that the computer will operate long enough to save valuable data. The photograph (*figure 7.1*) shows a variety of sizes and shapes of capacitors.

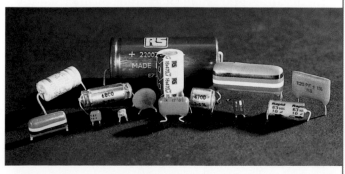

● **Figure 7.1** A variety of capacitors.

All capacitors have two leads, connected to two metal plates where the charge is stored. Between the plates is an insulating material called the dielectric. F*igure 7.2* shows a schematic version of the construction of a capacitor; in practice, many have a spiral 'Swiss-roll' form.

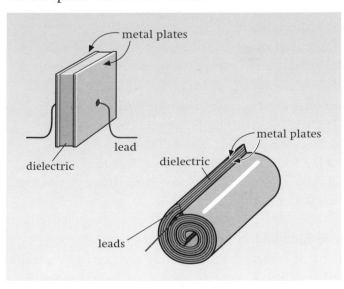

● **Figure 7.2** The construction of some capacitors.

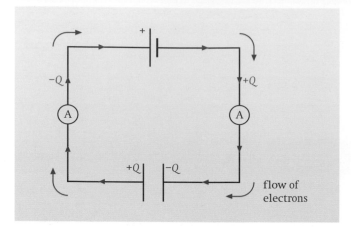

● **Figure 7.3** The flow of charge when a capacitor is charged up.

To charge up a capacitor, it must be connected to a voltage supply. This pushes electrons on to one plate; electrons are then repelled from the opposite plate, leaving it positively charged. Note that there is a flow of electrons all the way round the circuit until the capacitor is charged up to the supply voltage V (*figure 7.3*).

[Note: The convention is that current is the flow of positive charge. Here, it is free electrons that flow. Electrons are negatively charged; the current flows in the opposite direction to the electrons – see *figure 7.4*.]

If one plate of the capacitor stores charge $+Q$, then the other stores an equal and opposite charge $-Q$. We say that the charge stored is Q. To make the capacitor store more charge, we would have to use a higher voltage. If we connect the leads of the charged capacitor together, electrons flow back around the circuit and the capacitor is now discharged.

You can observe a capacitor discharging as follows: Connect the two leads of a capacitor to the terminals of a battery. Disconnect, and then reconnect the leads to a light-emitting diode (LED). It is best to have a protective resistor in series with the LED. The LED will glow as the capacitor discharges. This may last for some time, as only a small current will flow through the high resistance of the LED.

The meaning of capacitance

Look at some capacitors. They are marked with the value of their capacitance; as you might expect, capacitors of the same type but having greater

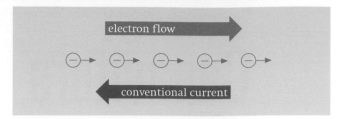

● **Figure 7.4** A flow of electrons to the right constitutes a conventional current to the left.

volume have greater capacitance. What do these numbers mean? Capacitance tells us about how good a capacitor is at storing charge. Since the amount of charge stored (Q) also depends on the voltage V used to charge up the capacitor, we have to take this into account. The equation that defines capacitance C is

$$C = Q/V \qquad \text{or} \qquad Q = CV$$

From the first form of this equation, you can see that:

> The capacitance of a capacitor is the charge stored per unit of potential difference across it.

The second form shows that the charge stored depends on two things: the capacitance C of the capacitor and the voltage V (double the voltage stores double the charge).

Units of capacitance

The unit of capacitance is the **farad**, F. From the equation that defines capacitance, you can see that this must be the same as the units of charge (coulombs, C) divided by volts (V):

$$1\,\text{F} = 1\,\text{C}\,\text{V}^{-1}$$

In practice, a farad is a large unit. Few capacitors are big enough to store 1 C when charged up to 1 V. If you look at some capacitors, you will see their values marked in picofarads or microfarads (pF or μF) (μ is Greek mu; sometimes manufacturers write uF or MFD):

$$1\,\text{pF} = 10^{-12}\,\text{F} \qquad 1\,\mu\text{F} = 10^{-6}\,\text{F}$$

Other markings on capacitors

Many capacitors are marked with their highest safe working voltage. If you exceed this value, then charge may leak across between the plates, and the dielectric will cease to be an insulator.

Some capacitors (electrolytic ones) must be connected correctly in a circuit. They have an indication to show which end must be connected to the positive of the supply. Failure to connect correctly will damage the capacitor, and can be dangerous.

SAQ 7.1

How much charge is stored by a 200 µF capacitor charged up to 15 V? Give your answer in microcoulombs (µC) and in coulombs (C).

SAQ 7.2

What is the capacitance of a capacitor that stores 0.001 C of charge when charged to 500 V? Give your answer in farads (F), microfarads (µF) and picofarads (pF).

SAQ 7.3

What is the average current required to charge a 50 µF capacitor to 10 V in 0.01 s?

Measuring capacitance

In order to determine the capacitance of a capacitor, you need to find out how much charge it stores at a particular voltage. (Remember that capacitance is the charge stored per unit potential difference.) One way to measure charge is to measure the current flowing into the capacitor as it charges up, and the time for which the current flows.

Figure 7.5 shows a suitable circuit for this. Because the current changes – it decreases gradually – it is necessary to record the current at regular intervals of time. This results in a graph like that in *figure 7.6*. The charge stored by the

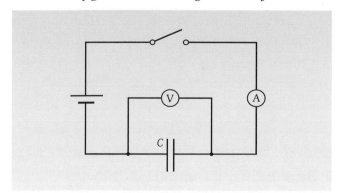

● **Figure 7.5** Circuit for measuring capacitance.

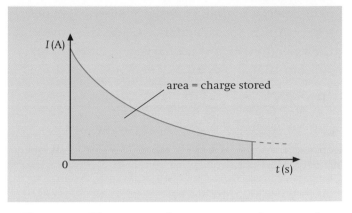

● **Figure 7.6** The area under a current–time graph represents the charge stored by a capacitor.

capacitor is the area under the graph. This is found by counting squares, or by cutting out and weighing the required area. (Weigh a complete sheet of graph paper to find the mass of one square.)

Note that this method is only suitable for fairly large values of capacitance, say, 100 µF or more; small capacitors store only a small amount of charge, so the current that flows when they are being charged is correspondingly small.

SAQ 7.4

A student charges up a capacitor C through a resistor, and records the current I flowing at intervals of 10 s. The results are shown below. The voltage across the capacitor after 60 s was 8.5 V. Plot a suitable graph, and use it to estimate the value of C.

t (s)	0	10	20	30	40	50	60
I (µA)	200	142	102	75	51	37	27

Energy stored in a capacitor

When you charge a capacitor, you use a power supply to push electrons on to one plate and off the other. The power supply does work on the electrons, so their potential energy increases. You recover this energy when you discharge the capacitor.

If you charge up a large capacitor (1000 µF or more) to 6 V, disconnect it from the supply, and then connect it across a 6 V lamp, you can see the energy as it is released from the capacitor. The lamp will flash briefly. Clearly, such a capacitor does not store much energy when it is charged.

The energy W that a capacitor stores depends on two things: its capacitance C and the potential difference to which it is charged, V. There is an equation that shows how W depends on C and V:

$$W = \tfrac{1}{2}CV^2$$

Suppose we charge a $2000\,\mu F$ capacitor to a p.d. of $10\,V$. How much energy is stored? Using $W = \tfrac{1}{2}CV^2$ we obtain

$$W = \tfrac{1}{2} \times 2000 \times 10^{-6} \times 10^2 = 0.1\,J$$

This is a small amount of energy – compare it with the energy stored by a rechargeable battery, typically of the order of $10\,000\,J$. A charged capacitor will not do to keep a personal stereo running for any length of time.

Because W depends on V^2, it follows that doubling the charging voltage means that four times as much energy is stored. (This comes about because, when you double the voltage, not only is twice as much charge stored, but it is stored at twice the voltage.)

Investigating energy stored

If you have a sensitive joulemeter (capable of measuring millijoules, mJ), you can investigate the equation for energy stored. A suitable circuit is shown in *figure 7.7*.

The capacitor is charged up when the switch connects it to the power supply. When the switch is altered, the capacitor discharges through the joulemeter. (It is important to wait for the capacitor to discharge completely.) The joulemeter will indicate the amount of energy released.

By using capacitors with different values of C, and by changing the charging voltage V, you can investigate how the energy stored W depends on C and V.

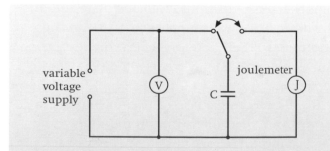

● **Figure 7.7** With the switch to the left, the capacitor charges up; to the right, it discharges through the joulemeter.

SAQ 7.5

Calculate the energy stored in each of the following cases:

a a $5000\,\mu F$ capacitor charged to $5\,V$;
b a $5000\,pF$ capacitor charged to $5\,V$;
c a $200\,\mu F$ capacitor charged to $230\,V$.

SAQ 7.6

Which stores more charge, a $100\,\mu F$ capacitor charged to $200\,V$ or a $200\,\mu F$ capacitor charged to $100\,V$? Which stores more energy? (You may be able to answer this question simply by considering the equations $Q = CV$ and $W = \tfrac{1}{2}CV^2$, rather than performing detailed calculations.)

SAQ 7.7

A $10\,000\,\mu F$ capacitor is charged to $12\,V$, and then connected across a lamp rated at $12\,V$, $36\,W$.

a How much energy is stored by the capacitor?
b If this energy was dissipated in the lamp at a steady rate, for how long could it keep the lamp fully lit?

Deriving the formula

In order to charge up a capacitor, work must be done to push electrons on to one plate and off the other (*figure 7.8*). At first, there is only a small amount of negative charge on the left-hand plate. Adding more electrons is relatively easy, because there is not much repulsion. As the charge stored increases, the repulsion between the electrons on the plate and the new electrons increases, and a greater amount of work must be done to increase the charge stored.

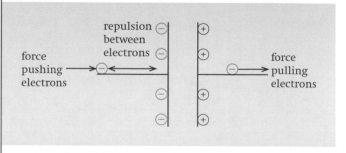

● **Figure 7.8** When a capacitor is charged, work must be done to push additional electrons against the repulsion of the existing electrons.

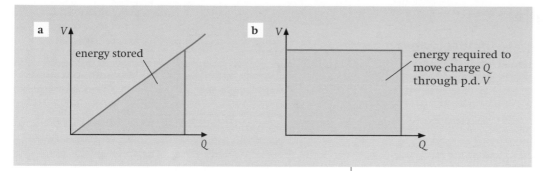

● **Figure 7.9** The area under a voltage–charge graph gives a quantity of energy. The area in **a** shows the energy stored in a capacitor; the area in **b** shows the energy required to drive a charge through a p.d.

This can be seen qualitatively in *figure 7.9a*. This graph shows how the p.d. *V* increases as the amount of charge stored *Q* increases. It is a straight line because *Q* and *V* are related by:

$$V = \frac{Q}{C}$$

We can use this graph to calculate the work done in charging up the capacitor.

First, consider the work done *W* in moving charge *Q* through a p.d. *V*. This is given by:

$$W = QV$$

(You studied this equation in chapter 11 of *Physics 1*.) From the graph of *Q* against *V* (*figure 7.9b*), we can see that the quantity *Q* × *V* is given by the area under the graph. If we apply the same idea to the capacitor graph (*figure 7.9a*), then the area under the graph is the shaded triangle, with an area of $\frac{1}{2}$base × height. Hence the work done in charging a capacitor to a particular p.d. is given by:

$$W = \frac{1}{2}QV$$

Substituting *Q* = *CV* into this equation gives two further equations:

$$W = \frac{1}{2}CV^2$$

and

$$W = \frac{1}{2}Q^2/C$$

You choose the appropriate version of the equation for *W* according to the information available to you.

These three equations tell us the work done in charging up the capacitor. This is equal to the energy stored by the capacitor, since this is the amount of energy released when the capacitor is discharged.

SAQ 7.8 _____

What is the gradient of the straight line shown in *figure 7.9a*?

SAQ 7.9 _____

The graph of *figure 7.10* shows how *V*

depends on *Q* for a particular capacitor. The area under the graph has been divided into strips to make it easy to calculate the energy stored. The first strip (which is simply a triangle) shows the energy stored when the capacitor is charged up to 1 V. The energy stored is $\frac{1}{2}QV = \frac{1}{2} \times 1\,\text{mC} \times 1\,\text{V} = 0.5\,\text{mJ}$.

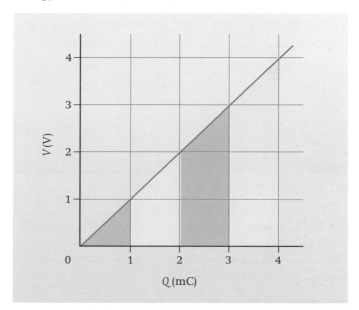

● **Figure 7.10** The energy stored by a capacitor is equal to the area under the voltage–charge graph.

a Copy the table and complete it by calculating the areas of successive strips, to show how *W* depends on *V*.

b Plot a graph of *W* against *V*. What shape does it have?

c What is the value of the capacitance *C*?

Q (mC)	*V* (V)	Area of strip ΔW (mJ)	Sum of areas *W* (mJ)
1	1	0.5	0.5
2	2	1.5	2.0
3			
4			

Capacitors in parallel

Capacitors are used in electric circuits to store charge and energy. Situations often arise where two or more capacitors are connected together in a circuit. In this section, we will look at capacitors connected in parallel. The next section deals with capacitors in series.

When two capacitors are connected in parallel (*figure 7.11*), their combined capacitance is simply the sum of their individual capacitances:

$$C_{total} = C_1 + C_2 \qquad (1)$$

This is because, when the two capacitors are connected together, they are equivalent to a single capacitor with larger plates. The bigger the plates, the more the charge that can be stored for a given voltage, and hence the greater the capacitance.

The charge Q stored by the two capacitors connected in parallel and charged to a potential difference V is simply given by:

$$Q = C_{total} \times V \qquad (2)$$

SAQ 7.10

a Calculate the capacitance of two 100 μF capacitors connected in parallel.

b Calculate the charge they store when charged to a p.d. of 20 V.

Deriving the formula

We can derive equation 1 by thinking about the charge stored by the two capacitors. As shown in *figure 7.12*, C_1 stores charge Q_1 and C_2 stores charge Q_2. Since the p.d. across each capacitor is V, we can write:

$$Q_1 = C_1V \quad \text{and} \quad Q_2 = C_2V$$

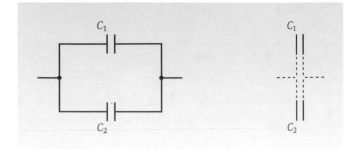

Figure 7.11 Two capacitors connected in parallel are equivalent to a single, larger capacitor.

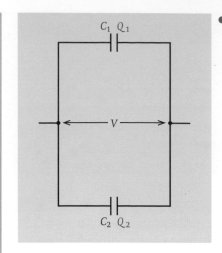

Figure 7.12 Two capacitors connected in parallel have the same p.d. across them, but store different amounts of charge.

The total charge stored is given by the sum of these:

$$Q = Q_1 + Q_2 = C_1V + C_2V$$

Since V is a common factor:

$$Q = (C_1 + C_2)V$$

Comparing this with $Q = C_{total}V$ gives the required $C_{total} = C_1 + C_2$. It follows that for three or more capacitors connected in parallel, we have:

$$C_{total} = C_1 + C_2 + C_3 + \dots$$

SAQ 7.11

Consider two capacitors, $C_1 = 200\,\mu F$ and $C_2 = 500\,\mu F$, charged up to a p.d. of 10 V. Following the steps of the argument above, calculate the charge stored by each individually and the total charge they store, and hence show that their combined capacitance when connected in parallel is 700 μF.

SAQ 7.12

A capacitor of value 50 μF is required, but the only values available to you are 10 μF, 20 μF and 100 μF (you may use more than one of each value). How would you achieve the required value? Give at least two answers.

Capacitors in series

In a similar way to the case of capacitors connected in parallel, we can consider two or more capacitors connected in series (*figure 7.13*). The combined capacitance of C_1 and C_2 is given by:

$$\frac{1}{C_{total}} = \frac{1}{C_1} + \frac{1}{C_2} \qquad (3)$$

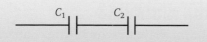

● **Figure 7.13** Two capacitors connected in series.

Here, it is the reciprocals of the capacitances that must be added to give the reciprocal of the total capacitance. For three or more capacitors connected in series, we have:

$$\frac{1}{C_{\text{total}}} = \frac{1}{C_1} + \frac{1}{C_2} + \frac{1}{C_3} + \dots$$

The following example shows the way in which these equations work.

Worked example

Calculate the combined capacitance of a 300 μF capacitor and a 600 μF capacitor connected in series.

The calculation should be done in two steps; this is relatively simple using a calculator with a '1/x' key. Substituting the values in equation 3 gives:

$$\frac{1}{C_{\text{total}}} = \frac{1}{C_1} + \frac{1}{C_2} = \frac{1}{300\,\mu F} + \frac{1}{600\,\mu F}$$

$$= \frac{1}{200\,\mu F}$$

Now take the reciprocals of both sides:

$$C_{\text{total}} = 200\,\mu F$$

Notice that the combined capacitance of two capacitors in series is less than either of the individual capacitances.

SAQ 7.13
Calculate the combined capacitance of three capacitors, 200 μF, 300 μF and 600 μF, connected in series.

SAQ 7.14
a What is significant about the combined capacitance of two *equal* capacitors connected in series? And of three equal capacitors in series?

b What is significant about the combined capacitance of two or more equal capacitors connected in parallel?

Deriving the formula

This follows the same principles as for the case of capacitors in parallel. *Figure 7.14* shows the situation. C_1 and C_2 are connected in series, and there is a p.d. V across them. This p.d. is divided (it is shared between the two capacitors), so that the p.d. across C_1 is V_1 and the p.d. across C_2 is V_2. It follows that:

$$V = V_1 + V_2$$

Now we must think about the charge stored by the combination of capacitors. In *figure 7.14*, you will see that both capacitors are shown as storing the same charge Q. How does this come about? When the voltage is first applied, charge $-Q$ arrives on the left-hand plate of C_1. This repels charge $-Q$ off the right-hand plate, leaving it with charge $+Q$. Charge $-Q$ now arrives on the left-hand plate of C_2, and this in turn results in charge $+Q$ on the right-hand plate.

Note that charge is not arbitrarily created or destroyed in this process – the total amount of charge in the system is constant. This is an example of the conservation of charge.

Notice also that there is a central isolated section of the circuit between the two capacitors. Since this is initially uncharged, it must remain so at the end. This requirement is satisfied, because there is charge $-Q$ at one end and $+Q$ at the other. Hence we conclude that capacitors connected in series store the same charge. This allows us to write equations for V_1 and V_2:

$$V_1 = \frac{Q}{C_1} \quad \text{and} \quad V_2 = \frac{Q}{C_2}$$

The combination of capacitors stores charge Q when charged to p.d. V, and so we can write:

$$V = \frac{Q}{C_{\text{total}}}$$

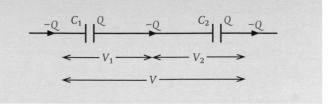

● **Figure 7.14** Capacitors connected in series store the same charge, but they have different p.d.s across them.

Substituting these in $V = V_1 + V_2$ gives:

$$\frac{Q}{C_{\text{total}}} = \frac{Q}{C_1} + \frac{Q}{C_2}$$

Cancelling the common factor of Q gives the required equation:

$$\frac{1}{C_{\text{total}}} = \frac{1}{C_1} + \frac{1}{C_2}$$

Comparing capacitors and resistors

It is helpful to compare the formulae for capacitors in series and parallel with the corresponding formulae for resistors (*table 7.1*).

Notice that the reciprocal formula applies to capacitors in series but to resistors in parallel. This comes from the definitions of capacitance and resistance. Capacitance tells us how good a capacitor is at storing charge for a given voltage, and resistance tells us how bad a resistor is at letting current through for a given voltage.

SAQ 7.15

The conductance G of a resistor tells us how *good* a resistor is at letting current through for a given voltage. It is the reciprocal of the resistance: $G = 1/R$. Write down equations for the combined conductance G_{total} of two resistors whose conductances are G_1 and G_2, connected **a** in series and **b** in parallel.

Capacitors	Resistors
in series	*in series*
$C_1 \quad C_2 \quad C_3$	$R_1 \quad R_2 \quad R_3$
store same charge	have same current
$\frac{1}{C_{\text{total}}} = \frac{1}{C_1} + \frac{1}{C_2} + \frac{1}{C_3} + \dots$	$R_{\text{total}} = R_1 + R_2 + R_3 + \dots$
in parallel	*in parallel*
C_1 C_2 C_3	R_1 R_2 R_3
have same p.d.	have same p.d.
$C_{\text{total}} = C_1 + C_2 + C_3 + \dots$	$\frac{1}{R_{\text{total}}} = \frac{1}{R_1} + \frac{1}{R_2} + \frac{1}{R_3} + \dots$

● **Table 7.1** Capacitors and resistors compared.

Capacitor networks

There are four ways in which three capacitors may be connected together. These are shown in *figure 7.15*. The combined capacitance of the first two arrangements (three capacitors in series, three in parallel) can be calculated using the formulae above. The other combinations must be dealt with in a different way:

- **Figure 7.15a**
  All in series – see above.
- **Figure 7.15b**
  All in parallel – see above.
- **Figure 7.15c**
  Calculate C_{total} for the two capacitors C_1 and C_2, which are connected in parallel, and then take account of the third capacitor C_3, which is connected in series.
- **Figure 7.15d**
  Calculate C_{total} for the two capacitors C_1 and C_2, which are connected in series, and then take account of the third capacitor C_3, which is connected in parallel.

These are the same approaches as would be used for networks of resistors.

SAQ 7.16

For each of the four circuits shown in *figure 7.15*, calculate the combined capacitance if each capacitor has a value of $100\,\mu\text{F}$.

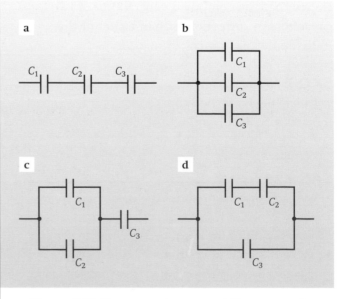

● **Figure 7.15** Four ways to connect three capacitors.

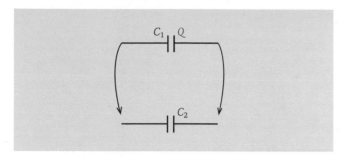

● **Figure 7.16** Capacitor C_1 is charged up and then connected across C_2.

SAQ 7.17

Given a number of $100\,\mu F$ capacitors, how might you connect networks to give the following values of capacitance:

a $400\,\mu F$;

b $25\,\mu F$;

c $250\,\mu F$?

Sharing charge, sharing energy

If a capacitor is charged up and then connected to a second capacitor (*figure 7.16*), what happens to the charge and the energy that it stores? Note that, when the capacitors are connected together, they are in parallel, because they have the same p.d. across them. Their combined capacitance C_{total} is equal to the sum of their individual capacitances. Now we can think about the charge stored, Q. This is shared between the two capacitors; the total amount of charge stored must remain the same, since charge is conserved. It is shared between the two capacitors in proportion to their capacitances. Now the p.d. can be calculated from $V = Q/C$, and the energy from $W = \frac{1}{2}CV^2$.

If we look at a numerical example, we find an interesting result.

Worked example

Consider two $100\,mF$ capacitors. One is charged to $10\,V$, disconnected from the power supply, and then connected across the other.

Initially we have:

charge stored $Q = 100\,mF \times 10\,V = 1000\,mC$

energy stored $W = \frac{1}{2}CV^2$

$$= \frac{1}{2} \times 100\,mF \times (10\,V)^2$$

$$= 5000\,mJ$$

After connecting together, we have:

combined capacitance $C_{total} = 200\,mF$

charge stored $= 1000\,mC$

p.d. $= \dfrac{1000\,mC}{200\,mF} = 5\,V$

energy stored $= \frac{1}{2} \times 200\,mF \times (5\,V)^2 = 2500\,mJ$

So, although the charge stored remains the same, the energy stored has fallen to half of its original value.

When capacitors are connected together, a current flows in the connecting wires, and energy is dissipated in overcoming their resistance. Energy is also dissipated as the current tends to oscillate back and forth in the wires, generating electromagnetic waves.

Figure 7.17 shows an analogy to this situation. Capacitors are represented by containers of water. A wide (high capacitance) container is filled to a certain level (p.d.). It is then connected to a container with a smaller capacitance, and the levels equalise. (The p.d. is the same for each.) Notice that the potential energy of the water has decreased, because the height of its centre of gravity above the base level has decreased. Energy is dissipated as heat, as there is friction both within the moving water and between the water and the container.

SAQ 7.18

A $20\,\mu F$ capacitor is charged up to $200\,V$ and then disconnected from the supply. It is then connected to a $5\,\mu F$ capacitor. Calculate:

a their combined capacitance;

b the charge they store;

c the p.d. across the combination;

d the energy dissipated when they are connected together.

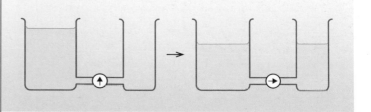

● **Figure 7.17** An analogy for the sharing of charge between capacitors.

SAQ 7.19

Draw a 'water container' diagram similar to that shown in *figure 7.17* to represent two capacitors of equal capacitance. One is filled to a high level, and then connected to the other.

a What is the final level of the water?

b What does this correspond to in the case of capacitors?

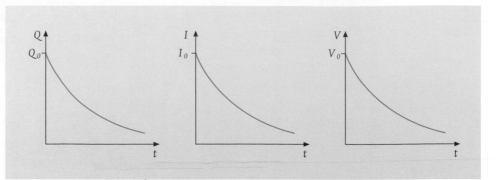

● **Figure 7.19** Graphs to show how three quantities vary during the discharge of a capacitor through a resistor: **a** charge, **b** current, and **c** p.d. across the capacitor

Each of these decreases during the discharge. As you can see from the graphs of *figure 7.19*, all three follow the same pattern of decrease. Each starts from a high initial value and decreases rapidly at first, and then more and more slowly. This pattern of decrease is known as **exponential decay**. (You may recognise this as the same pattern seen in radioactive decay, which we will look at in detail in chapter 14.)

Capacitor discharge

We have already had a brief look at the current that flows when a capacitor is discharged through a resistor (see *figure 7.6*). A suitable circuit for investigating this is shown in *figure 7.18*.

With the switch to the left, the capacitor is connected directly to the cell. There is no resistance in the circuit (other than the internal resistance of the cell) and so the capacitor charges up almost instantly.

Moving the switch to the right disconnects the capacitor from the cell. Now it is in a circuit with the resistor, of resistance R, and current can flow. The capacitor gradually discharges. It does not discharge instantly because the resistance in the circuit limits the current that flows.

There are three important quantities that change as charge flows from the capacitor:

- the charge stored, Q;
- the current flowing, I;
- the p.d. across the capacitor, V.

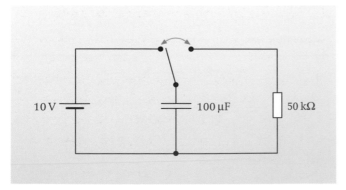

● **Figure 7.18** A circuit for investigating the discharge of a capacitor through a resistor.

Analysing the graphs

It is useful to get an understanding of the reasons behind the shapes of these three graphs. Why do they all follow the same pattern?

Initially, the capacitor is charged up. The electrons on one plate all repel one another. They want to get round to the positive plate. Connecting up via the resistor gives them the chance to start flowing round the circuit.

With a lot of charge stored by the capacitor, the p.d. is high, and so the current is high. As the charge of the capacitor decreases, the p.d. decreases and so the current decreases. This means that the charge decreases more slowly, the p.d. decreases more slowly, and the current decreases more slowly too. The consequence is that the slope of each graph gets less and less, although it never quite reaches zero.

We can explain the relationship between the two graphs in a more mathematical way using just two familiar equations:

$$Q = CV \qquad \text{and} \qquad V = IR$$

The first says that the charge Q is always just a constant (C) times the p.d. V. The second says that the p.d. V is always just a constant (R) times the current I. This allows us to find values of Q, V and I when we know the value of just one of them. For example, how can we know the initial values shown on the graphs of *figure 7.19*? (Initial values, when $t = 0$, are shown with a subscript zero.)

Since the capacitor is initially charged up by the 10 V cell:

initial p.d. V_0 = 10 V

From $Q = CV$ we can find the initial charge stored by the capacitor:

initial charge stored $Q_0 = CV_0$ = 100 μF × 10 V
= 1000 μC

Finally from $V = IR$ we can find the initial current that flows:

initial current $I_0 = V_0/R$ = 10 V/50 kΩ = 200 μA

Later, if the current flowing has halved to 100 μA, the p.d. and charge stored will both also have halved.

SAQ 7.20

For the circuit we have been discussing (*figure 7.18*), what will be the values of the current and the charge stored when the p.d. across the capacitor has dropped to 4 V?

Looking at gradients and areas

There are two more relationships that you should be aware of between the graphs of charge and current shown in *figure 7.19*.

1 The gradient of the charge–time graph is the current. At first, the gradient is steep: the current is high. Later, the gradient of the Q–t graph has decreased, and so the current must be less.

2 The area under the current–time graph represents the charge that has flowed from the capacitor. At first, the current is high, so the area under the graph is high: charge is leaving the capacitor quickly. Later, the current has decreased, so the area under the graph is increasing only slowly, and so the charge must be changing only slowly.

Look for both of these relationships between the current and charge graphs of *figure 7.19*.

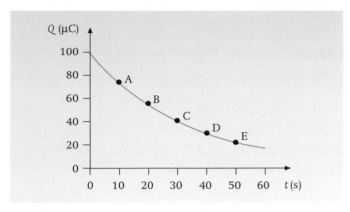

● **Figure 7.20** For SAQ 7.21.

SAQ 7.21

The graph of *figure 7.20* shows how the charge stored by a capacitor decreased as it was discharged through a resistor.

a By measuring the gradient of the graph at points A–E along its length, estimate the values of the current at these times.

b Using the values obtained, sketch a graph to show how the current changed as the capacitor discharged.

Discharge equations

The graphs of *figure 7.19* can be represented by equations. These involve a special number represented by the letter 'e' (for 'exponential'). Here is the equation that represents how the charge Q stored by a capacitor, of capacitance C, decreases with time t when it is discharged through a resistor of resistance R:

$$Q = Q_0\, e^{-t/CR}$$

At first, this equation may seem complex, but with a little practice its meaning becomes clear. It is best to start with a numerical example.

Worked example

A 1000 μF capacitor initially stores 20 mC of charge. It is discharged through a 500 kΩ resistor. How much charge does it store after 100 s?

Step 1: Write down the quantities that you know:
Q_0 = 20 mC
t = 100 s
C = 1000 μF = 1000 × 10⁻⁶ F
R = 500 kΩ = 500 × 10³ Ω

Step 2: We are going to calculate Q using the equation $Q = Q_0 \, e^{-t/CR}$. First, calculate the power to which 'e' is raised:

$$-t/CR = (-100 \, \text{s})/(1000 \times 10^{-6} \, \text{F} \times 500 \times 10^3 \, \Omega)$$
$$= -0.2$$

Note that it is necessary to express μF as 10^{-6} F, and so on. The answer to this part of the calculation is just a number, without units.

Step 3: Use the e^x key of your calculator to work out $e^{-0.2}$, and multiply by the value of Q_0.

$$Q = Q_0 \, e^{-0.2} = 16.4 \, \text{mC}$$

Here, we can keep the value of Q_0 in mC, and the final answer for Q will also be in mC.

With practice, you will be able to combine Steps 2 and 3 in a single calculation on your calculator.

SAQ 7.22

For the situation described in the worked example above, calculate the charge stored by the capacitor after 1000 s.

A general equation

As we have seen, the graphs for the decrease of current and p.d. have the same shape as the graph for charge. As you might expect, it follows that the equations for current and p.d. have the same form as the equation for charge. Here are all three:

charge	$Q = Q_0 \, e^{-t/CR}$
current	$I = I_0 \, e^{-t/CR}$
p.d.	$V = V_0 \, e^{-t/CR}$

Most people remember one of these equations, and know how to change between Q, I and V. The three equations are examples of a general equation of the form:

$$x = x_0 \, e^{-t/CR}$$

SAQ 7.23

The capacitor shown in *figure 7.21* is initially charged to 10 V. What will be the p.d. across it 1 min after the switch is closed?

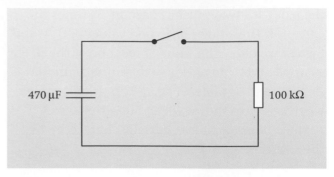

● **Figure 7.21** For SAQ 7.23.

SAQ 7.24

A 500 μF capacitor is charged to 200 V and connected across a 400 kΩ resistor.

a Calculate the initial current that flows through the resistor.

b Write an equation of the form $x = x_0 \, e^{-t/CR}$ to show how the current I decreases as the capacitor discharges.

c Use your equation to calculate values of I at intervals of 100 s. Copy and complete the table below to show your results.

d Plot a graph of your results.

Time t (s)	0	100	200	300	400	500
Current I (μA)						

Time constant τ

The quantity CR appears in the equations for the exponential decrease of charge, current and p.d. It should not be surprising that the values of C and R affect the discharge of a capacitor through a resistor.

■ With a large value of C, a lot of charge is stored. It takes longer for the charge to drain from the capacitor.

■ With a large value of R, the current flowing from the capacitor will be small. Again, it takes longer for the capacitor to discharge.

The quantity CR is called the **time constant** of the circuit – it is given the symbol τ (tau, Greek letter t):

time constant $\tau = CR$

The name 'time constant' reflects the fact that the unit of τ is seconds. The time constant is the time it takes for the current, charge or p.d. to fall to 1/e

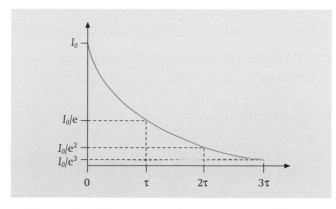

● **Figure 7.22** After time τ, the current has fallen to $1/e$ of its initial value; after $2 \times \tau$, to $1/e^2$; and so on.

of its initial value; that is, to about 37% of its initial value. After twice the time constant, the value will have fallen to $1/e^2$ of its initial value, and so on. *Figure 7.22* shows this. The graph will remind you of similar graphs to show the half-life of a radioactive substance.

Circuits in which a capacitor discharges through a resistor ('R–C circuits') are often used in electronic timers. At the start of a time interval, the capacitor is charged up. It gradually discharges, and eventually falls below a set value. This triggers a switching circuit to make an alarm sound, or to have some other effect.

Increasing the time constant of the R–C circuit makes the time interval longer. There are two ways to do this: by increasing C, or by increasing R.

SAQ 7.25

A 220 µF capacitor is discharged through a 100 Ω resistor. What is the time constant for this circuit? Give your answer in milliseconds (ms).

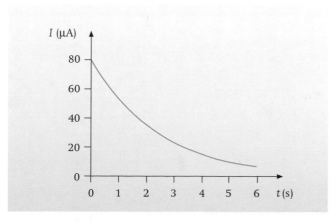

● **Figure 7.23** For SAQ 7.26.

SAQ 7.26

Understanding the idea of the time constant of an R–C circuit can form the basis for the measurement of an unknown capacitance. *Figure 7.23* shows the results of an experiment in which a capacitor C was discharged through a standard resistor of value $1000\,\Omega \pm 1\%$.

a From the graph, find the initial value of the current I_0.

b Calculate $1/e$ of this (i.e. $0.37 \times I_0$).

c From the graph, find the time when the current has fallen to this value. This time is the time constant τ.

d Use the equation $\tau = CR$ to deduce the value of C.

e Now use the graph to find the value of $2 \times \tau$, and deduce another value for C.

f Why is a standard resistor used in this experiment?

SUMMARY

◆ Capacitors are constructed from two metal sheets ('plates'), separated by an insulating material, the dielectric.

◆ Capacitors store charge, proportional to the p.d. between the plates. Capacitance is the charge stored per unit of p.d.; a farad is a coulomb per volt:
$$Q = CV, \qquad 1\,F = 1\,C\,V^{-1}$$

◆ Capacitors store energy; the energy stored W at p.d. V is
$$W = \tfrac{1}{2}QV = \tfrac{1}{2}CV^2 = \tfrac{1}{2}Q^2/C$$

◆ For capacitors connected in parallel and in series, the combined capacitances are as follows:
in parallel: $C_{total} = C_1 + C_2 + C_3 + ...$
in series: $1/C_{total} = 1/C_1 + 1/C_2 + 1/C_3 + ...$

◆ When a capacitor is discharged through a resistor, the charge, current and p.d. show an exponential decrease with time, which can be represented by equations of the form:
$$x = x_0\,e^{-t/CR}$$

◆ For an R–C circuit, the time constant $\tau = CR$. This is the time taken for charge, current and p.d. to fall to $1/e$ of their initial values.

Questions

1 You have three capacitors whose values are 100 pF, 200 pF and 600 pF. What are the greatest and least values of capacitance that you can make by connecting them together to form a network? How should they be connected in each case?

2 What is the capacitance of the network of capacitors shown in *figure 7.24*?

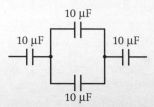
10 μF

10 μF   10 μF

10 μF

● **Figure 7.24** A capacitor network.

3 Three capacitors, each of capacitance 120 μF, are connected together in series. They are then connected to a 10 kV supply.
   a What is their combined capacitance?
   b How much charge do they store?
   c How much energy do they store?

4 In a photographic flashgun, a 0.2 F capacitor is charged by a 9 V battery. It is then discharged in a flash of duration 0.01 s. Calculate:
   a the charge and energy stored by the capacitor;
   b the average power dissipated during the flash;
   c the average current in the flash bulb;
   d the approximate resistance of the bulb.

5 A capacitor is discharged through a resistor; the current through the resistor varies according to the following equation:
$I = 0.5\,\text{mA} \times e^{-(0.02 \times t)\text{s}}$
   a What is the initial current flowing through the resistor (when $t = 0$)?
   b Calculate the current flowing after 30 s.
   c What is the time constant for this circuit?

6 A 100 μF capacitor is charged to 6 V. It is then discharged through a 500 kΩ resistor.
   a What is the time constant for this circuit?
   b Write down equations of the form $x = x_0\,e^{-t/CR}$ to show how the charge stored by the capacitor, the current through the resistor and the p.d. across it vary with time.
   c Calculate the current flowing after 1 minute.

CHAPTER 8

Electromagnetic forces

By the end of this chapter you should be able to:

1 recall and use $F = BIl \sin \theta$, with directions as interpreted by Fleming's left-hand (motor) rule, for the force on a current-carrying conductor in a uniform magnetic field;

2 recall and use $F = BQv \sin \theta$, for the force on a charge moving in a uniform magnetic field;

3 analyse the circular orbits of charged particles moving in a plane perpendicular to a uniform magnetic field by relating the electromagnetic force to the centripetal acceleration it causes.

Magnetic fields

So far we have considered how to think of two types of force (gravitational and electric) as fields of force. Now we will extend this to magnetic fields and the forces they exert on moving electrical charges.

Firstly, we will revise some ideas that were covered in *Physics 1*.

- Magnetic fields are produced by permanent magnets, and by electric currents (moving charges).
- Magnetic fields can be represented by field lines (just as gravitational and electric fields can). We think of magnetic flux flowing from north poles to south poles.
- The strength of a magnetic field is described in terms of its **flux density** B, measured in teslas.
- When a conductor of length l carrying a current I lies at right-angles to a magnetic field, a force F acts on it. The force is given by $F = BIl$.
- The relative directions of force, magnetic flux and current are given by **Fleming's left-hand (motor rule)** – see *figure 8.1*.
- The equation $F = BIl$ defines B and the tesla. We have $B = F/Il$, and $1\,\text{T} = 1\,\text{N}\,\text{A}^{-1}\,\text{m}^{-1}$.

The motor effect

The force on a current in a magnetic field is sometimes called 'the BIl force'. It is a very important

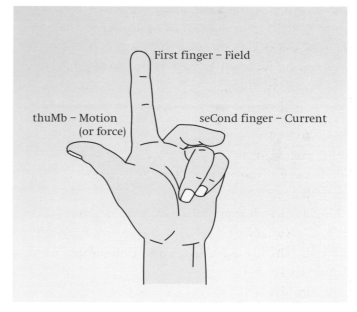

First finger – Field

thuMb – Motion (or force)

seCond finger – Current

● **Figure 8.1** The motor effect: Fleming's left-hand rule reminds us of the relative directions of force, current and magnetic flux.

force, because it is the basis of the motor effect, used in electric motors.

Now we must consider the situation where the current cuts across a magnetic field at an angle other than a right-angle. In *figure 8.2*, next page, the force gets weaker as the conductor is moved round from OA (angle $\theta = 90°$) to OB, to OC and finally to OD (there is no force when angle $\theta = 0°$). To calculate the force, we need to find the

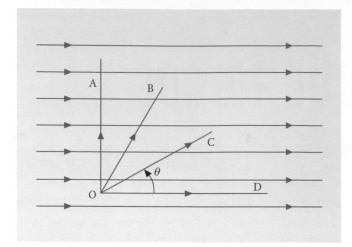

● **Figure 8.2** The force on a current depends on the angle it makes with the magnetic flux.

component of the current that is flowing across the field. This is $I \sin \theta$, and so the $F = BIl$ equation becomes

$$F = BIl \sin \theta$$

Note that the component of I parallel to the flux is $I \cos \theta$, but this does not contribute to the force; there is no force on a current flowing *parallel* to the magnetic flux.

Worked example

A conductor OC (see *figure 8.2*) of length 0.2 m lies at an angle $\theta = 25°$ to a magnetic field of flux density 0.05 T. It carries a current of 500 mA. What force acts on the conductor?

Step 1: Write down what you know, and what you want to know:

$B = 0.05$ T
$I = 500$ mA $= 0.5$ A
$l = 0.2$ m
$\theta = 25°$
$F = ?$

Step 2: Write down the equation, substitute values and solve:

$F = BIl \sin \theta$
  $= 0.05$ T $\times 0.5$ A $\times 0.2$ m $\times \sin 25° = 2.1 \times 10^{-3}$ N

Step 3: Give the direction of the force. The force acts at 90° to the field and the current, i.e. perpendicular to the page. The left-hand rule shows that it acts upwards, in to the page.

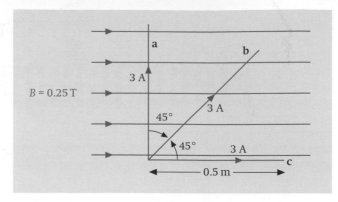

● **Figure 8.3** Three currents crossing a magnetic field − see SAQ 8.1.

SAQ 8.1

What force will be exerted on each of the currents shown in *figure 8.3*, and in what direction will it act?

Moving particles

The world of atomic physics is populated by a great variety of particles − electrons, protons, neutrons, positrons and more. Many of these particles are electrically charged, and their motion is influenced by electric and magnetic fields. Indeed, we use this fact to help us to distinguish one particle from another.

You can use your knowledge of how charged particles and electric currents are affected by fields to interpret diagrams of moving particles. You must bear in mind that, by convention, electric current is the flow of positive charge. When electrons are moving, the conventional current is regarded as flowing in the opposite direction (see *figure 7.4*).

● **Figure 8.4** An electron beam tube.

Observing the force

Electron beam tubes (*figure 8.4*) can be used to demonstrate the magnetic force on a moving charge. A beam of electrons is produced by an 'electron gun', and magnets or electromagnets can be used to apply a magnetic field.

You can use such an arrangement to observe the effect of changing the strength and direction of the field, and the effect of reversing the field. Note that you can seriously damage a television set by bringing a magnet close to the screen.

If you are able to observe a beam of electrons like this, you should find that the force on the electrons moving through the magnetic field can be correctly predicted using Fleming's left-hand rule. In *figure 8.5*, a beam of electrons is moving from right to left, into a region where a magnetic field is directed into the page. Since electrons are negatively charged, they represent a conventional current (flow of positive charge) from left to right. Fleming's left-hand rule predicts that, initially, the force on the electrons will be upwards, and the beam will be deflected up the page. As the direction of the beam changes, so does the direction of the force. It is always at 90° to the velocity of the electrons.

It is this force that gives rise to the motor effect. The electrons in a wire experience a force when they flow across a magnetic field, and they transfer the force to the wire itself.

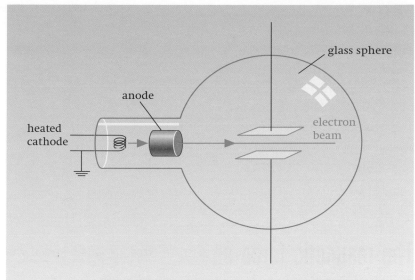

● **Figure 8.6** The construction of an electron beam tube.

Using electron beams

Televisions, oscilloscopes and computer monitors often make use of beams of electrons. Electrons are moved about using magnetic and electric fields, and the result can be a rapidly changing image on the screen.

The picture in *figure 8.6* shows the construction of a typical tube. The electron gun has a heated cathode. The positively charged anode attracts electrons from the cathode, and they pass through the anode to form a narrow beam in the space beyond. The direction of the beam can be changed using an electric field between two plates (as shown in *figure 8.6*), or a magnetic field created by electromagnetic coils.

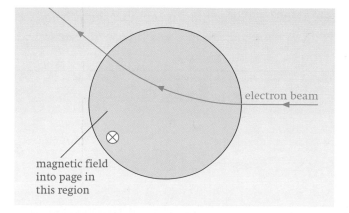

● **Figure 8.5** A beam of electrons is deflected as it crosses a magnetic field. The magnetic field into the page is represented by the blue cross in the circle.

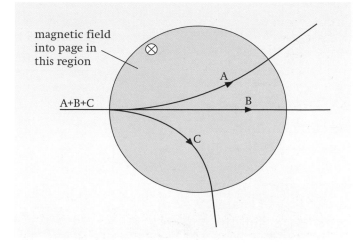

● **Figure 8.7** Three types of radiation passing through a magnetic field – see SAQ 8.2, next page.

SAQ 8.2

In the diagram in *figure 8.7*, radiation from a radioactive source is passing through a magnetic field. Which tracks are those of α-particles (alpha particles, +ve charge), β-particles (beta particles, −ve charge) and γ-rays (gamma-rays, no charge)?

The magnetic force on a moving charge

We can make an intelligent guess about the factors that determine the size of the force on a moving charge in a magnetic field (*figure 8.8*). It will depend on:

- the strength of the magnetic field (flux density), B;
- the charge on the particle, Q;
- the speed with which it is moving, v.

In the same way that we guessed the equation $F = BIl$, we can guess the equation for the force on a charge moving in a direction at right-angles to the magnetic field:

$$F = BQv$$

If the particle is moving at an angle θ to the magnetic field, this equation becomes

$$F = BQv \sin \theta$$

We can show that the two equations $F = BIl$ and $F = BQv$ are consistent with one another, as follows. Since current I is the rate of flow of charge, we can write $I = Q/t$. Substituting in $F = BIl$ gives

$$F = BQl/t$$

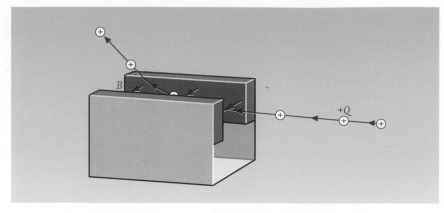

● **Figure 8.8** The path of a charged particle is curved in a magnetic field.

Now, l/t is the speed v of the moving particle, and so we can write

$$F = BQv$$

For an electron, whose charge is $-e$, the force on it is

$$F = -Bev$$

(The force on a moving charge is sometimes called 'the Bev force', and it is really no different from 'the BIl force'.)

It is important to note that the force F is always at right-angles to the particle's velocity v, and its direction can be found using the left-hand rule (*figure 8.9*).

SAQ 8.3

A beam of electrons, moving at $10^6 \, \text{m s}^{-1}$, is directed through a magnetic field of flux density 0.5 T. Calculate the force on each electron if **a** the beam is at right-angles to the magnetic flux, and **b** if it is at an angle of 45° to the flux.

(Note: magnitude of electron charge $e = 1.6 \times 10^{-19} \, \text{C}$.)

SAQ 8.4

Positrons are particles identical to electrons, except that their charge is positive (+e). Suggest how a magnetic field could be used to separate a mixed beam of positrons and electrons.

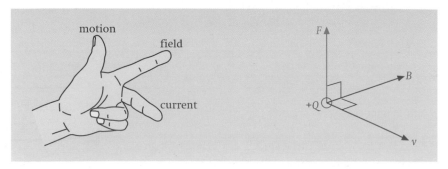

● **Figure 8.9** Fleming's left-hand rule, applied to a moving positive charge.

Orbiting charges

Because the force F is always perpendicular to v, a charged particle moving in a magnetic field will travel along a circular path. We can describe F as a centripetal force, because it is always directed towards the centre of the circle.

Figure 8.10 shows a fine-beam tube. In this tube, a beam of fast-moving electrons is produced by an electron gun. This is similar to the cathode and anode shown in *figure 8.6*, but in this case the beam is directed vertically upwards as it emerges from the gun. It enters the spherical tube, which sits in a uniform horizontal magnetic field. The beam is thus at right-angles to the field, and the Bev force pushes it round in a circle.

The fact that the Bev force acts as a centripetal force gives us a clue as to how we can calculate the radius of the orbit of a charged particle in a magnetic field. Any centripetal force can be written as

centripetal force $= mv^2/r$

and we can equate this to Bev:

$Bev = mv^2/r$

Cancelling and rearranging to find r gives

$r = mv/Be$

Studying this equation shows the following:

- faster-moving particles move in bigger circles;
- particles with greater masses also move in bigger circles (they have more inertia);

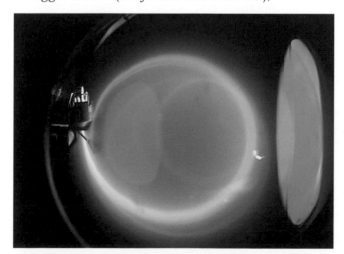

- a stronger field makes the particles move in tighter circles (smaller r).

This is made use of in a variety of scientific applications, such as particle accelerators. In a mass spectrograph, chemists separate ions of different masses and charges by passing them through a magnetic field. The greater the mass and the smaller the charge, the less the ions are deflected by the field.

Worked example

Electrons moving at $8 \times 10^6\,\mathrm{m\,s^{-1}}$ move at 90° to a magnetic field of flux density 0.001 T. What will be the radius of their orbit? [For an electron, charge $e = 1.6 \times 10^{-19}$ C and mass $= 9.1 \times 10^{-31}$ kg.]

We have

$r = mv/Be$

Substituting and solving gives

$$r = \frac{9.1 \times 10^{-31}\,\mathrm{kg} \times 8 \times 10^6\,\mathrm{m\,s^{-1}}}{(0.001\ \mathrm{T} \times 1.6 \times 10^{-19}\,\mathrm{C})} = 0.0455\,\mathrm{m}$$

$$= 4.55\,\mathrm{cm}$$

SAQ 8.5

Look at the photograph of the electron beam in the fine-beam tube (*figure 8.10*). In which direction is the magnetic field (front–to–back, or back–to–front)?

SAQ 8.6

The electrons in the circular beam shown in *figure 8.10* all travel round in the same orbit. What does this tell you about their mass, charge and speed?

SAQ 8.7

An electron beam in a vacuum tube is directed at right–angles to a magnetic field, so that it travels along a circular path. Predict the effect on the size and shape of the path that would be produced (separately) by each of the following changes:

a increasing the magnetic field;
b reversing the magnetic field;
c slowing down the electrons;
d tilting the beam, so that the electrons have a component of velocity along the magnetic field.

● **Figure 8.10** In this fine-beam tube, a beam of electrons is bent around into a circular orbit by a magnetic field. (The beam is shown up by the presence of a small amount of gas in the tube.)

Investigation

A deflection tube (*figure 8.11*) is designed to show a beam of electrons passing through a combination of electric and magnetic fields. By adjusting the strengths of the fields, you can balance the two forces on the electrons, and the beam will remain horizontal.

To find the speed of the electrons emerging from the anode, you need to know the cathode–anode voltage, V_{ca}. An individual electron has charge $-e$, and an amount of work $e \times V_{ca}$ is done on it in accelerating it from the cathode to the anode. This is its kinetic energy:

$$eV_{ca} = \tfrac{1}{2}m_e v^2$$

If the electron beam remains straight, it follows that the electric and magnetic forces on each electron are balanced:

$$eV/d = Bev$$

where V/d is the electric field strength between the two deflection plates.

Combining these two equations (to eliminate v) gives

$$\frac{e}{m_e} = \frac{V^2}{2V_{ca}B^2d^2}$$

If you can measure the voltages V and V_{ca}, the flux density B and the plate separation d, you can now find the charge/mass ratio of an individual electron. Since we know the electron charge $-e = -1.6 \times 10^{-19}$ C, you can also use this experiment to find the electron mass m_e.

In this experiment, there are three variables that you might consider changing. Draw up a plan showing the following points:

■ What factors will you vary?
■ How will you vary them in a systematic way?
■ What will you measure?
■ How will you record and process your results?
■ What patterns will you expect to see in your results?

Carry out the investigation, and use your results to find values for e/m_e and m_e.

[Note: The magnetic field is provided by two coils, called Helmholtz coils (*figure 8.12*), which give a very uniform field in the space between them. Each coil has N turns and they are separated by a distance r, which is equal to the radius of one of the coils. To find the strength of the magnetic field, you need to measure the current I flowing through them. Then the flux density B is given by $B = 9.05 \times 10^{-7} \times NI/r$.]

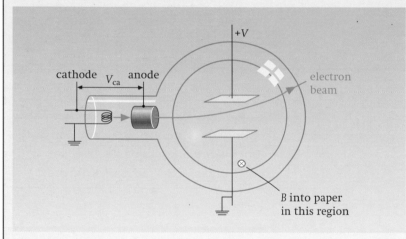

● **Figure 8.11** The path of an electron beam in a deflection tube.

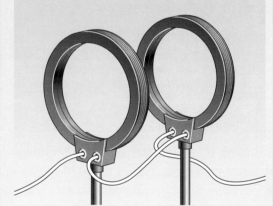

● **Figure 8.12** A pair of Helmholtz coils is used to give a uniform magnetic field.

SUMMARY

◆ The force on a current-carrying conductor in a magnetic field is given by $F = BIl \sin \theta$.

◆ This arises from the force exerted by the field on the moving charges within the conductor, given by $F = BQv \sin \theta$.

◆ The direction of the force is given by Fleming's left-hand rule.

◆ Because the force is always at right-angles to the velocity of the moving charge, it can act as a centripetal force. Hence charged particles moving at right-angles to a magnetic field follow circular orbits.

Question

1 Use your knowledge of the forces on charged particles to work out where the electron beam will strike the screen in the tube shown in *figure 8.13*. Break the problem into small steps as follows.
[Note: electron charge $-e = -1.6 \times 10^{-19}$ C; electron mass $m_e = 9.11 \times 10^{-31}$ kg.]

a Electrons are attracted from the cathode to the anode by the potential difference between them. Calculate the kinetic energy gained by an electron as it accelerates from the cathode to the anode, and use this value to calculate the speed of the electron.

b In this tube, the electron beam is deflected by the electric field between two parallel plates. Calculate the strength of the field, and the force on a single electron.

c The horizontal component of the electron's velocity is not affected by the electric field. Why is this? Calculate the time the electron takes to travel through the space between the plates.

d The electrons are accelerated upwards by the electric force on them. Calculate their acceleration, and use your answer to deduce the upward component of the electron's velocity as it emerges from the space between the plates.

e From your knowledge of the components of the electron's velocity, calculate the angle ϕ.

f Calculate how far up the screen the beam will strike.

g Explain how your answer would differ if the anode–cathode voltage was increased, and if the voltage between the deflecting plates was increased.

h The beam can be restored to its horizontal path if a magnetic field is applied in the region between the two parallel plates. Calculate the flux density B needed to do this. In what direction must the magnetic field act?

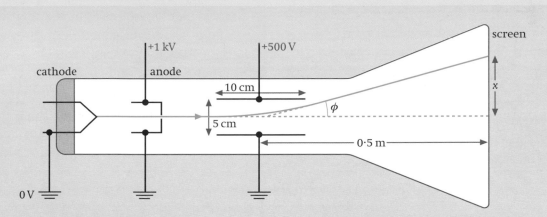

● **Figure 8.13** A cathode-ray tube.

CHAPTER 9

Electromagnetic induction

By the end of this chapter you should be able to:

1 define magnetic flux and the weber;

2 recall and use $\Phi = BA$;

3 define magnetic flux linkage, $N\Phi$;

4 recall and use Faraday's law of electromagnetic induction;

5 recall and use the equation

magnitude of induced e.m.f. = rate of change of flux linkage;

6 recall and use Lenz's law to determine the direction of an induced e.m.f.;

7 describe, explain and interpret simple applications of electromagnetic induction.

Generating electricity

Most of the electricity we use is generated by electromagnetic induction. This process goes on in the generators at work in power stations and, on a much smaller scale, in bicycle dynamos. It is the process whereby a conductor and a magnetic field are moved relative to each other to induce or generate a current or voltage.

● **Figure 9.1** These giant wind turbines drive generators, which use electromagnetic induction to produce electricity.

Here are some simple experiments in which you can observe some of the features of electromagnetic induction. In each case, try to predict what you will observe before you try the experiment.

■ **Experiment 1**

Connect a small electric motor to a moving-coil voltmeter (*figure 9.2*). Spin the shaft of the motor and observe the deflection of the meter. What happens when you spin the motor more slowly? What happens when you stop?

Usually, we connect a motor to the voltage provided by a power supply, and it turns. In this experiment, you have turned the motor and it generates a voltage. A generator is like a motor working in reverse.

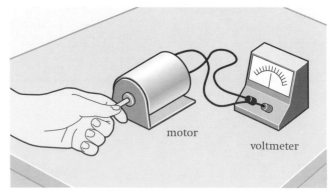

motor

voltmeter

● **Figure 9.2** A motor works in reverse as a generator.

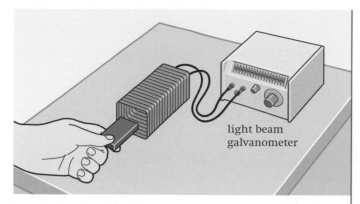

● **Figure 9.3** A moving magnet near a coil generates a small current.

■ **Experiment 2**

Connect a solenoid to a sensitive microammeter, such as a light beam galvanometer (*figure 9.3*). Move a bar magnet in towards the coil. Hold it still, and then remove it. How does the deflection on the meter change? Try different speeds, and the other pole of the magnet. Try weak and strong magnets.

With the same equipment, move the coil towards the magnet and observe the deflection of the meter.

■ **Experiment 3**

Connect a long wire to the sensitive meter. Move the middle section up and down between the poles of a horseshoe magnet (*figure 9.4*). Double up the wire so that twice as much passes through the magnetic field. What happens to the meter reading? How can you form the wire into a loop to give twice the deflection on the meter?

In all these experiments, you have seen an electric current generated or induced. In each case, there is a magnetic field and a conductor. When you move the magnet or the conductor, the induced current flows. When you stop, the current stops.

Explaining electromagnetic induction

Magnetic flux

You have seen that relative movement of a conductor and a magnetic field induces a current to flow in the conductor, if the conductor is part of a complete circuit. (In the experiments above, the meter was used to complete the circuit.) Now we need to think about how to explain these observations, using what we know about magnetic fields.

Start by thinking about a simple bar magnet. It creates a magnetic field in the space around it. We represent this field by lines of force (*figure 9.5*). It can help to think of these as lines of magnetic flux. 'Flux' means something that flows, and we picture magnetic flux flowing out of the north pole of the magnet, round to the south pole.

(The idea of flux is very useful, particularly to electrical engineers, who often trace the flow of magnetic flux around a magnetic circuit, just as we can trace the flow of electric current around an electric circuit.)

Now think about what happens when a wire is moved into the magnetic field (*figure 9.6*, next page). As it moves, it cuts across the magnetic flux. Remove the wire from the field, and again it must cut across the flux, but in the opposite direction.

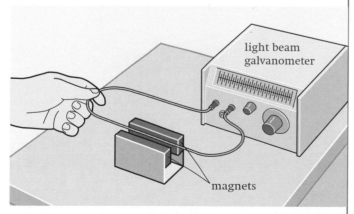

● **Figure 9.4** Investigating the current induced when a wire moves through a magnetic field.

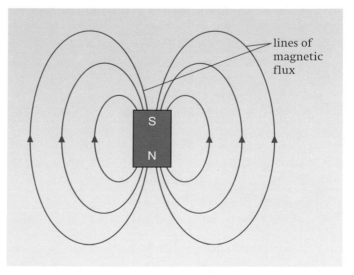

● **Figure 9.5** Magnetic flux around a permanent bar magnet.

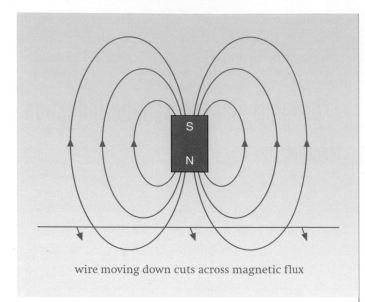

wire moving down cuts across magnetic flux

● **Figure 9.6** Inducing a current by moving a conductor through a magnetic field.

We think of this cutting of flux by a conductor as the effect that gives rise to an induced current flowing in the conductor. It doesn't matter whether the conductor is moved through the field, or the magnet is moved past the conductor, the result is the same – an induced current flows.

The effect is magnified if we use a coil of wire. Each bit of wire cuts across the magnetic flux, and so each contributes to the induced current. For a coil of N turns, the effect is N times greater than for a single turn of wire.

Another way to think of this is to talk about the flux that 'links' the coil (*figure 9.7*). When the coil is outside the field, no flux links it. When it is inside the field, flux links it by flowing through it.

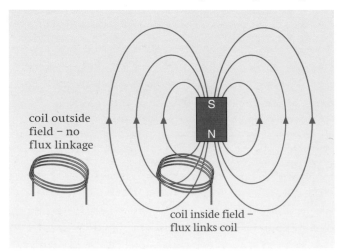

coil outside field – no flux linkage

coil inside field – flux links coil

● **Figure 9.7** The flux linking a coil changes as it is moved in to and out of a magnetic field.

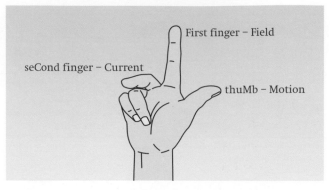

First finger – Field

seCond finger – Current

thuMb – Motion

● **Figure 9.8** Fleming's right-hand (dynamo) rule.

Moving the coil in to or out of the field changes the flux linkage, and this induces a current.

Current direction

How can we predict the direction in which an induced current will flow? For the motor effect in chapter 8, we used Fleming's left-hand (motor) rule. Electromagnetic induction is like the mirror image of the motor effect. Instead of a current flowing across a magnetic field and movement resulting, we have movement of a conductor across a magnetic field, and a current results. So you should not be too surprised to find that we use the mirror image of the left-hand rule: **Fleming's right-hand (dynamo) rule**.

The three fingers represent the same things again (*figure 9.8*):

■ thuMb – Motion
■ First finger – Field
■ seCond finger – Current

In the example shown in *figure 9.9*, the conductor is being moved downwards across the magnetic flux, which is flowing as shown, from north to south. The induced current flows in the conductor

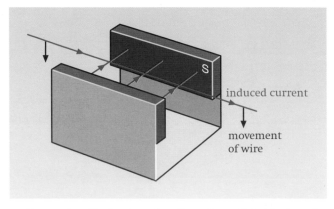

induced current

movement of wire

● **Figure 9.9** Deducing the direction of the induced current.

as shown. Check this with your own right hand. You should also check that reversing the movement or the field will result in the current flowing in the opposite direction.

Induced e.m.f.

Because a conductor is not always part of a complete circuit, the induced current cannot always flow all the way round a circuit. Instead, positive charge will accumulate at one end of the conductor, leaving the other end negatively charged. We have created a voltage between the ends of the conductor.

Is this voltage a potential difference or an e.m.f.? (Recall the distinction between these two types of voltage, which was discussed in *Physics 1*.)

Since we could connect the ends of the conductor so that it made a current flow through some other component, such as a lamp, which would light up, it must be an e.m.f. – a source of electrical energy. *Figure 9.10* shows how the induced current gives rise to an induced e.m.f. Notice that, within the conductor, current flows from negative to positive, in the same way that it does inside a battery or any other source of e.m.f.

From the three experiments in the previous section, you should see that the size of the induced e.m.f. depends on several factors.

For a *straight wire*:
- the strength of the magnetic field;
- the length of the wire;
- the speed of movement of the wire.

For a *coil of wire*:
- the strength of the magnetic field;

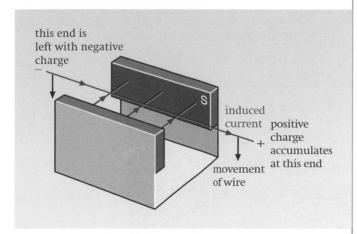

● **Figure 9.10** A voltage is induced across the ends of the conductor.

this end is left with negative charge

induced current

positive charge accumulates at this end

movement of wire

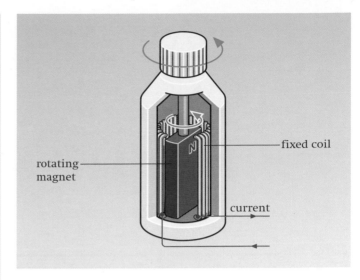

rotating magnet

fixed coil

current

● **Figure 9.11** In a bicycle dynamo, a permanent magnet rotates inside a fixed coil of wire.

- the area of the coil;
- the number of turns of wire;
- the rate at which the coil turns in the field.

You should be able to see that, for the coil, all of these factors contribute to the rate at which the flux linking the coil changes.

SAQ 9.1

Use the idea of magnetic flux to explain how a bicycle dynamo (*figure 9.11*) generates electricity.

SAQ 9.2

Use the idea of magnetic flux linkage to explain why, when a magnet is moved into a coil, the e.m.f. induced depends on the strength of the magnet and the speed at which it is moved.

SAQ 9.3

The coil in *figure 9.12*, (see next page) is rotating in a uniform magnetic field. In which direction will the induced current flow in side AB, and in side CD? Which terminal, X or Y, will become positive?

SAQ 9.4

When an aircraft flies from east to west, its wings are an electrical conductor cutting across the Earth's magnetic flux. In the Northern Hemisphere, which wingtip will become positively charged? Why will this wingtip be negative in the Southern Hemisphere?

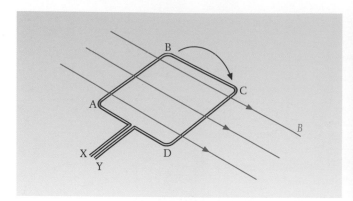

● **Figure 9.12** A coil rotates in a magnetic field.

SAQ 9.5

In an experiment to investigate the factors that affect the magnitude of an induced e.m.f., a student moves a wire back and forth between two magnets, as shown in *figure 9.13*. Explain why the e.m.f. generated in this way is much smaller than if the wire is moved up and down in the field.

SAQ 9.6

In the type of generator found in a power station (*figure 9.14*), a large electromagnet is made to rotate inside a fixed coil. An e.m.f. of 25 kV is generated; this is an alternating voltage of frequency 50 Hz. What factors do you think would affect the magnitude of the e.m.f.? What factor determines the frequency?

Calculating magnetic flux

So far in this chapter we have looked at the ideas of electromagnetic induction in a qualitative way.

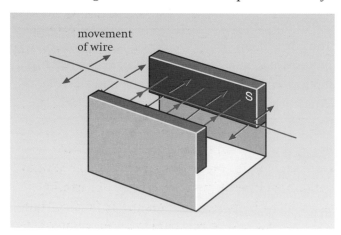

● **Figure 9.13** A wire is moved horizontally in a horizontal magnetic field.

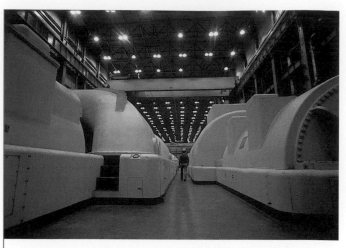

● **Figure 9.14** The generators of this power station produce electricity at an induced e.m.f. of 25 kV.

Now we will see how to calculate the value of the induced e.m.f., and look at a general way of determining its direction.

In *Physics 1*, we saw how magnetic flux density B is defined from the equation $F = BIl$. Now we can go on to define magnetic flux as a quantity.

We can think of **flux density** as a measure of how closely spaced the lines of magnetic flux are; in other words, how concentrated they are as they pass through a particular area – the amount of flux per square metre. Now we can say that the total amount of flux Φ (Φ is the Greek capital letter phi) is equal to the flux density B multiplied by the area A through which it is flowing (*figure 9.15*). So

$$\Phi = BA \qquad \text{or} \qquad B = \Phi/A$$

Note that the magnetic flux lines are perpendicular to area A; otherwise we would have to consider the component of B perpendicular to A. The unit of magnetic flux is the weber, Wb. From the

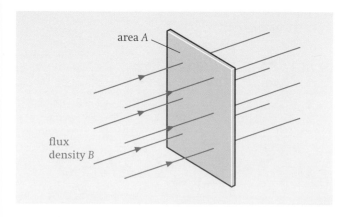

● **Figure 9.15** Defining flux Φ. The lines of magnetic flux are perpendicular to area A.

second form of the equation, we can see how teslas and webers are related:

$$1\,T = 1\,Wb\,m^{-2}$$

That is, one tesla is one weber of flux passing through one square metre.

Similarly, for a coil having N turns, we can define the magnetic flux linking the coil, the **flux linkage**, as

$$\text{flux linkage} = N\Phi = BAN$$

Worked examples.

1 The magnetic flux density through the centre of a solenoid of cross-sectional area $5\,cm^2$ is $0.01\,T$. How much flux passes through the solenoid?

We have $B = 0.01\,T$ and $A = 5\,cm^2 = 5 \times 10^{-4}\,m^2$. Hence

$$\Phi = BA = 0.01\,T \times 5 \times 10^{-4}\,m^2$$
$$= 5 \times 10^{-6}\,Wb$$

2 How much flux links a coil of area $0.1\,m^2$ and having 250 turns (*figure 9.16*), when it is placed at right-angles to a uniform magnetic field of flux density $2 \times 10^{-3}\,T$?

We have $B = 2 \times 10^{-3}\,T$, $A = 0.1\,m^2$ and $N = 250$ turns.
Hence

$$N\Phi = BAN = 2 \times 10^{-3}\,T \times 0.1\,m^2 \times 250$$
$$= 0.05\,Wb$$

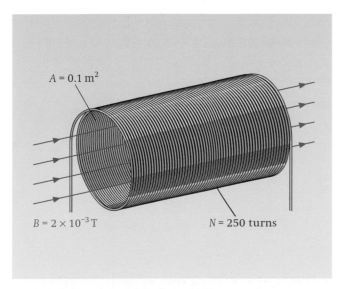

● **Figure 9.16** Magnetic flux linking a coil.

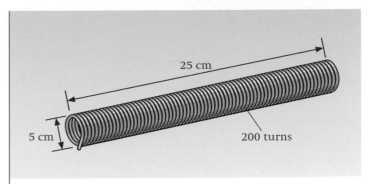

● **Figure 9.17** Solenoid for SAQ 9.9.

SAQ 9.7
A bar magnet produces a uniform flux density of $0.15\,T$ at the surface of its N pole. If the pole measures $1\,cm \times 1.5\,cm$, how much flux does this pole produce?

SAQ 9.8
In the British Isles, the vertical component of the Earth's magnetic field has a flux density of $5.0 \times 10^{-5}\,T$. If the area of the British Isles is $2.9 \times 10^{11}\,m^2$, how much magnetic flux passes through?

SAQ 9.9
A solenoid is wound on a tubular former of diameter $5.0\,cm$ and length $25\,cm$ (*figure 9.17*). There are 200 turns of wire. When a current of $2\,A$ is made to flow through it, the flux density at the centre of the coil is $2.0 \times 10^{-3}\,T$. How much flux passes through the coil?

SAQ 9.10
A rectangular coil, $5\,cm \times 7.5\,cm$, and having 120 turns, is at right-angles to a magnetic field of flux density $1.2\,T$. Calculate the flux that links the coil.

Faraday's law

Earlier in this chapter, we saw that electromagnetic induction occurs whenever a conductor cuts across lines of magnetic flux – for example, when a coil is rotated in a magnetic field so that the flux linking the coil changes. The value of the induced e.m.f. is proportional to the rate at which flux is cut.

We can write this in mathematical symbols, relating the e.m.f. E to the rate at which flux Φ is cut, dΦ/dt:

$$E \propto \frac{d\Phi}{dt}$$

In the SI system of units, the constant of proportionality in this relationship is −1, which gives us a simple equation to use to calculate E

$$E = -\frac{d\Phi}{dt}$$

In words, this equation says that the induced e.m.f. is equal to the rate at which magnetic flux is cut. (The reason for the minus sign, which represents Lenz's law, will be dealt with in the next section.)

For a coil having N turns of wire, the e.m.f. will be N times greater than for a single turn:

$$E = -N\frac{d\Phi}{dt}$$

Thus the e.m.f. induced in a coil is equal in magnitude to the rate of change of the flux linking the coil:

magnitude of induced e.m.f.
= rate of change of flux linkage

Faraday's law of electromagnetic induction is a general statement of this:

> The magnitude of the induced e.m.f. is proportional to the rate of change of magnetic flux linkage.

Worked examples

1 A straight wire of length 0.2 m moves at a steady speed of 3 m s⁻¹ at right-angles to a magnetic field of flux density 0.1 T. What will be the e.m.f. induced across the ends of the wire?

To determine the e.m.f. E, we need to find the rate at which the wire is cutting flux; in other words, how much flux it cuts each second. *Figure 9.18* shows that, in 1 s, the wire travels 3 m, and so the area A of flux that it cuts is $3 \, m \times 0.2 \, m = 0.6 \, m^2$.

Hence $A = 0.6 \, m^2$ and $B = 0.1 \, T$. So the amount of flux Φ cut in this time is

$$\Phi = BA = 0.1 \, T \times 0.6 \, m^2 = 0.06 \, Wb$$

This is the amount of flux cut in 1 s, i.e. the rate at

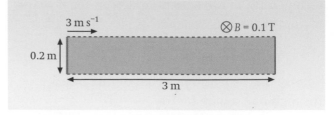

● **Figure 9.18** A moving conductor cuts across magnetic flux.

which flux is cut. By Faraday's law, this is equal to the induced e.m.f. Hence $E = 0.06 \, V$.

2 (This example shows one way in which the flux density of a magnetic field can be measured – *figure 9.19*.) A coil of wire having 2500 turns and of area 1 cm² is placed between the poles of a magnet so that the magnetic flux passes perpendicularly through the coil. The flux density of the field is 0.5 T. The coil is pulled rapidly out of the field in a time of 0.1 s. What average e.m.f. is induced across the ends of the coil?

When the coil is pulled from the field, the flux linking it falls to zero. We have to calculate the flux linking the coil when it is in the field.

$$N\Phi = BAN = 0.5 \, T \times 1 \times 10^{-4} \, m^2 \times 2500$$
$$= 0.125 \, Wb$$

Since the flux linkage falls from this value to zero in 0.1 s, we can calculate the rate of change of flux linkage, which is equal to the induced e.m.f.:

magnitude of induced e.m.f.
= rate of change of flux linkage

$$E = -N \, d\Phi/dt = 0.125 \, Wb \, / \, 0.1 \, s = 1.25 \, V$$

(Note that, in this example, we have assumed that the flux linking the coil falls steadily to zero during the time interval of 0.1 s. Our answer is thus the average value of the e.m.f.)

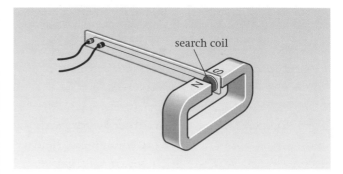

● **Figure 9.19** A search coil can be moved in to and out of a magnetic field to detect magnetic flux.

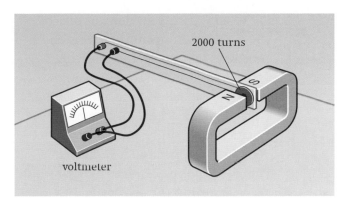

● **Figure 9.20** Using a search coil to measure flux.

SAQ 9.11

A wire of length 10 cm is moved through a distance of 2 cm in a direction at right-angles to its length in the space between the poles of a magnet, and perpendicular to the magnetic flux, where the flux density is 1.5 T. If this takes 0.5 s, calculate the average e.m.f. induced in the wire.

SAQ 9.12

An aircraft of wingspan 40 m flies horizontally at a speed of 300 m s^{-1} in an area where the vertical component of the Earth's magnetic field is 5×10^{-5} T. Calculate the e.m.f. generated between the aircraft's wingtips.

SAQ 9.13

Figure 9.20 shows a small coil of wire, having 2000 turns and of area 1 cm^2, placed between the poles of a powerful magnet. The ends of the coil are connected to a voltmeter. The coil is then pulled out of the magnetic field, and the voltmeter records an average e.m.f. of 0.4 V over a time interval of 0.2 s. What is the flux density between the poles of the magnet?

Lenz's law

We use Faraday's law to calculate the magnitude of an induced e.m.f. Now we can go on to think about the direction of the e.m.f.; in other words, which end of a wire or coil moving in a magnetic field becomes positive, and which becomes negative.

Fleming's right-hand rule gives the direction of an induced current. This is a particular case of a more general law, Lenz's law, which will be explained in this section. First, we will see how the motor effect and the dynamo effect are related to each other.

The origin of electromagnetic induction

So far, we have not given an explanation of electromagnetic induction. You have seen, from the experiments at the beginning of this chapter, that it does occur, and you know the factors that affect it. But why does an induced current flow?

Figure 9.21 gives an explanation. A straight wire XY is being pushed downwards through a horizontal magnetic field of strength B. Now, think about the free electrons in the wire. They are moving downwards, so they are in effect an electric current. Of course, because electrons are negatively charged, the conventional current is flowing upwards.

We now have a current flowing across a magnetic field, and the motor effect will therefore come into play. Using Fleming's left-hand rule, we can find the direction of the force on the electrons. The diagram shows that the electrons will be pushed in the direction from X to Y. So a current has been induced to flow in the wire; the direction of the conventional current is from Y to X.

Now we can check that Fleming's right-hand rule gives the correct directions for motion, field and current, which indeed it does.

So, to summarise, an induced current flows because the electrons are pushed by the motor effect. Electromagnetic induction is simply a consequence of the motor effect.

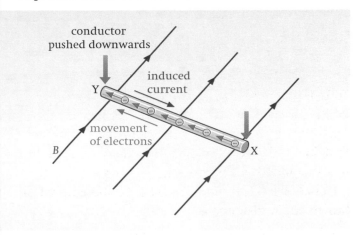

● **Figure 9.21** Showing the direction of induced current flow.

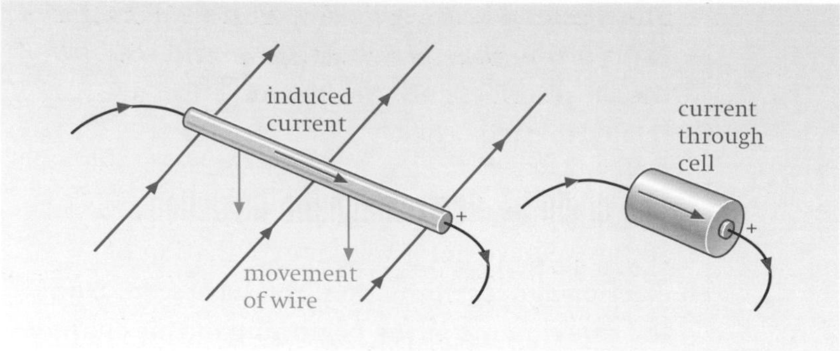

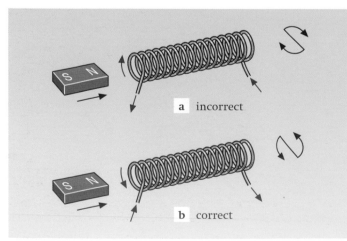

• **Figure 9.22** A moving conductor in a magnetic field is a source of e.m.f., equivalent to a cell.

Positive and negative

In *figure 9.21*, electrons are found to accumulate at Y. This end of the wire is thus the negative end of the e.m.f., and X is positive. If the wire was connected to an external circuit, electrons would flow out of Y, round the circuit, and back into X. *Figure 9.22* shows how the moving wire is equivalent to a cell (or any other source of e.m.f.).

Forces and movement

Electromagnetic induction is how we generate most of our electricity. We turn a coil in a magnetic field, and the mechanical energy we put in is transferred to electrical energy. By thinking about these energy transfers, we can deduce the direction in which an induced current will flow.

Figure 9.23 shows one of the experiments from earlier in this chapter. The north pole of a magnet is being pushed towards a coil of wire. An induced current flows in the coil, but which way round does it flow? The diagram shows the two possibilities.

a incorrect

b correct

• **Figure 9.23** Moving a magnet towards a coil: which way does the induced current flow?

When the current flows in the coil, it becomes an electromagnet. One end becomes the N pole, the other the S pole. In *figure 9.23a*, the current flows so that the end nearest the approaching N pole becomes a S pole. These poles will attract one another, and you could let go of the magnet and it would be dragged into the coil. The magnet would accelerate into the coil, the induced current would increase further, and the force of attraction between the two would also escalate.

In this situation, we would be putting no energy in to the system, but the magnet would be gaining kinetic energy, and the current would be gaining electrical energy. A nice trick if you could do it, but against the principle of conservation of energy!

It follows that *figure 9.23b* must show the correct situation. As the magnet is pushed towards the coil, the induced current flows so that the end of the coil nearest the magnet becomes a N pole. The two poles repel one another, and you have to do work to push the magnet in to the coil. The energy transferred by your work is transferred to electrical energy of the current.

SAQ 9.14

Use these ideas to explain what happens if **a** you stop pushing the magnet towards the coil, and **b** you pull the magnet away from the coil.

Figure 9.24 shows how we can apply the same thinking to a straight wire being moved through a magnetic field. An induced current flows in the wire, but in which direction? Since this is a case of a current flowing across a magnetic field, a force will act on it (the motor effect), and we can use Fleming's left-hand rule to deduce its direction.

First we will consider what happens if the induced current flows in the wrong direction. This is shown in *figure 9.24a*. The left-hand rule shows that the force that results would be in the direction in which we are trying to move the wire. The wire would thus be accelerated, the current would increase, and again we would be getting both kinetic and electrical energy for no energy input.

The induced current must flow as in *figure 9.24b*. The force that acts on it due to the motor effect

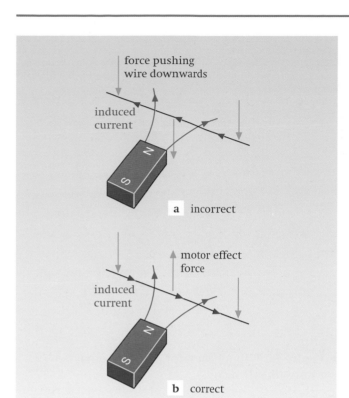

● **Figure 9.24** Moving a conductor through a magnetic field: which way does the induced current flow?

pushes against you as you try to move the wire through the field. You have to do work to move the wire, and hence to generate electricity.

SAQ 9.15 _____

Draw a diagram to show the directions of the induced current and of the opposing force if you now try to move the wire shown in *figure 9.24* upwards through the magnetic field.

A general law

Lenz's law summarises this general principle. Induced currents flow in such a way that they always produce a force that opposes the motion that is being used to produce them. If they flowed the opposite way, we would be getting energy for nothing. Here is a statement of **Lenz's law**:

> Any induced current will flow (or an induced e.m.f. will be established) in a direction so as to produce effects which oppose the change that is producing it.

The idea of this opposition to change is encapsulated in the minus sign in the equation for Faraday's law:

$$E = -N\frac{d\Phi}{dt}$$

SAQ 9.16 _____

A bar magnet is dropped vertically downwards through a long solenoid, which is connected to an oscilloscope (*figure 9.25*). The oscilloscope trace shows how the e.m.f. induced in the coil varies as the magnet accelerates downwards.

a Explain why an e.m.f. is induced in the coil as the magnet enters it (section AB of the trace).

b Explain why no e.m.f. is induced while the magnet is entirely inside the coil (section BC).

c Explain why section CD shows a negative trace, why the peak e.m.f. is greater over this section, and why CD represents a shorter time interval than AB.

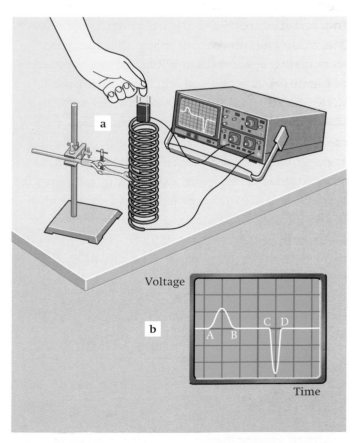

● **Figure 9.25** **a** A bar magnet falls through a long coil. **b** The oscilloscope trace shows how the induced voltage varies with time.

SAQ 9.17

SAQ 9.17

You can turn a bicycle dynamo by hand, and cause the lamps to light up. Use the idea of Lenz's law to explain why it is easier to turn the dynamo when the lamps are switched off than when they are on.

Using electromagnetic induction

An induced e.m.f. can be generated in a variety of ways. What they all have in common is that a conductor is cutting across magnetic flux. (In some cases, the conductor moves; in others, the flux moves.)

We can generate electricity by spinning a coil in a magnetic field. This is equivalent to using an electric motor backwards. *Figure 9.26* shows such a coil in several different orientations as it spins. Notice that the coil is cutting flux rapidly when it is horizontal – one side is cutting down through the flux, the other is cutting upwards. In this position, we get a large induced e.m.f. When the coil is vertical, it is travelling along the lines of flux. No flux is being cut, and so the induced e.m.f. is zero. As the coil continues round, it begins to cut lines of flux in the opposite direction (i.e. the side which was cutting upwards through flux is now cutting downwards). The induced e.m.f. is now reversed.

Hence, for a coil like this we get a varying e.m.f. – this is how alternating current is generated. In practice, it is simpler to keep the large coil fixed and spin an electromagnet inside it (*figure 9.27*). A bicycle dynamo (see *figure 9.11*) is similar, but in this case a permanent magnet is made to spin inside a fixed coil. This makes for a very robust device.

Another use of electromagnetic induction is in transformers. An alternating current in the primary coil produces a varying magnetic field in

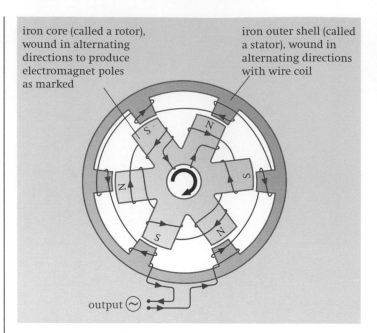

iron core (called a rotor), wound in alternating directions to produce electromagnet poles as marked

iron outer shell (called a stator), wound in alternating directions with wire coil

output ⊘

● **Figure 9.27** In a generator, an electromagnet rotates inside a coil.

the core (*figure 9.28*). The secondary coil is also wound round this core, so the flux linking the secondary coil is constantly changing. Hence a varying e.m.f. is induced across the secondary.

SAQ 9.18

Explain why, if a transformer is connected to a steady (d.c.) supply, no e.m.f. is induced across the secondary coil.

SAQ 9.19

Figure 9.29 represents a coil of wire ABCD being rotated in a uniform horizontal magnetic field. Copy and complete the diagram to show the direction of the induced current flowing in the coil, and the directions of the forces on sides AB and CD that oppose the rotation of the coil.

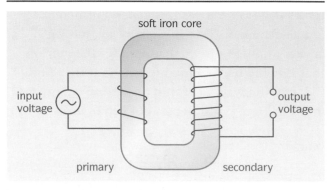

soft iron core

input voltage

output voltage

primary

secondary

● **Figure 9.28** A transformer consists of two coils linked by an iron core.

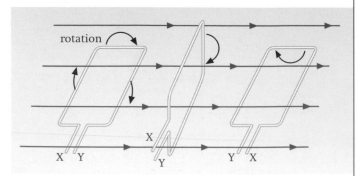

rotation

X Y   X   Y X
         Y

● **Figure 9.26** A coil rotating in a magnetic field.

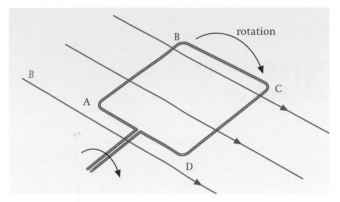

● **Figure 9.29** A coil rotating in a magnetic field.

SAQ 9.20

Does a bicycle dynamo generate alternating or direct current? Justify your answer.

SAQ 9.21

The peak e.m.f. induced in a rotating coil in a magnetic field depends on four factors: magnetic flux density B, area of the coil A, number of turns N, and rate of rotation ω. Use the ideas of Faraday's and Lenz's laws to explain why the e.m.f. should be proportional to each of these quantities.

SUMMARY

◆ In a magnetic field of flux density B, the flux passing normally through an area A is given by $\Phi = BA$.

◆ The flux linking a coil of N turns is the flux linkage, $N\Phi$.

◆ Flux and flux linkage are measured in webers (Wb).

◆ When a conductor moves so that it cuts across magnetic flux, an e.m.f. is induced across its ends. When the flux linking a coil changes, an e.m.f. is induced in it.

◆ The e.m.f. is proportional to the rate of change of flux linkage (Faraday's law), and the induced e.m.f. acts in such a direction to produce effects to oppose the change producing it (Lenz's law).

◆ Electromagnetic induction has many applications, including dynamos, generators and transformers.

Questions

1 *Figure 9.30* shows a magnet placed next to a wire. The ends of the wire are connected to a sensitive galvanometer that will detect any induced current flowing in the wire. The student tries two ways of inducing a current in the wire. Firstly, she moves the wire upwards past the magnet. Secondly, she moves the magnet upwards past the wire.

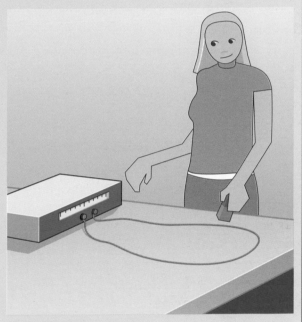

● **Figure 9.30** Investigating an induced current – see question 1

a Will the current flow in the same direction in each of these experiments, or in opposite directions? Justify your answer.

b The student now tries to increase the induced current that flows. Suggest *two* ways in which she might do this.

2 A square coil of 100 turns of wire has sides of length 5 cm. It is placed in a magnetic field of flux density 20 mT, so that the flux is perpendicular to the plane of the coil.

a Calculate the flux linking the coil.

b The coil is now pulled from the magnetic field in a time of 0.1 s. Calculate the average e.m.f. induced in it.

CHAPTER 10

Thermal physics

By the end of this chapter you should be able to:

1 show an awareness that the internal energy of a system is determined by the state of the system;

2 show an awareness that the internal energy of a system can be expressed as the sum of a random distribution of kinetic and potential energies of its molecules;

3 relate a rise in temperature of a body to an increase in internal energy;

4 define and use specific heat capacity, and show an awareness of the principle of its measurement by an electrical method;

5 recall and use $\Delta Q = mc\,\Delta\theta$;

6 describe melting and boiling in terms of energy input without a change in temperature;

7 define and use specific latent heat, and show an awareness of the principle of its measurement;

8 recall and use $\Delta Q = \Delta m\,L$.

A particle model

In science, we use models. We try to explain many different phenomena using a few simple models – for example, the *wave model* is used to explain sound, light, the behaviour of electrons in metals, the energy levels of electrons in atoms and so on. In this chapter, we are going to look at the *particle model* of matter in order to see some of the different aspects of the behaviour of matter that it can explain.

Macroscopic and microscopic

We live in a macroscopic world. '*Macro*' means large, and our large-scale world includes rocks, trees, buildings, people and other animals, the atmosphere, planets and so on. We can simplify this complex world by focusing on particular materials – metals, stone, plastic, water, air. We can make measurements of many macroscopic properties of these materials – density, temperature, strength, viscosity, elasticity,

● **Figure 10.1** This image, made using a scanning tunnelling microscope, shows atoms of gold (orange) on a graphite surface (green).

pressure. However, in science, we are always looking for underlying explanations.

You will be familiar with a microscopic description of matter as being made up of particles. '*Micro*' means small, and these tiny particles may be atoms (*figure 10.1*) or ions or molecules. By developing a simple picture of the way in which these particles behave, we can arrive at explanations of many of the macroscopic properties of matter listed above.

There is a great deal of satisfaction for a scientist in the way in which a simple microscopic model can explain a very diverse range of macroscopic phenomena. Nowadays we have techniques for showing up the particles from which matter is made, at least at the level of atoms and molecules. But bear in mind that many of these ideas were developed long before there was any possibility of 'seeing' atoms. In fact, until recently, a textbook like this might well have said that, because atoms are so small, there was no hope of ever seeing an individual atom. Inventions like the scanning tunnelling microscope (*figure 10.2*) have changed all this.

The kinetic model

The model that we are going to use to describe matter is based on the following assumptions:

■ Matter is made up of tiny particles.
■ These particles tend to attract one another.

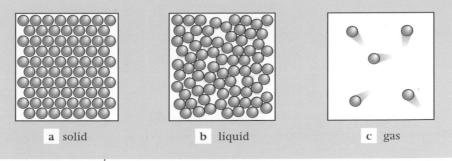

● **Figure 10.3** Typical arrangements of atoms in **a** a solid, **b** a liquid and **c** a gas.

■ The particles tend to move about.
(The word '*kinetic*' means moving.)

For simplicity, we picture the particles as small, hard spheres. *Figure 10.3* shows the three states of matter, solid, liquid and gas, as represented by this model. We describe the differences between these three states in terms of three criteria:

■ The *spacing* of the particles – how far apart are they, on average?
■ The *ordering* of the particles – are they arranged in an orderly or a random way?
■ The *motion* of the particles – are they moving quickly, slowly or not at all?

You should be familiar with the idea that, as a material changes from solid to liquid to gas, there is a change from close spacing to greater spacing, from order to disorder, and from restricted motion to free, fast motion.

SAQ 10.1

Figure 10.3 illustrates how the kinetic model represents solids, liquids and gases. (These diagrams are two-dimensional representations only.) Explain how the diagrams represent the differences in spacing, ordering and motion of particles between the three states of matter.

Modifying the model

The kinetic model we have described so far is very useful, but it cannot explain everything. It often has to be modified to explain particular observations. The change in density of ice when it melts is a case in point.

Our model suggests that, when a solid melts, the particles from which it is made become

● **Figure 10.2** This scanning tunnelling microscope is capable of showing details of the arrangement of atoms on a scale as small as 10^{-10} m.

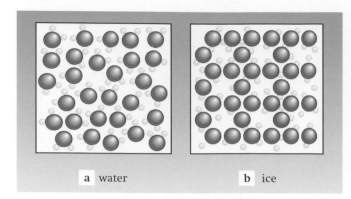

a water   b ice

● **Figure 10.4** The molecules of water occupy less space   **a** as a liquid than   **b** as a solid.
In ice the water molecules form a more regular hexagonal arrangement.

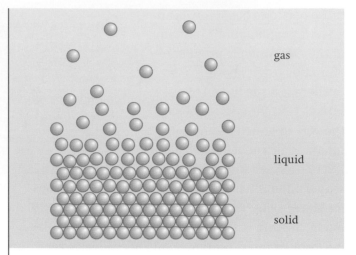

gas

liquid

solid

● **Figure 10.5** Changes of state.

slightly more disordered and further apart on average. We would thus expect a liquid to be less dense than the corresponding solid. This is generally the case, but there are exceptions. Ice is less dense than water, for example, and iron also expands when it freezes.

We have to modify the model. For water, we picture the particles as being some shape other than spherical (*figure 10.4*). When liquid water becomes solid ice, the particles pack in such a way that there is more empty space, and so the solid is less dense than the liquid.

Changes of state

Many solid materials, when heated, undergo a change of state. They first become a liquid, and then a gas. Some materials change directly from the solid state into a gas. (Some solids dissociate into simpler substances when heated, but we are not concerned here with such chemical changes.)

Figure 10.5 represents these changes of state at the molecular level. We will consider first what happens when a solid melts. The particles of the solid gain enough energy to break some of the bonds with their neighbours; they adopt a more disordered arrangement, and usually their average spacing increases. The particles are more free to move around within the bulk of the material. The solid has melted.

As the liquid is heated further, the particles become more disordered, further apart and faster moving. Eventually, at the boiling point, the particles have sufficient energy to break free from

their neighbours. They are now much farther apart, moving rapidly about in a disordered state. The liquid has boiled to become a gas.

When a liquid boils at atmospheric pressure, its volume increases by a factor of about 1000. In the liquid state, the molecules were closely packed; now they are occupying 1000 times as much space. It follows that about 99.9% of the volume of a gas is empty space. If the diameter of a single molecule is d, it follows that the average separation of molecules in the gas is about $10d$.

Energy changes

Energy is needed to raise the temperature of a solid, to melt it, to heat the liquid and to boil it. Where does this energy go to? It is worth taking a close look at a single change of state and thinking about what is happening on the molecular scale.

Figure 10.6a shows a suitable arrangement. A test-tube containing octadecanoic acid (a white, waxy substance at room temperature) is warmed in a water bath. At 80 °C, the substance is a clear liquid. The tube is then placed in a rack and allowed to cool. Its temperature is monitored, either with a thermometer or with a temperature probe and data-logger. *Figure 10.6b* shows typical results.

The temperature drops rapidly at first, then more slowly as it approaches room temperature. The important section of the graph is in the region BC. Here, the temperature remains steady for some time. The clear liquid is gradually returning to its white, waxy solid state. It is

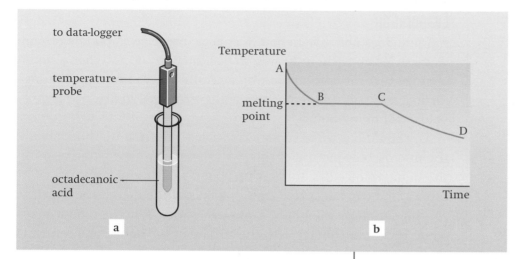

● **Figure 10.6 a** Apparatus for obtaining a cooling curve, and **b** typical results.

essential to note that heat is still being lost even though the temperature is not decreasing. When no liquid remains, the temperature starts to drop again.

From the graph, we can deduce the melting point of octadecanoic acid. This is a technique used to help identify substances by finding their melting points.

Heating ice

In some ways, it is easier to think of this experiment in reverse. What happens when we heat a substance?

Imagine taking some ice from the deep freeze. Put the ice in a well-insulated container and heat it at a steady rate. Its temperature will rise; eventually we will have a container of steam. *Figure 10.7* shows the results we might expect if we could carry out this idealised experiment. We will

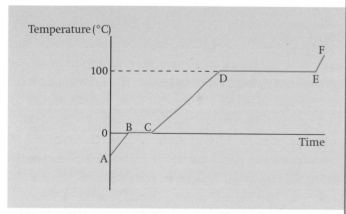

● **Figure 10.7** A temperature–time graph for water, heated at a steady rate.

consider the different sections of this graph in some detail, in order to see where the energy is going at each stage. (Remember that we are putting energy in at a steady rate.) We need to think about the kinetic and potential energies of the molecules. If they move around more freely and faster, their kinetic energy has increased; if they break free of their neighbours and become more disordered, their potential energy has increased.

■ **Section AB**
The ice starts below 0°C; its temperature rises. The molecules gain energy and vibrate more and more. Their vibrational energy is increasing.

■ **Section BC**
The ice melts at 0°C. The molecules become more disordered. Their potential energy is increasing.

■ **Section CD**
The ice has become water. Its temperature rises towards 100°C. The molecules move increasingly rapidly. Their kinetic energy is increasing.

■ **Section DE**
The water is boiling. The molecules are becoming completely separate from one another. Their movement becomes very disorderly. Their potential energy is increasing.

■ **Section EF**
The steam is being heated above 100°C. The molecules move even faster. Their kinetic energy is increasing.

From this analysis, you should realise that a change of state involves the following: there must be an input of energy; the temperature does not change; the molecules are breaking free of one another; their potential energy is increasing.

In between the changes of state: the input of energy raises the temperature of the substance; the molecules move faster; their kinetic energy is increasing.

The hardest point to appreciate is that you can put energy in to the system without its temperature rising. This happens during any change of state; the energy goes to breaking the bonds between neighbouring molecules.

It may help to think of temperature as a measure of the average kinetic energy of the molecules. When you put a thermometer in some water to measure its temperature, the water molecules collide with the thermometer and share their kinetic energy with it. At a change of state, there is no change in kinetic energy, so there is no change in temperature.

Notice that melting the ice (section BC) takes much less energy than boiling the same amount of water (section DE). This is because, when a solid melts, the molecules are still bonded to most of their immediate neighbours. When a liquid boils, each molecule breaks free of all of its neighbours. Melting may involve the breaking of one or two bonds per molecule, whereas boiling involves breaking eight or nine.

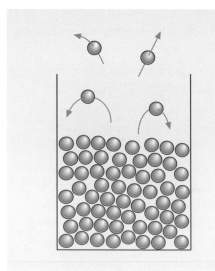

● **Figure 10.8** Fast-moving molecules leave the surface of a liquid.

Evaporation

A liquid does not have to boil to change into a gas. A puddle of rainwater dries up without having to be heated to 100 °C. When a liquid changes to a gas without boiling, we call this **evaporation**. The gas formed is called a **vapour** – this is the term used to describe a gas below its boiling point.

Any liquid has some vapour associated with it. If we think about the microscopic picture of this, we can see why (*figure 10.8*). Within the liquid, molecules are moving about. Some move faster than others, and can break free from the bulk of the liquid. They form the vapour above the liquid. Some molecules from the vapour may come back into contact with the surface of the liquid, and return to the liquid. However, there is a net outflow of energetic molecules from the liquid, and eventually it will evaporate away completely.

You may have had your skin swabbed with alcohol or ether before an injection. You will have noticed how cold your skin becomes as the volatile liquid evaporates. Similarly, you can become very cold if you get wet and stand around in a windy place. This cooling of a liquid is a very important aspect of evaporation.

When a liquid evaporates, it is the most energetic molecules that are most likely to escape. This leaves molecules with a below-average kinetic energy. Since temperature is a measure of the average kinetic energy of the molecules, it follows that the temperature of the evaporating liquid must fall.

SAQ 10.2

Use the kinetic model of matter to explain the following:
a If you leave a pan of water on the stove for a long time, it does not all boil away as soon as the temperature reaches 100 °C.
b It takes less energy to melt a 1 kg block of ice at 0 °C than to boil away 1 kg of water at 100 °C.
c When a dog is overheated, it pants. (Don't try to explain this to the dog!)

Internal energy

All matter is made up of particles, which we will refer to here as molecules. Matter can have energy. For example, if we lift up a stone, it has gravitational potential energy. If we throw it, it has kinetic energy. Kinetic and potential energies are the two general forms of energy. We consider the stone's potential and kinetic energies to be properties or attributes of the stone itself; we calculate their values (mgh and $\frac{1}{2}mv^2$) using the mass and speed of the stone.

Now think about another way in which we could increase the energy of the stone: we could heat it (*figure 10.9*). Now where does the energy from the heater go? The stone's gravitational potential

● **Figure 10.9** Increasing the internal energy of a pebble.

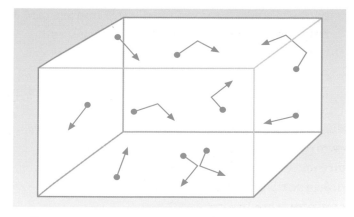

● **Figure 10.10** The molecules of a gas have both kinetic and potential energies.

and kinetic energies do not increase; it is not higher or faster than before. The energy seems to have disappeared into the stone.

Of course, you already know the answer to this. The stone gets hotter, and that means that the molecules which make up the stone have more energy, both kinetic and potential. They vibrate more and faster, and they move further apart. This energy of the molecules is known as the **internal energy** of the stone. We can define internal energy thus:

> The internal energy of a system is the sum of the randomly distributed kinetic and potential energies of its molecules.

Molecular energy

Earlier in this chapter, where we studied the phases of matter, we saw how solids, liquids and gases could be characterised by differences in the arrangement, order and motion of their molecules. We could equally have said that, in the three phases, the molecules have different amounts of kinetic and potential energies.

Now, it is a simple problem to find the internal energy of some matter. We add up the kinetic and potential energies associated with all the molecules in the matter.

For example, we consider the gas shown in *figure 10.10*. There are ten molecules in the box; each has kinetic and potential energy, and we can work out what all of these are and add them together. The principle at least is simple, and this example should serve to explain what we mean by the internal energy of a gas.

Changing internal energy

There are two obvious ways in which we can increase the internal energy of some gas: we can heat it, or we can do work on it (compress it).

■ **Heating a gas** (*figure 10.11a*)
The walls of the container become hot, and so its molecules vibrate more vigorously. The molecules of the cool gas strike the

walls, and bounce off faster. They have gained kinetic energy, and we say the temperature has risen.

■ **Doing work on a gas** (*figure 10.11b*)
In this case, a wall of the container is being pushed inwards. The molecules of the

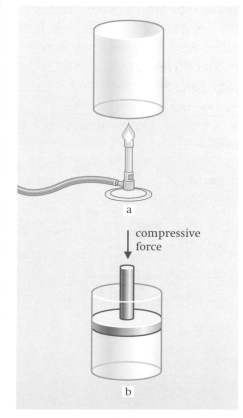

● **Figure 10.11** Two ways to increase the internal energy of a gas: **a** by heating it, and **b** by compressing it.

cool gas strike a moving wall, and bounce off faster. They have gained kinetic energy, and again the temperature has risen. This explains why a gas gets hotter when it is compressed. (We have already discussed why gases get cooler when they expand.)

There are other ways in which the internal energy of a system can be increased; by passing an electric current through it, for example. However, doing work and heating are all we need to consider here.

Calculating energy changes

So far, we have considered the effects of heating a substance in qualitative terms, and we have given an explanation in terms of a kinetic model of matter. Now we will look at the amount of energy needed to change the temperature of something, and to produce a change of state.

Specific heat capacity

If we heat some matter so that its temperature rises, the amount of energy we must supply depends on three things: the mass m of the material we are heating; the temperature rise $\Delta\theta$ we wish to achieve (Δ is Greek capital delta); and the material itself. Some materials are easier to heat than others – it takes more energy to raise the temperature of 1 kg of water by 1 °C than to raise the temperature of 1 kg of alcohol by the same amount.

We can represent this in an equation. The amount of energy ΔQ that must be supplied is given by

$$\Delta Q = mc\,\Delta\theta$$

where c is the specific heat capacity of the material. Rearranging this equation gives

$$c = \Delta Q/m\,\Delta\theta$$

Hence

> The **specific heat capacity** of a substance is numerically equal to the amount of energy required to raise the temperature of 1 kg of the substance by 1 K (or by 1 °C).

(The word 'specific' here means 'per unit mass', i.e. per kg.) From this form of the equation, you

Substance	$c\,(\mathrm{J\,kg^{-1}\,K^{-1}})$
aluminium	880
copper	380
lead	126
glass	500–680
ice	2100
water	4180
sea-water	3950
ethanol	2500
mercury	140

● **Table 10.1** Values of specific heat capacity c measured at 0 °C.

should be able to see that the units of c are $\mathrm{J\,kg^{-1}\,K^{-1}}$ (or $\mathrm{J\,kg^{-1}\,{}^{\circ}C^{-1}}$). *Table 10.1* shows some values of specific heat capacity.

Specific heat capacity is related to the gradient of the sloping sections of the graph shown earlier in *figure 10.7*. The steeper the gradient, the faster the substance heats up, and hence the lower its specific heat capacity must be.

Specific latent heat

In a similar way, we can think about the amount of energy we must supply to melt or boil a substance. In this case, we do not need to concern ourselves with temperature rise, since the temperature stays constant during a change of state. We can write an equation for the energy ΔQ that must be supplied to melt or boil a mass m of a substance:

$$\Delta Q = mL$$

Here L is the specific latent heat of the substance. Rearranging gives

$$L = \Delta Q/m$$

Hence

> The **specific latent heat** of a substance is numerically equal to the energy that must be supplied to change the state of 1 kg of the substance without any change in temperature.

For melting, you may see this called the specific latent heat of fusion.

The word 'latent' means 'hidden', and refers to the fact that, when you melt something, its

Substance	Melting L (J kg^{-1})	Boiling L (J kg^{-1})
ice, water	334 000	2 260 000
ethanol	110 000	840 000
benzene	127 000	394 000
mercury	69 000	1 100 000
aluminium	412 000	
iron	270 000	
copper	205 000	
lead	25 000	

● **Table 10.2** Values of specific latent heat.

temperature does not rise and the heat that you have put in seems to have disappeared. *Table 10.2* shows some values of specific latent heat.

We shall now give two worked examples. In these, values for *c* and *L* are taken from *tables 10.1* and *10.2*.

Worked examples

1 When 26 400 J of energy is supplied to a 2 kg block of aluminium, its temperature rises from 20°C to 35°C. Find the specific heat capacity of aluminium.

We are going to use the equation $c = \Delta Q/m\Delta\theta$. We need to write down the quantities that we know:

$\Delta Q = 26\,400$ J
$m = 2$ kg
$\Delta\theta = (35 - 20)\text{K} = 15$ K

Substituting gives

$c = 26\,400\text{ J}/(2\text{ kg} \times 15\text{ K}) = 880\text{ J kg}^{-1}\text{K}^{-1}$

2 How much energy must be supplied to change 2.0 kg of ice at −10°C to steam at 100°C?

Here we have four separate calculations to perform, corresponding to raising the temperature of the ice to 0°C, melting it, heating the water to 100°C, and boiling the water. You should be able to identify the four terms in the equation that follows:

$\Delta Q = 2\text{ kg} \times 2100\text{ J kg}^{-1}\text{K}^{-1} \times 10\text{ K}$
$\quad + 2\text{ kg} \times 334\,000\text{ J kg}^{-1}$
$\quad + 2\text{ kg} \times 4180\text{ J kg}^{-1}\text{K}^{-1} \times 100\text{ K}$
$\quad + 2\text{ kg} \times 2\,260\,000\text{ J kg}^{-1}$
$\quad = 42\,000\text{ J} + 668\,000\text{ J} + 836\,000\text{ J}$
$\quad + 4\,520\,000\text{ J}$
$\quad = 6\,066\,000\text{ J}$

Notice that three-quarters of the energy is required to boil the water when it has reached 100°C.

Ice, water, steam

Water is an unusual substance. We have already noted that it expands when it freezes – that is why ice floats on water. It also has an unusually high specific heat capacity. This means that water heats up and cools down relatively slowly. This makes water very suitable for the liquid in central heating systems.

Another consequence is that the sea cools down relatively slowly in the winter, compared to the land. Also it warms up relatively slowly in the summer. In the British Isles, we are surrounded by the sea, which helps to keep us warm in the winter and cool in the summer. In central Europe, far from the sea, temperatures fall more dramatically in the winter and rise higher in the summer. This is the origin of the difference between a maritime climate and a continental climate. If the sea was made of alcohol, the British climate would vary more between the seasons. You can probably imagine some other important consequences!

You will need to use data from *tables 10.1* and *10.2* above to answer SAQs 10.3 to 10.6.

SAQ 10.3
How much energy must be supplied to raise the temperature of 5 kg of water from 20°C to 100°C?

SAQ 10.4
Which requires more energy, heating a 2 kg block of lead by 30 K, or heating a 4 kg block of copper by 5 K?

SAQ 10.5
A well-insulated 1 kg block of iron is heated using a 50 W heater for 5 min. Its temperature rises from 22°C to 55°C. Find the specific heat capacity of iron.

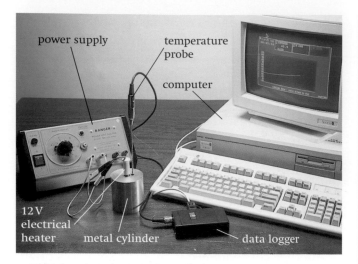

● **Figure 10.12** A practical arrangement for determining the specific heat capacity of a metal.

SAQ 10.6

A 10 g block of ice at 0 °C is put into a glass containing 100 g of water at 20 °C. How much energy is taken in by the ice in melting? What will the temperature of the water be, once the ice has all melted?

Measuring specific heat capacity

How can we measure the specific heat capacity of a material? The principle is simple: supply a known amount of energy to a known mass of the material, and measure the rise in its temperature. *Figure 10.12* shows one practical way of doing this for a metal.

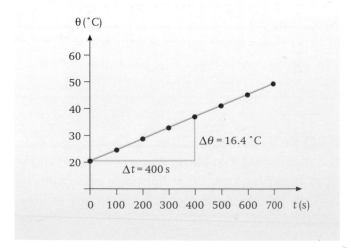

● **Figure 10.13** Temperature–time graph for an aluminium block as it is heated.

The metal is in the form of a cylindrical block of mass 1 kg. An electrical heater is used to supply the energy. This is because we can easily determine the amount of energy supplied – more easily than if we heated the metal with a Bunsen flame, for example. An ammeter and voltmeter are used to make the necessary measurements.

A thermometer or temperature sensor is used to monitor the block's temperature as it is heated. The block must not be heated too quickly; we want to be sure that the energy has time to spread throughout the metal.

The block should be insulated by wrapping it in a suitable material – this is not shown in the illustration. It would be possible in principle to determine c by making just one measurement of temperature change, but it is better to record values of the temperature as it rises and plot a graph of temperature against time. The method of calculating c is illustrated in the worked example.

Worked example

An experiment to determine the specific heat capacity c of a 1.00 kg aluminium block is carried out; the block is heated using an electrical heater. Measurements of current and p.d. show that the heater's power is 50 W. Measurements of the rising temperature of the block are represented by the graph shown in *figure 10.13*. Calculate a value for c.

Step 1: Write down the equation that relates energy change to specific heat capacity:

$$\Delta Q = mc\,\Delta\theta$$

Step 2: Divide both sides by a time interval Δt:

$$\Delta Q/\Delta t = mc\,\Delta\theta/\Delta t$$

The quantity on the left-hand side, $\Delta Q/\Delta t$, is simply the rate at which energy is supplied, i.e. the power of the heater (50 W). The quantity $\Delta\theta/\Delta t$ that appears on the right-hand side is the rate of rise of temperature of the block, i.e. the gradient of the θ–t graph.

Step 3: Substitute values, rearrange and solve:

$$50\,\text{W} = 1.00\,\text{kg} \times c \times 0.041\,°\text{C s}^{-1}$$
$$c = 50\,\text{W}/(1.00\,\text{kg} \times 0.041\,°\text{C s}^{-1})$$
$$= 1220\,\text{J kg}^{-1}\,\text{K}^{-1}$$

Sources of error

This experiment can give reasonably good measurements of specific heat capacities. As noted earlier, it is desirable to have a relatively low rate of heating, so that heat spreads throughout the block. If the block is heated rapidly, different parts may be at different temperatures.

Insulation is also vital. Inevitably, some energy will escape to the surroundings. This means that *more* energy must be supplied to the block for each degree rise in temperature, and so the final result will be too high. One way around this is to cool the block below room temperature before beginning to heat it. Then, as its temperature rises past room temperature, heat losses will be zero in principle, because there is no temperature difference between the block and its surroundings.

SAQ 10.7

At higher temperature, the graph shown in *figure 10.13* deviates increasingly from a straight line. Suggest an explanation for this.

SAQ 10.8

In measurements of the specific heat capacity of a metal, energy losses to the surroundings are a source of error. Is this a systematic error or random error? Justify your answer.

SAQ 10.9

In an experiment to measure the specific heat capacity of water, a student used an electrical heater to heat some water. His results are shown below. Calculate a value for the heat capacity of water, and comment on any likely sources of error in the result.
mass of beaker = 150 g
mass of beaker + water = 672 g
current to heater = 3.9 A
p.d. across heater = 11.4 V
initial temperature = 18.5 °C
final temperature = 30.2 °C
time taken = 13 min

Measuring specific latent heat

You can measure the specific latent heat of a material in a similar way to its specific heat capacity: heat it electrically. The difference here is that we are looking for a change of state, not a rise in temperature.

Figure 10.14 shows one method of measuring the latent heat of vaporisation (boiling) of water. An electric kettle is part-filled with water, and placed on an electronic balance. The kettle is switched on and allowed to boil continuously. (The automatic cut-off has been over-ridden.) The mass of the kettle, which decreases as water boils away, is monitored. Knowing the power rating of the kettle, the specific latent heat can be deduced as follows:
We have

$$\Delta Q = L\,\Delta m$$

Dividing both sides by a time interval Δt, we obtain

$$\Delta Q/\Delta t = L\,\Delta m/\Delta t$$

Here $\Delta Q/\Delta t$ is the rate at which energy is supplied (the power of the kettle); and $\Delta m/\Delta t$ is the rate of loss of mass. Hence

$$L = \text{power}/(\text{rate of loss of mass})$$

SAQ 10.10

An electric kettle is rated at 3 kW. It is filled with 800 g of water. It is switched on and comes to the boil. If it continues to boil, estimate how long it will take for all of the water to boil away. Why is your answer only an estimate?

[Specific latent heat of vaporisation of water = 2.26 MJ kg^{-1}]

● **Figure 10.14** Measuring the latent heat of boiling of water.

SAQ 10.11

In an experiment to measure the specific heat capacity of a liquid, we would have to take account of the heat that is needed to raise the temperature of the container. In the experiment described above to determine *L* for water, the water is contained in a kettle.

a Why do we not have to be concerned about energy supplied to the material of the kettle?

b Energy escapes from the kettle to the surroundings. How will this affect the result obtained for *L*?

SUMMARY

◆ The kinetic model of matter allows us to explain behaviour (e.g. changes of state) and macroscopic properties (e.g. specific heat and latent heat) in terms of the behaviour of molecules.

◆ The internal energy of a system is the sum of the kinetic and potential energies associated with the molecules that make up the system.

◆ If the temperature of an object increases, there is an increase in its internal energy.

◆ Internal energy also increases during a change of state, but there is no change in temperature.

◆ The specific heat capacity *c* of a substance is numerically equal to the energy required to raise the temperature of 1 kg by 1 K.

◆ The energy transferred in raising the temperature of a substance is given by $\Delta Q = mc\,\Delta\theta$.

◆ The specific latent heat *L* of a substance is numerically equal to the energy required to change the state of 1 kg of the substance without any change in temperature.

◆ The energy transferred in changing the state of a substance is given by $\Delta Q = L\,\Delta m$.

Questions

1   How much energy must be supplied to change 1 kg of ice at 0 °C into 1 kg of steam at 100 °C?

   [Specific latent heat of melting of ice
   = 334 kJ kg^{-1}
   Specific latent heat of boiling of water
   = 2.26 MJ kg^{-1}
   Specific heat capacity of water
   = 4180 J kg^{-1} K^{-1}]

2   A block of paraffin wax was heated gently, at a steady rate. Heating was continued after the wax had completely melted. The graph of *figure 10.15* shows how the material's temperature varied during the experiment.

   a For each section of the graph (AB, BC and CD), say what state the material was in.

   b For each section, say whether the material's internal energy was increasing, decreasing or remaining constant.

   c Consider the two sloping sections of the graph. State whether the material's specific heat capacity is greater when it is a solid or when it is a liquid. Justify your answer.

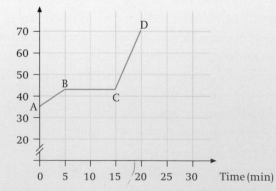

● **Figure 10.15** Temperature variation of a sample of wax, heated at a constant rate.

CHAPTER 11

Ideal gases

By the end of this chapter you should be able to:

1 appreciate that one mole (1 mol) is 6.02×10^{23} particles and that 6.02×10^{23} mol^{-1} is the Avogadro constant N_A;

2 demonstrate knowledge that there is an absolute scale of temperature that does not depend upon the physical property of any particular substance, i.e. the thermodynamic scale;

3 appreciate that, on the thermodynamic (Kelvin) scale, absolute zero is the temperature at which all substances have a minimum internal energy;

4 show familiarity with temperatures measured in kelvin and degrees Celsius;

5 recall and use the ideal gas equation $pV = nRT$, where n is the amount of gas in moles;

6 recall that the mean kinetic energy of a molecule of an ideal gas is proportional to the thermodynamic temperature.

Gases

We picture the particles that make up a gas as being fast-moving. They bounce off the walls of their container (and off each other) as they travel around at high speed. But how do we know that these particles are moving like this?

It is much harder to find ways of visualising the particles of a gas than those of a solid, simply because they are moving about in such a disordered way, and because most of a gas is empty space. However, the movement of gas particles was investigated as long ago as the 1820s, by an English botanist, Robert Brown. He was investigating the motion of pollen grains; it is easier in the laboratory to look at the movement of smoke grains.

Observing Brownian motion

The oxygen and nitrogen molecules that make up most of the air are far too small to see; they are much smaller than the wavelength of light. So we have to look at something bigger, and see the

effect of the air molecules. In this experiment (*figure 11.1*), the smoke cell contains air into which a small amount of smoke has been introduced.

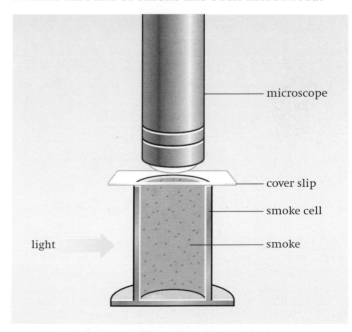

microscope

cover slip

smoke cell

light

smoke

● **Figure 11.1** Experimental arrangement for observing Brownian motion.

The cell is lit from the side, and the microscope is used to view the smoke grains.

The smoke grains show up as tiny specks of reflected light, but they are too small to see any detail of their shape. What is noticeable is the way they move. If you can concentrate on a single grain, you will see that it follows a somewhat jerky and erratic path. This is a consequence of the grain suffering repeated collisions with air molecules. Since the air molecules are much smaller than the smoke grain, we can deduce that they must be moving much faster than the smoke grain if they are to affect it in this way.

[Note that you may observe that all of the smoke grains in your field of view have a tendency to travel in one particular direction. This is a consequence of convection currents in the air. Also, you may have to adjust the focus of the microscope to keep track of an individual grain, as it moves up or down in the cell.]

Figure 11.2 shows the sort of path followed by a particle showing Brownian motion. In fact, this is from a paper by the French physicist Jean Perrin, published in 1911. He was looking at the movement of a pollen grain suspended in water. He

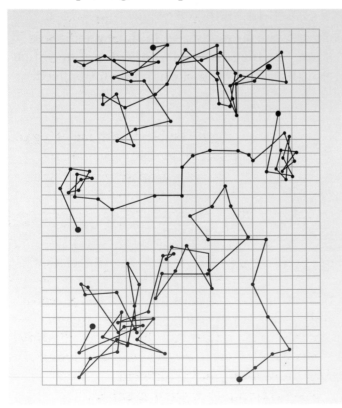

● **Figure 11.2** Brownian motion of a particle, as drawn by the French scientist Perrin.

recorded its position every 30 s; the grid spacing is approximately 3 μm. From this he could deduce the average speed of the grain, and hence work out details of the movement of water molecules.

SAQ 11.1

Consider a smoke grain, mass M and speed V. It is constantly buffeted by air molecules, mass m and speed v. It is reasonable to assume that the smoke grain will have kinetic energy approximately equal to the kinetic energy of a single air molecule $(\text{KE} = \frac{1}{2}mv^2)$. Show that, since $M \gg m$ (M is much greater than m), it follows that the air molecules must be moving much faster than the smoke grain ($v \gg V$).

Fast molecules

For air at standard temperature and pressure (STP), the average speed of the molecules is about 400 m s^{-1}. At any moment, some are moving faster than this, and others more slowly. If we could follow the movement of a single air molecule, we would find that, some of the time, its speed was greater than this average; at other times it would be less. The velocity of an individual molecule changes every time it collides with anything else.

This value for molecular speed is reasonable. It is comparable to (but greater than) the speed of sound in air (approximately 330 m s^{-1} at STP). If the molecules were moving much faster than this, they would be approaching escape velocity, and the atmosphere would have escaped from the Earth's gravitational field long ago.

Explaining pressure

A gas exerts pressure on any surface with which it comes into contact. Pressure is a macroscopic property, defined as the force exerted per unit area of the surface.

The pressure of the atmosphere at sea level is approximately 100 000 Pa. The surface area of a typical person is 2 m^2. Hence the force exerted on them by the atmosphere is 200 000 N. This is approximately the weight of 200 000 apples! Fortunately, air inside the body presses outwards with an equal and opposite force, so we do not collapse under the influence of this large force.

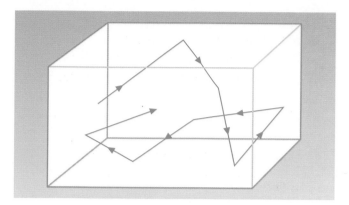

● **Figure 11.3** The path of a single molecule in an otherwise empty box.

We can explain the macroscopic phenomenon of pressure by thinking about the behaviour of the microscopic particles that make up the atmosphere. *Figure 11.3* shows the movement of a single molecule of air in a box. It bounces around inside, colliding with the various surfaces of the box. At each collision, it exerts a small impulse on the box. The pressure on the box is a result of the impulses exerted by the vast number of molecules in the box.

Of course, because of the great difference in scale between ourselves and the air molecules that are constantly battering us, we do not observe a multiplicity of tiny impulses. Instead, the pressure of the atmosphere is a constant effect, which we do not notice under normal circumstances.

The gas laws and absolute zero

We are going to picture a container of gas, such as the box shown in *figure 11.4*. There are four properties of this gas that we might measure: pressure, temperature, volume and mass.

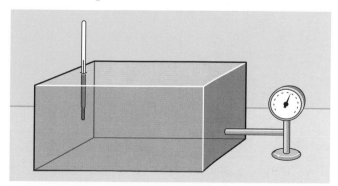

● **Figure 11.4** A gas has four measurable properties, which are all related to one another: pressure, temperature, volume and mass.

■ **Pressure**
This is the force exerted normally per unit area by the gas on the walls of the container. It is measured in pascals, Pa (1 Pa = 1 N m^{-2}).

■ **Temperature**
This might be measured in °C, but in practice it is more useful to use the thermodynamic (Kelvin) scale of temperature. This scale starts at absolute zero, an idea that is discussed in detail below.

■ **Volume**
This is measured in m^3.

■ **Mass**
This is measured in g or kg. In practice, it is more useful to consider the **amount** of gas measured in moles.

> One **mole** of any substance is the amount of that substance which contains the same number of particles (atoms, molecules etc.) as there are in 0.012 kg of carbon-12.

One mole of any substance is equal to the relative molecular mass of the substance measured in grams. For example, one mole of oxygen O_2 has a mass of about 32 g. A mole of any gas contains a standard number of molecules (the Avogadro constant, 6.02×10^{23} mol^{-1}, approximately). It turns out that, if we consider equal numbers of moles of two different gases under the same conditions, their properties are the same.

Boyle's law

This law relates the pressure and volume of a gas. If a gas is compressed (pressure increased), its volume decreases. Pressure p and volume V are inversely related. We can write **Boyle's law** as:

> The volume of a fixed mass of gas is inversely proportional to its pressure, provided the temperature remains constant.

Note that this law relates two variables, pressure and volume, and it requires that the other two, mass and temperature, remain constant. If either changed as the pressure of the gas was changed, then the result would be different.

Boyle's law can be written as either a proportionality or an equation:

$$p \propto 1/V \quad \text{or} \quad pV = \text{constant}$$

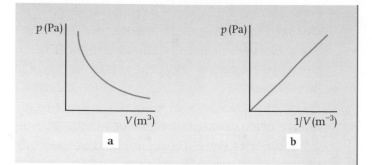

● **Figure 11.5** Graphical representations of the relationship between pressure and volume of a gas (Boyle's law).

We can also represent Boyle's law as a graph, as shown in *figure 11.5*. A graph of p against $1/V$ is a straight line passing through the origin, showing direct proportionality.

Charles' law

This law describes how the volume of a gas depends on its temperature, and can be investigated using apparatus like that shown in *figure 11.6*.

As the water bath is heated, the trapped air expands and its volume increases in proportion to the temperature change. Notice that the pressure of the air remains constant throughout. This arrangement can be used to find values of volume and temperature between 0 °C and 100 °C, and an idealised set of results are represented in *figure 11.7*.

This graph does not show that the volume of a gas is proportional to its temperature on the Celsius scale. If a gas contracted to zero volume at 0 °C, the atmosphere would condense on a cold day, and we would have a great deal of difficulty in breathing! However, the graph *does* show that there is a temperature at which the volume of a gas does, in principle, shrink to zero. This temperature is found by extrapolating the graph to zero volume (the dashed line), and it is roughly −273 °C. This is a fundamental temperature, below which it is impossible to go, and it is known as **absolute zero**.

Figure 11.7 also shows how we can renumber the temperature scale, starting at absolute zero, 0 K. Now 0 °C becomes 273.15 K and 100 °C becomes 373.15 K. This graph shows clearly that

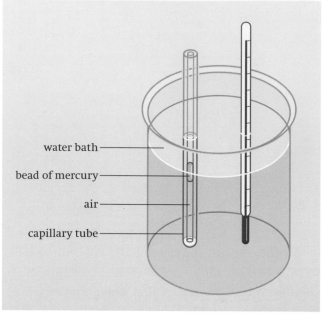

● **Figure 11.6** Apparatus for investigating Charles' law.

volume V of the gas is proportional to its absolute temperature, measured on the thermodynamic (Kelvin) scale. We can write **Charles' law** as:

> The volume of a fixed mass of gas is directly proportional to its absolute temperature, provided its pressure remains constant.

We can write this as a proportionality or as an equality:

$$V \propto T \qquad \text{or} \qquad V/T = \text{constant}$$

Note again that the other two variables, mass and pressure, must remain fixed for this law to hold.

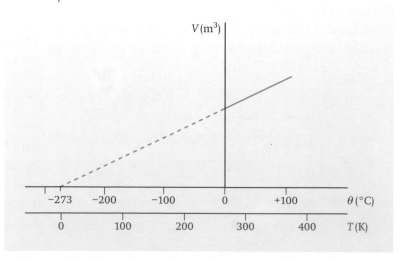

● **Figure 11.7** The volume of a gas increases as its temperature increases.

The pressure law

This law describes how the pressure of a gas changes as the temperature changes. Again, we have to consider the absolute temperature of the gas. The relationship between pressure p and thermodynamic temperature T is shown as a graph in *figure 11.8*. Again, we have direct proportionality. We can write the **pressure law** as:

> The pressure of a fixed mass of gas is directly proportional to its absolute temperature, provided its volume remains constant.

This can be written as:

$$p \propto T \qquad \text{or} \qquad p/T = \text{constant}$$

If we combine all three laws, we can arrive at a single equation for a fixed mass of gas:

$$\frac{pV}{T} = \text{constant}$$

This is useful because very often we have situations where all three variables, p, V and T, are changing at the same time. For example, if you increase the pressure on a gas, its volume will decrease and its temperature will increase.

The thermodynamic (Kelvin) scale

The Celsius scale of temperature is based on the properties of water. It takes two fixed points, the melting point of pure ice and the boiling point of pure water, and divides the range between them into 100 equal intervals.

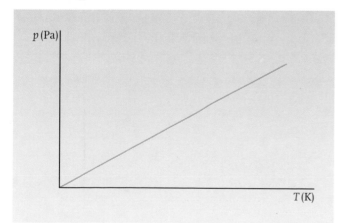

● **Figure 11.8** Graphical representation of the relationship between pressure and temperature for a gas.

There is nothing intrinsically special about these two fixed points. In fact, both change if the pressure changes or if the water is impure. The Kelvin scale is a better scale in that one of its fixed points, absolute zero, has a greater significance than either of the Celsius fixed points.

Absolute zero is a very significant temperature; we have arrived at it by considering the behaviour of gases, but its significance is greater than this. It is not possible to have a temperature lower than 0 K. Sometimes it is suggested that, at this temperature, matter has no energy left in it. This is not strictly true; it is more correct to say that, for any matter at absolute zero, it is impossible to *remove* any more energy from it. Hence absolute zero is the temperature at which all substances have the minimum internal energy.

We use different symbols to represent temperatures on these two scales: θ for the Celsius scale, and T for the thermodynamic (Kelvin) scale. To convert between the two scales, we use these relationships:

$$\theta\,(^{\circ}\text{C}) = T\,(\text{K}) - 273.15$$
$$T\,(\text{K}) = \theta\,(^{\circ}\text{C}) + 273.15$$

For most practical purposes, we round off the conversion factor to 273 as shown in the conversion chart (*figure 11.9*).

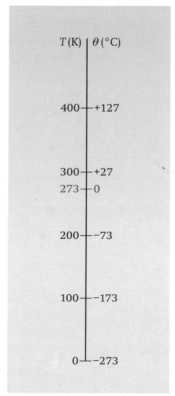

● **Figure 11.9**
A conversion chart relating temperatures on the thermodynamic (Kelvin) and Celsius scales.

The **thermodynamic scale** is sometimes known as the Kelvin scale of temperature. It is different from other scales of temperature, such as the Celsius and Fahrenheit scales, because it does not depend on somewhat variable properties of substances such as the melting and boiling points of water. It has two fixed points:

- absolute zero, which is defined as 0 K;
- the triple point of water, the temperature at which ice, water and water vapour can co-exist, which is defined as 273.16 K.

So the gap between absolute zero and the triple point of water is divided into 273.16 equal divisions. Each division is 1 K.

Ideal gases

The laws that we have considered above are based on experimental observations of gases such as air, helium, nitrogen, etc., at temperatures and pressures around room temperature and pressure. In practice, if we change to more extreme conditions, such as low temperatures or high pressures, gases start to deviate from these laws. For example, *figure 11.10* shows what happens when nitrogen is cooled down towards absolute zero. At first, the graph of volume against temperature follows a good straight line. However, as it approaches the temperature at which it condenses, it deviates from ideal behaviour, and at 77 K it condenses to become liquid nitrogen.

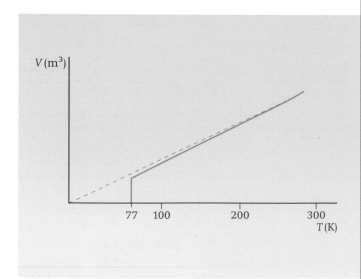

- **Figure 11.10** A real gas (in this case, nitrogen) deviates from the behaviour predicted by Charles' law at low temperatures.

Thus we have to attach a proviso to the gas laws discussed above. We say that these laws apply to an ideal gas; when we are dealing with real gases, we have to be aware that their behaviour may be significantly different from that suggested by these laws.

An **ideal gas** is thus defined as one that obeys all three laws; in other words, pV/T = constant for a fixed mass of the gas at all values of pressure, volume and temperature.

SAQ 11.2
a Convert each of the following temperatures from the Celsius scale to the thermodynamic scale: 0 °C, 20 °C, 120 °C, 500 °C, 223 °C, −200 °C.
b Convert each of the following temperatures from the thermodynamic scale to the Celsius scale: 0 K, 20 K, 100 K, 300 K, 373 K, 500 K.

SAQ 11.3
Use the gas laws to explain the following observations:
a The pressure in a car tyre increases on a hot day.
b A toy balloon shrinks when placed in a fridge.

SAQ 11.4
The electrical resistance of a pure copper wire is mostly due to the vibrations of the copper atoms. *Table 11.1* shows how the resistance of a piece of copper wire is found to change as it is heated. Draw a graph to show these data, and use it to deduce a value for absolute zero. (Start the temperature scale of your graph at −300 °C.) Explain why the resistance of copper should be zero at this temperature.

Temperature (°C)	Resistance (Ω)
10	3120
50	3600
75	3900
100	4200
150	4800
220	5640
260	6120

- **Table 11.1** Resistance of a copper wire.

Ideal gas equation

It is possible to write a single equation embodying all three gas laws, and taking into account the amount of gas being considered. For n moles of an ideal gas, we have

$pV = nRT$

This equation is known as the **ideal gas equation** or the **equation of state** for an ideal gas; it is an equation that relates all of the four variable quantities that were discussed at the beginning of the previous section. The constant of proportionality R is called the **universal gas constant**, and its value is

$R = 8.31\,\text{J}\,\text{mol}^{-1}\text{K}^{-1}$

Note that it doesn't matter what gas we are considering – it could be a very light gas like hydrogen, or a much heavier one like carbon dioxide. So long as it is behaving as an ideal gas, we can use the same equation of state with the same constant R.

Calculating n

Sometimes we know the mass of gas we are concerned with, and then we have to be able to find how many moles this represents. To do this, we use this relationship:

$$\text{number of moles} = \frac{\text{mass (g)}}{\text{molar mass (g mol}^{-1})}$$

For example, how many moles are there in 1.6 kg of oxygen?

molar mass of oxygen = $32\,\text{g}\,\text{mol}^{-1}$
number of moles = $1600\,\text{g}/32\,\text{g}\,\text{mol}^{-1} = 50\,\text{mol}$

Worked examples

1 Find the volume occupied by 1 mol of an ideal gas at standard temperature and pressure.

Here we have the following values:

$p = 1.013 \times 10^5\,\text{Pa}$
$T = 273\,\text{K}$
$n = 1$

Substituting in the equation of state gives

$V = nRT/p$
$= 1 \times 8.31\,\text{J}\,\text{mol}^{-1}\text{K}^{-1} \times 273\,\text{K}/(1.013 \times 10^5\,\text{Pa})$

$= 0.0224\,\text{m}^3$
$= 22.4\,\text{dm}^3$

This value, the volume of one mole of gas at standard temperature and pressure, is well worth remembering. It is certainly known by all chemists.

2 A car tyre contains $0.02\,\text{m}^3$ of air at 27 °C and at a pressure of 3×10^5 Pa. What is the mass of the air in the tyre? (Molar mass of air = 28.8 g.)

Here, we need first to calculate the number of moles of air using the equation of state. We have:

$p = 3 \times 10^5\,\text{Pa}$
$V = 0.02\,\text{m}^3$
$T = 27\,°\text{C} = 300\,\text{K}$

So, from the equation of state:

$n = pV/RT$
$= \dfrac{3 \times 10^5\,\text{Pa} \times 0.02\,\text{m}^3}{8.31\,\text{J}\,\text{mol}^{-1}\text{K}^{-1} \times 300\,\text{K}}$
$= 2.41\,\text{mol}$

Now we can calculate the mass of air:

mass = number of moles × molar mass
$= 2.41\,\text{mol} \times 28.8\,\text{g}\,\text{mol}^{-1} = 69.4\,\text{g}$

SAQ 11.5
How many moles are there in 100 g of nitrogen? (Molar mass of N_2 = 28 g.) What volume does this mass occupy at standard temperature and pressure? (STP = 0 °C, 1.013×10^5 Pa.)

SAQ 11.6
At what temperature would 1 kg of oxygen occupy $1\,\text{m}^3$ at a pressure of 10^5 Pa? (Molar mass of O_2 = 32 g.)

SAQ 11.7
A cylinder of hydrogen has a volume of $0.1\,\text{m}^3$. Its pressure is found to be 20 atmospheres at 20 °C. What mass of hydrogen does it contain? If it was filled with oxygen instead to the same pressure, how much oxygen would it contain? (Molar mass of H_2 = 2 g, of O_2 = 32 g; 1 atmosphere = 10^5 Pa.)

Temperature and molecular energy

The equation of state for an ideal gas relates four macroscopic properties of a gas – pressure, volume, temperature and amount of gas. How does this relate to our microscopic picture of a gas? We picture a gas as being made up of a large number of fast-moving molecules (or atoms). They rush around in a rather haphazard way, colliding with one another and with the walls of their container. Collisions with the walls give rise to the pressure of the gas on the container; at higher temperatures, the molecules move faster.

Imagine taking the temperature of a hot gas using a mercury-in-glass thermometer. You place the bulb of the thermometer in the gas. The molecules of the gas collide with the bulb, sharing their energy with it. Eventually, the gas and the bulb are at the same temperature and you can read the temperature from the scale. At a higher temperature, the gas molecules have greater kinetic energy; they give more energy to the bulb and the mercury rises higher. Hence the reading on the thermometer is an indication of the kinetic energy of the gas molecules.

In fact, the following can be shown:

> The mean translational kinetic energy of a molecule of an ideal gas is proportional to the thermodynamic temperature.

(You may wish to recall this as: mean KE $\propto T$.) We need to consider two of the terms in this statement. Firstly, we talk about *translational* KE. This is the energy that the molecule has because it is moving along; a molecule made of two or more atoms may also spin or tumble around, and is then said to have rotational kinetic energy – see *figure 11.11*.

Secondly, we talk about *mean* (or average) translational KE. There are two ways to find the average translational KE of a molecule of a gas: add up all the KEs of the individual molecules of the gas and calculate the average. Alternatively, watch an individual molecule over a period of time as it moves about, colliding with other molecules and the walls of the container, and calculate its average KE over this time. Both should give the same answer.

Mass, energy and temperature

Since mean KE $\propto T$, it follows that if we double the thermodynamic temperature of an ideal gas (e.g. from 300 K to 600 K), we double the mean KE of its molecules. It doesn't follow that we have doubled their speed; because KE $\propto v^2$, their speed has increased by a factor of $\sqrt{2}$.

Air is a mixture of several gases: nitrogen, oxygen, carbon dioxide etc. In a sample of air, the mean KE of the nitrogen molecules is the same as that of the oxygen molecules and that of the carbon dioxide molecules. This comes about because they are all repeatedly colliding with one another, sharing their energy. Carbon dioxide molecules have greater mass than oxygen molecules; since their mean translational KE is the same, it follows that the carbon dioxide molecules move more slowly than the oxygen molecules.

SAQ 11.8

Show that, if the average speed of the molecules in an ideal gas is doubled, the absolute temperature of the gas increases by a factor of 4.

SAQ 11.9

Air consists of molecules of oxygen and nitrogen. A nitrogen molecule has less mass than an oxygen molecule. In a particular sample of air, which would you expect to have the greater average speed? Explain your answer.

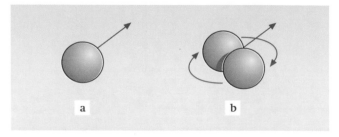

● **Figure 11.11 a** A monatomic molecule has translational kinetic energy. **b** A diatomic molecule can have both translational and rotational kinetic energy.

SUMMARY

- Temperatures on the thermodynamic (Kelvin) and Celsius scales of temperature are related by $T\,(\text{K}) = \theta\,(°\text{C}) + 273.15$.

- At absolute zero, all substances have a minimum internal energy.

- The gas laws are summarised by the equation of state for an ideal gas, $pV = nRT$, with temperatures measured on the thermodynamic scale.

- The mean translational kinetic energy of a molecule of an ideal gas is proportional to the thermodynamic temperature.

Questions

(universal gas constant $R = 8.31\,\text{J}\,\text{mol}^{-1}\,\text{K}^{-1}$)

1 At what temperature (in K) will 1 mol of a gas occupy $1\,\text{m}^3$ at a pressure of $10^4\,\text{Pa}$?

2 A fixed mass of gas expands to twice its original volume at a constant temperature. How do the following change:
   a the pressure of the gas;
   b the mean translational kinetic energy of its molecules?

3 Calculate the volume of 5 mol of an ideal gas at a pressure of $10^5\,\text{Pa}$ and a temperature of $200\,°\text{C}$.

CHAPTER 12

Atomic structure

By the end of this chapter you should be able to:

1 demonstrate a qualitative understanding of the α-particle scattering experiment and the evidence that this provides for the existence, charge and small size of the nucleus;

2 distinguish between nucleon (mass) number and proton (atomic) number;

3 understand that an element can exist in various isotopic forms, each with a different number of neutrons;

4 use the usual notation for the representation of nuclides;

5 demonstrate a qualitative understanding of the diffraction of X-rays, electrons and neutrons and the evidence that this provides for crystal structure and the spacing of atoms;

6 demonstrate a qualitative understanding of high-energy electron scattering and the evidence that this provides for the radius of the nucleus;

7 show an awareness of the relative sizes of nuclei, atoms and molecules.

Looking inside the atom

The idea that matter is composed of very small particles called **atoms** was first suggested by the Greeks some two thousand years ago. However, it was not until the middle of the nineteenth century that any ideas about the *inside* of the atom were proposed.

It was the English scientist J. J. Thomson (*figure 12.1*) who suggested that the atom is a neutral particle made of a positive charge with lumps of negative charge (electrons) in it. At the time he was also investigating the nature of the particles in cathode rays (produced when an electrically charged plate is heated), and he presented his conclusions at the Royal Institution on 30 April 1897. He could not measure the charge and mass of the cathode ray particles separately, but it was clear that a new particle, probably much smaller than the hydrogen atom, had been discovered. Thomson called this particle a 'corpuscle' and used this term for many years even after the name **electron** had been given to it by most other physicists. Since atoms are neutral

● **Figure 12.1** J. J. Thomson at work.

and physicists had discovered a negatively charged part of an atom, it meant that there were both positive and negative charges in an atom. We now call this the **plum pudding model** of the atom (positive pudding with negative plums!).

Other experiments show that the electron has a mass of 9.11×10^{-31} kg (m_e) and a charge of -1.6×10^{-19} C ($-e$).

Rutherford scattering and the nucleus

Early in the twentieth century, many physicists were investigating the recently discovered phenomenon of radioactivity, the process whereby nuclei emit radiation. One kind of radiation they found consisted of what they called α-particles (alpha-particles). These α-particles were known to be smaller than atoms, and had relatively high energies, and therefore they were useful in experiments designed to discover what atoms were made of.

In 1906, while experimenting with the passage of α-particles through a thin mica sheet, Rutherford (*figure 12.2*) noticed that most of the α-particles passed straight through. In 1911 he carried out a further series of experiments with Geiger and Marsden at the University of Manchester using gold foil in place of the mica. They fired α-particles at a piece of gold foil only 10^{-6} m thick. Most of the α-particles went straight through, some were deflected slightly, but about

● **Figure 12.2** Ernest Rutherford (on the right) in the Cavendish Laboratory, Cambridge, England. He had a loud voice that could disturb sensitive apparatus and so the notice was a joke aimed at him.

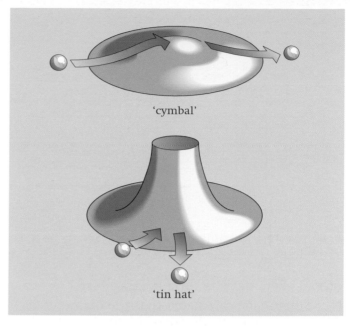

● **Figure 12.3** An analogy for Rutherford's experiment.

1 in 20 000 were deflected through an angle of more than 90°, so that they appeared to bounce back off the foil. When Geiger told Rutherford of the results, Rutherford wrote: 'It was quite the most incredible event that has happened to me in my life. It was almost as incredible as if you fired a 15 inch shell at a piece of tissue paper and it came back and hit you.' This gave Rutherford the idea that atoms might be mostly empty space with a central **nucleus** that only affected the α-particles when they came close to it.

A very simple analogy (or model) of the experiment is shown in *figure 12.3*. When you roll a ball-bearing down a slope towards the 'cymbal', it can be deflected; but even if it is rolled directly at the cymbal's centre, it does not come back but rolls over it and carries on to the other side. However, using the 'tin hat' shape, with a much narrower but higher central bulge, any ball-bearings rolled close to the centre will be markedly deflected, and those rolled directly towards it will come straight back. The shape of the cymbal represents the shape of the electric field of an atom in the 'plum pudding' model: low central intensity and spread out. The 'tin hat' represents that for the nuclear model: high central intensity and concentrated.

The paths of an α-particle near a nucleus are shown in *figure 12.4*. Rutherford reasoned that the large deflection of the α-particle must be due to a very small charged nucleus with a very large

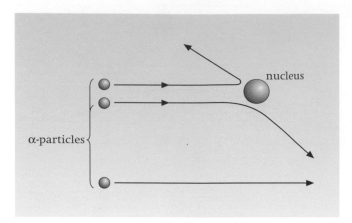

● **Figure 12.4** Possible paths of an α-particle near a nucleus.

electric field near its surface. From his experiments he calculated that the diameter of the gold nucleus was about 10^{-14} m. It has since been shown that the very large deflection of the α-particle is due to the electrostatic repulsion between the positive charges of the α-particle and the positive charges in the nucleus of the atom. The closer the path of the α-particle gets to the nucleus, the greater will be this repulsion.

SAQ 12.1
Rutherford's scattering experiments were done in an evacuated container. Why was this necessary?

The structure of the nucleus
The nucleus is small and positively charged, but what is it made up of? After Rutherford had described the size and mass of the nucleus, scientists carried out experiments to see what it was made from. They discovered two kinds of particles.

Discovery of the proton
The first subnuclear particle to be identified was the proton, discovered by Rutherford in 1919. He used the apparatus shown in *figure 12.5*. Alpha-particles were passed through some nitrogen gas in a cylinder and flashes of light were seen on a screen. Rutherford knew that these flashes

were produced by the impact of particles on the screen. A sheet of aluminium foil in front of the screen prevented any α-particles reaching it, so there must have been some other kind of particle emitted by the foil when the α-particles hit the foil. Measurements were made of the deflection of the penetrating particles that passed between the foil and the screen, and these measurements proved that they were particles smaller than most nuclei and with a charge (shown by other experiments to be positive) equal in size to that of the electron. These particles were called **protons**.

Discovery of the neutron
Rutherford had shown that nuclei contained charged protons, and then in 1932 Chadwick discovered the neutron. This was an electrically neutral particle with a slightly greater mass than that of the proton. He did this by bombarding beryllium with α-particles emitted from polonium (*figure 12.6*). A penetrating neutral radiation was produced by the beryllium, and when this radiation fell on a piece of paraffin wax, protons with high energy were emitted by the paraffin. The neutral radiation was difficult to detect, but the protons emitted as a result of this neutral radiation were quite easily detected. The conclusion was that the penetrating neutral radiation consisted of uncharged particles that could pass easily through matter without a large transfer of energy, since particles with no charge

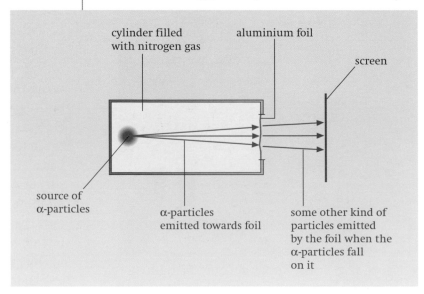

● **Figure 12.5** A schematic diagram of the apparatus used in the discovery of the proton.

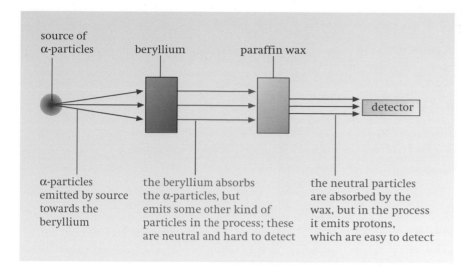

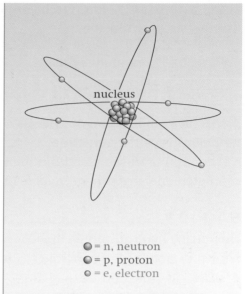

= n, neutron
= p, proton
= e, electron

- **Figure 12.6** A schematic diagram of the apparatus used in the discovery of the neutron.

- **Figure 12.7** A simple model of the atom.

produce virtually no ionisation of matter. Chadwick called these particles **neutrons**. Neutrons collide elastically with atoms, transferring more energy to a light atom than to a heavy one. For this reason, neutron radiation is especially damaging to human tissue.

SAQ 12.2

Explain carefully why neutron radiation is so dangerous to humans.

A simple atom model

We have discussed protons and neutrons in the atom, but what about the electrons? They orbit the nucleus in a cloud, some closer to and some further from the centre of the nucleus. This fact and the experiments and discoveries covered in this chapter so far suggest a model for the atom like the one shown in *figure 12.7*. From this model it looks as though all matter, including ourselves, is mostly empty space. For example, if we scaled up the hydrogen atom so that the nucleus was the size of a 1 cm diameter marble, the orbiting electron would be a grain of sand some 800 m away!

Particle	Nature	Relative mass (proton = 1)*	Charge†
proton	proton	1	$+e$
neutron	neutron	1	0
electron	electron	0.0005	$-e$
alpha (α)	helium nucleus ‡	4	$+2e$

* The numbers given for the masses are approximate.
† $e = 1.6 \times 10^{-19}$ C.
‡ Notice that the α-particle is in fact a helium nucleus. It contains two protons and two neutrons.

- **Table 12.1** Summary of the particles that we have met so far in this chapter.

Nucleons and electrons

We will start this section with a summary of the particles mentioned so far (*table 12.1*). All nuclei, except the lightest form of hydrogen, contain protons and neutrons, and each nucleus is described by the number of protons and neutrons that it contains. Protons and neutrons in a nucleus are collectively called **nucleons**. For example, in a nucleus of gold, there are 79 protons and 118 neutrons, giving a total of 197 nucleons altogether. The total number of nucleons in a nucleus is called the **nucleon number** (mass number) A. This is equal to the sum of the number of neutrons in the nucleus, the **neutron number** N, and the number of protons, the **proton number** (atomic number) Z, i.e.

$$A = N + Z$$

Any nucleus can be represented by the symbol for the element along with the nucleon number and proton number as shown below:

$$\begin{smallmatrix} \text{nucleon number} \\ \text{proton number} \end{smallmatrix} \text{element symbol} \qquad {}^{A}_{Z}X$$

oxygen ${}^{16}_{8}O$ gold ${}^{197}_{79}Au$ uranium ${}^{235}_{92}U$

A specific combination of protons and neutrons in a nucleus is called a **nuclide**.

The proton and nucleon numbers of some common elements are shown in *table 12.2*.

SAQ 12.3

How many neutrons are in the following nuclei shown in *table 12.2*: **a** nitrogen, **b** bromine, **c** silver, **d** gold and **e** mercury?

You can see from *table 12.2* that, as the nuclei get heavier, so the ratio of the number of neutrons to the number of protons gets larger. For example, for light elements such as hydrogen, helium, carbon and oxygen the ratio is 1, for iron it is 1.15 and for uranium it has risen to 1.59. After this it starts to fall again for the artificial elements with Z > 92. A graph of neutron number against proton number for the naturally occurring elements is shown in *figure 12.8*.

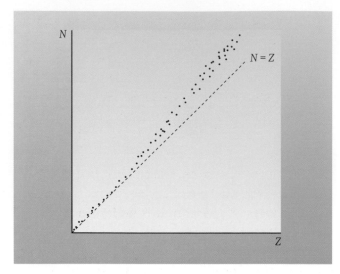

● **Figure 12.8** A graph of neutron number N against proton number Z for the naturally occurring elements.

SAQ 12.4

What charges have the following, in terms of *e*: **a** proton, **b** neutron, **c** nucleus, **d** molecule and **e** α-particle?

Isotopes and their uses

Although atoms of the same element may be identical chemically, their nuclei may be slightly different. The number of protons in the nucleus of an atom determines what element it is; helium always has 2 protons, carbon 6, oxygen 8, neon 10, radium 88, uranium 92 and so on.

However, the number of neutrons in a given element can vary. Take neon as an example. Three different naturally occurring forms of neon are:

${}^{20}_{10}Ne$ ${}^{21}_{10}Ne$ ${}^{22}_{10}Ne$

The first has 10 neutrons in the nucleus, the second 11 and the third 12. These three types of neon are called **isotopes** of neon.

Element	Nucleon number	Proton number	Element	Nucleon number	Proton number
hydrogen	1	1	bromine	79	35
helium	4	2	silver	107	47
lithium	7	3	tin	120	50
beryllium	9	4	iodine	130	53
boron	11	5	caesium	133	55
carbon	12	6	barium	138	56
nitrogen	14	7	tungsten	184	74
oxygen	16	8	platinum	195	78
neon	20	10	gold	197	79
sodium	23	11	mercury	202	80
magnesium	24	12	lead	206	82
aluminium	27	13	bismuth	209	83
chlorine	35	17	radium	226	88
calcium	40	20	uranium	238	92
iron	56	26	plutonium	239	94
nickel	58	28	americium	241	95

● **Table 12.2** Proton and nucleon numbers of some nuclides.

Each isotope has the same number of protons (for neon this is 10) but a different number of neutrons. The word 'isotope' comes from the Greek *isotopos* (same place), because all isotopes of the same element have the same place in the Periodic Table of elements.

Any atom is electrically neutral (it has no net positive or negative charge), so the number of orbiting electrons must equal the number of protons in the nucleus of the atom. If an atom gains or loses an electron, it is no longer electrically neutral and is called an **ion**.

For an atom, the number of protons (and hence the number of orbiting electrons) determines the chemical properties of the atom. The number of protons and the number of neutrons determine the nuclear properties. It is important to realise that, since the number of protons, and therefore the number of electrons, in isotopes of the same element are identical, they will all have the same chemical properties but different nuclear properties.

Hydrogen has three important isotopes, $^1_1$H, $^2_1$H (deuterium) and $^3_1$H (tritium) (*figure 12.9*). $^1_1$H and deuterium occur naturally, but tritium has to be made. Deuterium and tritium form the fuel of many fusion research reactors. Hydrogen is the most abundant element in the Universe (*figure 12.10*), because it consists of just one proton and

● **Figure 12.10** The Horsehead Nebula in Orion. The large coloured regions are expanses of dust and gas, mostly hydrogen, that are ionised by nearby stars and emit light. The dark 'horse head' is where the areas of gas and dust remain in atomic form and block out the light from behind.

one electron, and this is the simplest structure possible for an atom.

The relative atomic masses of isotopes will also be different. There are differences too in some of their physical properties, such as density and boiling point. For example, heavy water, water containing deuterium, has a boiling point of 104 °C under normal atmospheric pressure.

Table 12.3 gives details of some other common isotopes.

SAQ 12.5

There are seven naturally occurring isotopes of mercury with nucleon numbers (relative abundances) of 196 (0.2%), 198 (10%), 199 (16.8%), 200 (23.1%), 201 (13.2%), 202 (29.8%) and 204 (6.9%).

a What are the proton and neutron numbers for each isotope?

b Suggest what the average relative atomic mass of naturally occurring mercury might be.

SAQ 12.6

Group the following imaginary elements A–H into isotopes and name them using the Periodic Table:

	A	B	C	D	E	F	G	H
Proton number	20	23	21	22	20	22	22	23
Nucleon number	44	50	46	46	46	48	50	51

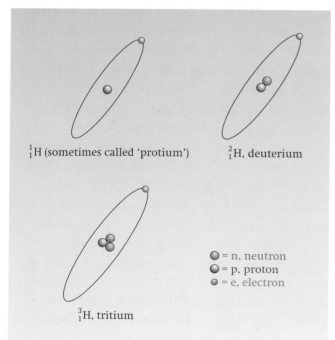

$^1_1$H (sometimes called 'protium')

$^2_1$H, deuterium

$^3_1$H, tritium

● = n, neutron
● = p, proton
● = e, electron

● **Figure 12.9** The isotopes of hydrogen.

Element	A	Z	N
hydrogen	1	1	0
	2	1	1
carbon	12	6	6
	14	6	8
oxygen	16	8	8
	18	8	10
neon	20	10	10
	21	10	11
potassium	39	19	20
	40	19	21
strontium	88	38	50
	90	38	52
caesium	135	55	80
	137	55	82
lead	206	82	124
	208	82	126
radium	226	88	138
	228	88	140
uranium	235	92	143
	238	92	146

● **Table 12.3** Some common isotopes.

SAQ 12.7

A nucleus of strontium has a nucleon number of 90 and a proton number of 38. Describe the structure of the strontium nucleus.

SAQ 12.8

An element has several isotopes.
a How do their nuclei differ?
b In what ways are their nuclei the same?

Structure of the nucleus and the strong nuclear force

As you know from earlier in this chapter, there are two kinds of particle in the nucleus of an atom: protons, which carry a unit positive charge; and neutrons, which are uncharged. It is therefore quite surprising that the nucleus holds together at all – you would expect the electrostatic repulsions from all those positively charged protons to blow it apart. The fact that this does not happen is very good evidence for the existence of another attractive force between the nucleons. This is

called the **strong nuclear force**. It only acts over very short distances (10^{-14} m), and it is what holds the nucleus together.

In small nuclei the strong force from all the nucleons reaches most of the others in the nucleus, but as we go on adding protons and neutrons the balance becomes much finer. The longer-range electrostatic force affects the whole nucleus, but the short-range strong nuclear force of any particular nucleon only affects those nucleons around it – the rest of the nucleus is unaffected. In a large nucleus the nucleons are not held together so tightly, and this can make the nucleus unstable. However, the more protons there are in a nucleus, the greater the electric forces between them, and we need a few extra neutrons to help 'keep the protons apart'. This is why heavy nuclei have more neutrons than protons.

The variation of neutron number with proton number is shown in *figure 12.8*. You can see that for light elements these two numbers are the same, but they become very different for heavy elements. Adding more neutrons helps to keep the nucleus stable; but when the number of protons is greater than 83, adding more neutrons is not enough, and all elements with a proton number of greater than 83 become less stable.

Most atoms that make up our world are stable; that is, they do not change as time goes by, which is quite fortunate really! However, some are less stable and give out radiation. Whether or not an atom is unstable depends on the numbers of protons and neutrons in its nucleus. Hydrogen-1 (1p), helium-4 (2p,2n), carbon-12 (6p,6n) and oxygen-16 (8p,8n) are all stable – but add extra neutrons and the situation changes.

For example, add a neutron to helium-4 and you get helium-5, a very unstable nucleus. Carbon-14, with two neutrons more than the stable isotope carbon-12, is used in carbon dating. The radioactive isotope carbon-14 ($^{14}_{6}$C) is present in very small quantities in all natural substances containing carbon-12. The amount of carbon-14 present in living material, in a plant or animal, is kept constant, because the living 'thing' is continually taking in other materials containing carbon-14 (for example, in the food that animals eat). When the plant or animal dies, the amount

● **Figure 12.11** Carbon dating is used to measure the ages of historical artefacts, such as this Egyptian mummy.

of carbon-14 reduces because it emits radiation. The quantity of carbon-14 in a substance can be measured quite accurately, and so the age of the substance can be determined (*figure 12.11*).

Uses of isotopes

■ Archaeological and geological dating
■ Medical – diagnostic and treatment
■ Fluid flow tracking and measurement
■ Sterilisation of foodstuffs
■ Fertiliser tracers
■ Nuclear power sources for spacecraft

The scale of things

Rutherford's α-particle scattering experiment showed the existence of a charged nucleus at the heart of the atom, which is much smaller than the atom as a whole. Further experiments showed that the charge is positive. Since then, many different techniques have been developed to look at atoms and the particles of which they are made. These techniques usually rely on directing a beam of particles or electromagnetic radiation at a target and observing how the beam is scattered or diffracted.

[There is no real difference between the terms 'scattering' and 'diffraction'. In *scattering*, we picture particles in the beam being deflected by the particles of the target. In *diffraction*, we picture waves in the beam being diffracted as they pass around or between particles in the target. Hence Rutherford's α-particle experiment is an example of scattering, but when we shine a beam of electrons on to a piece of crystalline material, we say that it is diffracted. You should remember that particles show wave-like behaviour and that waves can behave like particles: this is wave–particle duality.]

Here are some examples of such probing experiments, and the information they can give us.

■ **X-ray diffraction**
A beam of X-rays is directed at a crystal. The atoms of the crystal form a regularly spaced array. The spacings between planes of atoms are similar to the wavelength of the X-rays, and so the X-rays are diffracted. (Recall that the diffraction effect is greatest when the wavelength of the waves matches the spacing causing the diffraction.)

Figure 12.12 shows an example of a diffraction pattern obtained when X-rays are diffracted by a single crystal. The pattern of the dots, and their spacing, can be used to determine the arrangement and spacings of the atoms in the

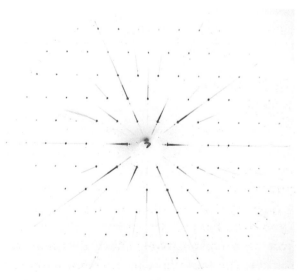

● **Figure 12.12** X-ray diffraction pattern for a single crystal of palladium complex.

crystal. If the material is polycrystalline or non-crystalline, the dots will be blurred, or smeared into rings.

■ **Electron diffraction**
As we saw in *Physics 1*, a beam of electrons can be diffracted by the planes of atoms in a crystalline material. This technique can provide similar evidence to that provided by X-ray diffraction.

■ **Neutron diffraction**
Neutrons are uncharged, so they do not readily interact with the electrons that orbit the nucleus of an atom. However, they are magnetic. They can therefore interact with atoms of magnetic elements such as iron, or with the nuclei of atoms, which are also magnetic because of the neutrons they contain.

Neutron diffraction provides information about the pattern in which the nuclei within a solid material are arranged, and their average separations.

■ **High-energy electron scattering**
This technique is used to probe into the nucleus. A nucleus is much smaller than an atom, and so a probe with a much smaller wavelength is needed. The de Broglie equation shows how to achieve this:

wavelength = (Planck constant)/momentum
$$\lambda = h/mv$$

By increasing the momentum of the electrons, their wavelength can be decreased. Since the diameter of a nucleus is roughly 10^5 times smaller than that of an atom, the electrons' momentum must be increased by a factor of 10^5. Large particle accelerators are needed to achieve such high energies – *figure 12.13* shows one such accelerator.

In high-energy electron scattering, electrons are diffracted as they pass around an atomic

● **Figure 12.13** The Stanford Linear Accelerator in California. Electrons are accelerated to speeds close to the speed of light as they travel down the long, straight track; they are then directed at a variety of targets in the laboratories at the end.

nucleus. This can show up the diameters of different nuclei. As you might expect, the greater the nucleon number A, the greater the diameter of the nucleus.

Orders of magnitude

The experimental techniques summarised above show the following:

■ radius of proton ~ radius of neutron ~ 10^{-15} m
■ radius of nucleus ~ 10^{-15} m to 10^{-14} m
■ radius of atom ~ 10^{-10} m
■ radius of molecule ~ 10^{-10} m to 10^{-6} m

(Some molecules, such as large protein molecules, are very large indeed – compared to an atom!)

Note that the radii of nuclear particles are often quoted in femtometres (fm), where 1 fm = 10^{-15} m.

SUMMARY

◆ The α-particle scattering experiment provides evidence for the existence of a small, charged nucleus at the centre of the atom.

◆ Most of the mass of an atom is concentrated in its nucleus.

◆ The nucleus consists of protons and neutrons, and is surrounded by a cloud of orbiting electrons.

◆ The number of protons and neutrons in the nucleus of an atom is called its nucleon number (A).

◆ The number of protons in the nucleus of an atom is called its proton number (Z).

◆ Isotopes are atoms of the same element (with the same proton number) but with different neutron numbers.

◆ Different isotopes (or nuclides, if referring to the nucleus only) can be represented by the notation: ^A_ZX.

◆ Diffraction and scattering techniques, using beams of X-rays, electrons and neutrons, provide information about the arrangement and separations of atoms in crystalline materials.

◆ High-energy electron scattering experiments can give evidence of the dimensions of the nucleus.

Questions

1 In Rutherford's experiment, α-particles were directed at a thin gold foil. A small fraction of the α-particles were back-scattered. Explain how this result would be affected if each of the following changes was (separately) made.
   a A thicker foil was used.
   b Higher-energy α-particles were used.
   c A silver foil was used – the atomic number of silver is less than that of gold.

2 Electron diffraction can be used to investigate both the arrangement of atoms and the dimensions of nuclei. Explain how changing the energy of the electrons can be used to achieve this.

3 Uranium has atomic number 92. Two of its common isotopes have nucleon numbers 235 and 238. How many neutrons are there in a nucleus of each of these isotopes?

CHAPTER 13

Nuclear physics

By the end of this chapter you should be able to:

1 appreciate that nuclear processes involve the conservation of charge;

2 represent simple nuclear reactions by nuclear equations;

3 describe the processes of nuclear fission and nuclear fusion, and appreciate that these reactions involve a release of energy;

4 appreciate the equivalence between mass and energy, as applying to all energy changes;

5 recall and use $\Delta E = \Delta m\, c^2$;

6 illustrate graphically the variation with nucleon number of binding energy per nucleon, and describe the relevance of binding energy per nucleon to nuclear fission and to nuclear fusion;

7 appreciate that nuclear processes involve the conservation of mass–energy;

8 express mass in kilograms and in atomic mass units, and energy in joules and in electron-volts.

Nuclear processes

Radioactivity was discovered at the end of the nineteenth century. The next decades saw an increasing understanding of radioactivity as just one of several nuclear processes, along with nuclear fission and nuclear fusion. The second half of the twentieth century saw increasing applications of these processes, in nuclear power and nuclear weapons (see *figure 13.1*), so that people talked of 'the nuclear age'.

These processes were predicted following Einstein's development of his theories of relativity, with his famous equation $\Delta E = \Delta m\, c^2$. In this chapter, we will look at fission and fusion processes as sources of energy and see how Einstein's equation can explain the release of energy that occurs during them.

● **Figure 13.1** Our understanding of nuclear physics has proved to be a mixed blessing. Nuclear weapons dominated global politics for much of the twentieth century.

Nuclear fission

In Nature, we find nuclei with proton numbers up to Z = 92 (uranium). However, the most massive of these, beyond Z = 83, are unstable, and are gradually decaying away. In chapter 14, we will look in more detail at the nature of this radioactive decay.

However, there is another way in which massive, unstable nuclei such as uranium and plutonium ($Z = 94$) can become more stable. They can split apart into two, more stable fragments; this process is called **nuclear fission**. Usually, fission occurs when a neutron collides with a large, unstable nucleus (*figure 13.2*). The neutron is absorbed, making the nucleus even more unstable, and the nucleus then splits into two. Several neutrons are also released. (These neutrons may go on to cause the fission of other large nuclei. A chain reaction is set up; use is made of this in nuclear power stations and in nuclear explosions.)

We can represent nuclear fission by nuclear equations. Here is the equation for the fission shown in *figure 13.2*:

$$^1_0n + ^{235}_{92}U \rightarrow ^{92}_{36}Kr + ^{141}_{56}Ba + 3^1_0n$$

In words, this says that a single neutron ^1_0n collides with a uranium nucleus $^{235}_{92}U$. Fission occurs, resulting in isotopes of krypton and barium, and three neutrons are also released. (A neutron is represented by ^1_0n. A proton is shown as ^1_1p or ^1_1H.)

For this equation to be balanced, we require that both the proton number and the nucleon number are conserved; that is, the total number of protons (representing positive charge) must be the same on both sides of the equation, because we cannot create or destroy charge in a nuclear reaction. Similarly, the total number of nucleons must be the same on both sides. We can check like this:

- for Z $92 + 0 = 36 + 56 + 3 \times 0$
- for A $235 + 1 = 92 + 141 + 3 \times 1$

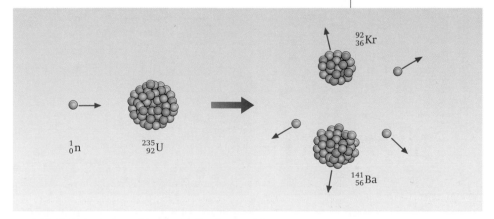

● **Figure 13.2** In induced nuclear fission, a neutron collides with a uranium nucleus, causing it to become unstable, so that it splits into two large fragments. More neutrons are released.

SAQ 13.1

Show that the following equation is correctly balanced:

$$^{235}_{92}U + ^1_0n \rightarrow ^{138}_{54}Xe + ^{95}_{38}Sr + 3^1_0n$$

SAQ 13.2

In a nuclear fission event, the large nucleus usually splits into two unequal fragments; sometimes two neutrons are released, sometimes three or four. Complete the following equations by ensuring that both proton number and nucleon number are conserved. (In **b**, the missing element is an isotope of krypton, Kr.)

a $^{239}_{94}Pu + ^1_0n \rightarrow ^{145}_{56}Ba + ^{93}_{38}Sr + ?$

b $^{239}_{94}Pu + ^1_0n \rightarrow ^{147}_{58}Ce + ? + 3^1_0n$

SAQ 13.3

A light nucleus can become unstable if it is bombarded with nuclear radiation. Copy and complete the equation below to find the particle released when a nucleus of $^{14}_7N$ captures an α-particle ^4_2He:

$$^{14}_7N + ^4_2He \rightarrow ^{17}_8O + ?$$

Nuclear fusion

Massive nuclei tend to be unstable, and they can become more stable through the process of fission. In a similar way, light nuclei can become more stable by joining together in the process of **nuclear fusion**. As a general rule, middle-sized nuclei tend to be the most stable. This will be discussed in more detail in the next section.

Figure 13.3 (overleaf) shows two light nuclei, both isotopes of hydrogen, fusing to form a helium nucleus. The equation for this is:

$$^2_1H + ^1_1H \rightarrow ^3_2He$$

Note that, as before, both Z and A are conserved.

● **Figure 13.3** In nuclear fusion, two light nuclei join together to make a more stable nucleus.

Often in fusion reactions, the result is not a single particle, but two or more. For example:

$$^2_1H + ^2_1H \rightarrow ^3_1H + ^1_1H$$

In the process of nuclear fusion, light nuclei are becoming more stable. Energy is released. This is the source of energy that keeps stars (such as the Sun) shining for billions of years. It is also hoped that one day we will be able to have fusion reactors for generating electricity. Prototype reactors, such as the Joint European Torus (JET) at Culham in Oxfordshire (*figure 13.4*), suggest that controllable fusion reactions may one day be within our technological grasp.

SAQ 13.4
Complete the following equation for a fusion reaction in which *three* particles result:

$$^3_2He + ^3_2He \rightarrow ^4_2He + ?$$

SAQ 13.5
In one of the fusion reactions that occur in the Sun, the most stable isotope of carbon, $^{12}_6C$, is formed from the fusion of a proton with a nucleus of an isotope of nitrogen, $^{15}_7N$. Write a balanced equation for this reaction. What other new element is formed?

Explaining fission and fusion
In both fission and fusion, unstable nuclei have become more stable. Energy is released. In order to explain these processes, we need to be able to say where this energy comes from. One answer lies in the origins of the nuclei we are considering. Take, for example, uranium. The Earth's crust contains uranium. In some places, it is sufficiently concentrated to make it worth while extracting it for use as the fuel in fission reactors (*figure 13.5*). This uranium has been part of the Earth since it was formed, 4500 million years ago.

The Earth formed from a swirling cloud of dust and gas, at the same time that the Sun itself was forming. These materials condensed under the force of gravitational attraction. But where did they come from in the first place? It is believed that heavy elements (such as uranium) were formed in supernovae. At some time in the distant past, an ageing star collapsed and then blew itself apart in an explosion of awesome scale. At the

● **Figure 13.4** The JET torus at the Culham Laboratory in Oxfordshire is a European experiment to solve some of the problems associated with maintaining controlled nuclear fusion as a source of energy.

● **Figure 13.5** Uranium, the fuel used in nuclear reactors, comes from mines such as the Ranger mine in Australia's Northern Territory.

very high temperatures that resulted, there was sufficient energy available for light nuclei to fuse to form the heaviest nuclei, which we now find if we dig in the Earth's crust. It is this energy, from an ancient stellar explosion, that is released when a large nucleus undergoes fission.

Mass and energy

We can extend this explanation by asking: 'How can we calculate the amount of energy released in fission or fusion?' To find the answer to this, we need to think first about the masses of the particles involved.

We will start by considering a stable nucleus, $^{12}_{6}$C. This consists of six protons and six neutrons. Fortunately for us, because we have a lot of this form of carbon in our bodies, this is a very stable nuclide. This means that the nucleons are bound tightly together. It takes a lot of energy to pull them apart.

Figure 13.6 shows the results of an imaginary experiment in which we have done just that. On the left-hand side of the balance is a $^{12}_{6}$C nucleus. On the right-hand side are six protons and six neutrons, the result of dismantling the nucleus. The surprising thing is that the balance is tipped to the right. The separate nucleons have *more* mass than the nucleus itself. This means that the law of conservation of mass has been broken. We have violated what was thought to be a fundamental law of Nature, something that was held to be true for hundreds of years. How can this be?

Notice that, in dismantling the $^{12}_{6}$C nucleus, we have had to do work. The nucleons attract one

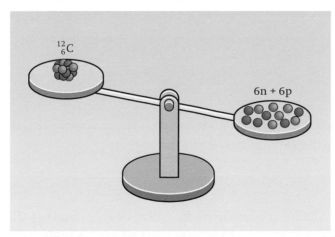

another with nuclear forces, and these are strong enough to make the nucleus very stable. So we have put energy in to the system to pull the nucleus apart. Where has this energy gone?

At the same time, we have the mystery of the appearing mass. There is more mass when we have pulled the nucleons apart than when they are bound together.

You probably already know that these two problems, disappearing energy and appearing mass, can be solved together. We say that 'energy has turned into mass'. If we let the separate protons and neutrons recombine to make a $^{12}_{6}$C nucleus, the extra mass will disappear and the missing energy will be released. This 'mass–energy conversion' explains where the energy comes from in nuclear fusion.

A better way to express this is to treat mass and energy as aspects of the same thing. Rather than having separate laws of conservation of mass and conservation of energy, we can combine these two. The total amount of mass and energy together in a system is constant. There may be conversions from one to the other, but the total amount of 'mass–energy' remains constant.

Einstein's equation

If we are saying that the total amount of 'mass–energy' in a closed system remains constant, we need to know how to add mass (in kg) to energy (in J). Albert Einstein produced his famous equation, which allows us to do this. The energy ΔE equivalent to mass Δm is given by

$$\Delta E = \Delta m \, c^2$$

where c is the speed of light in free space. The value of c is approximately $3 \times 10^8 \, \mathrm{m \, s^{-1}}$, but its precise value has been fixed as

$$c = 299\,792\,458 \, \mathrm{m \, s^{-1}}$$

(Recall that the symbol Δ means 'a change in' a quantity; so ΔE means a change in energy E, and Δm means a change in mass m.) Now if we know the total mass of particles before a nuclear reaction, and their total mass after the reaction, we can work out how much energy is released. *Table 13.1* gives the relative masses of the particles shown in *figure 13.6*. (These are measured on a

● **Figure 13.6** The mass of a nucleus is less than the total mass of its component protons and neutrons.

Particle	Relative mass	Mass (10^{-27} kg)
$^{1}_{1}$P	1.007 276	1.672 623
$^{1}_{0}$n	1.008 665	1.674 929
$^{12}_{6}$C	12.000 000	19.926 483

● **Table 13.1** Masses of some particles.

standard scale where the mass of $^{12}_{6}$C is defined as 12 exactly – see later in this chapter.) The masses are also given in kg.

The first thing to notice about these data is that, although the relative mass of $^{12}_{6}$C is precisely 12, the mass of an individual proton or neutron is slightly more than 1. So the total mass of six protons and six neutrons is clearly greater than the mass of $^{12}_{6}$C.

Secondly, notice that the masses are not much greater than 1. Nuclear masses are measured to a high degree of precision, often to seven or eight significant figures, because it is the small differences *between* values that are important.

We can use the mass values in kg to calculate the mass that is seen as energy when nucleons combine to form a nucleus. So for our particles in *figure 13.6*:

$$\text{mass before} = (6 \times 1.672\,623$$
$$+ 6 \times 1.674\,929) \times 10^{-27}\,\text{kg}$$
$$= 20.085\,312 \times 10^{-27}\,\text{kg}$$
$$\text{mass after} = 19.926\,483 \times 10^{-27}\,\text{kg}$$

mass difference
$$\Delta m = (20.085\,312 - 19.926\,483) \times 10^{-27}\,\text{kg}$$
$$= 0.158\,829 \times 10^{-27}\,\text{kg}$$

Thus there is a very small loss of mass Δm when the nucleons combine to form the nucleus. This lost mass reappears as a small amount of energy, ΔE, related to Δm by

$$\Delta E = \Delta m\,c^2$$

Now we can calculate the energy released:

$$\Delta E = \Delta m\,c^2$$
$$= 0.158\,829 \times 10^{-27}\,\text{kg} \times (2.997\,925\,310\,8\,\text{m s}^{-1})^2$$
$$= 1.43 \times 10^{-11}\,\text{J}$$

This may seem like a small amount of energy, but it is a lot on the scale of an atom. For comparison, the amount of energy released in a chemical reaction involving a single carbon atom would

typically be of the order of 10^{-18} J, more than a million times smaller.

SAQ 13.6

a Calculate the energy released if a $^{4}_{2}$He nucleus is formed from separate protons and neutrons.

b Calculate also the energy released per nucleon. Mass values are given in *table 13.2*.

SAQ 13.7

Use the relative mass values given in *table 13.3* to explain why the fusion reaction

$$^{4}_{2}\text{He} + {}^{4}_{2}\text{He} \rightarrow {}^{8}_{4}\text{Be}$$

is unlikely to occur, unless some extra energy is supplied.

Binding energy and stability

We can now begin to see why some nuclei are more stable than others. If a nucleus is formed from separate nucleons, energy is released. In order to pull the nucleus apart, energy must be put in; in other words, work must be done against the forces holding the nucleons together. The more energy involved in this, the more stable is the nucleus.

The energy needed to pull a nucleus apart into separate nucleons is called the **binding energy** of the nucleus. Take care: this is *not* energy stored in the nucleus; on the contrary, it is the energy that must be put in to the nucleus in order to pull it apart. In the example of $^{12}_{6}$C discussed above, we calculated the binding energy from the mass

Particle	Mass (10^{-27} kg)
$^{1}_{1}$P	1.672623
$^{1}_{0}$n	1.674929
$^{4}_{2}$He	6.644661

● **Table 13.2** Masses of some particles.

Particle	Relative mass
$^{4}_{2}$He	4.001506
$^{8}_{4}$Be	8.003111

● **Table 13.3** Relative masses of some particles.

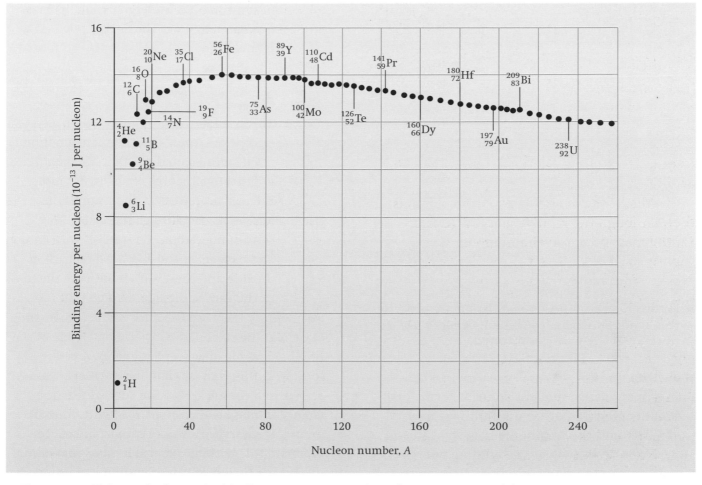

● **Figure 13.7** This graph shows the binding energy per nucleon for common nuclei. The nucleus becomes more stable as binding energy increases.

difference between the mass of the $^{12}_{6}$C nucleus and the masses of the separate protons and neutrons.

In order to compare different nuclides, we need to consider the binding energy per nucleon. *Figure 13.7* shows the binding energy per nucleon for stable nuclei. This is a graph plotted against A; the greater the value, the more tightly bound are the nucleons that make up the nucleus.

If you examine this graph, you will see that the general trend is for light nuclei to have low binding energies. For nuclides with $A >$ 20 approximately, there is not much variation in binding energy.

In fact, the greatest value of binding energy per nucleon is found for $^{56}_{26}$Fe. This isotope of iron requires the most energy per nucleon

to dismantle it into separate nucleons.

Notice the anomalous position of $^{4}_{2}$He, which lies off the main curve of the graph. This nucleus (two protons and two neutrons, the same as an α-particle) is very stable. Other common stable nuclei include $^{12}_{6}$C and $^{16}_{8}$O, which can be thought of as three or four α-particles bound together (*figure 13.8*).

Binding energy, fission and fusion

We can use the binding energy graph to help us decide which nuclear processes – fission, fusion, radioactive decay (chapter 14) – are likely to occur (*figure 13.9*).

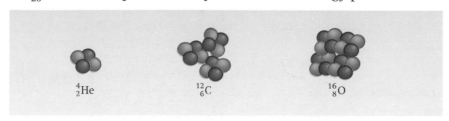

● **Figure 13.8** Light, stable nuclei are formed when α-particles are bound together.

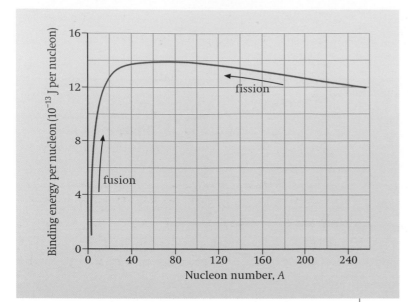

y-axis: Binding energy per nucleon (10^{-13} J per nucleon)

x-axis: Nucleon number, A

fission

fusion

● **Figure 13.9** Both fusion and fission are processes that tend to increase the binding energy per nucleon of the particles involved.

■ **Fission**

When a massive nucleus splits, it forms two smaller fragments. For uranium, we have $A = 235$, and the fragments have $A = 140$ and 95, typically. If we look at the binding energy curve, we see that these two products have greater binding energy than the original uranium nucleus. Hence, if the uranium nucleus splits in this way, energy will be released.

■ **Fusion**

In a similar way, if two light nuclei fuse, the final binding energy will be greater than the original value. There is a problem with the anomalous value for ^4_2He. This makes it difficult for two of these nuclei to fuse; you worked this out from the particles' masses in SAQ 13.7.

SAQ 13.8

Use the binding energy graph to explain why fission is unlikely to occur with light nuclei ($A < 20$), and why fusion is unlikely to occur for heavier nuclei ($A > 40$).

Mass–energy conservation

We have seen how to apply the equation $\Delta E = \Delta m\,c^2$ in the nuclear processes of fusion and fission. Large amounts of energy may be released in these processes. For example, if all of the nuclei in 1 kg

of uranium-235 undergo fission, its mass decreases by 0.9 g. The energy released ΔE is then:

$$\Delta E = \Delta m\,c^2 = 0.9 \times 10^{-3}\,\text{kg} \times (3 \times 10^8\,\text{m s}^{-1})^2$$
$$= 8.1 \times 10^{13}\,\text{J}$$

This is a lot of energy – more than a typical European citizen's lifetime consumption.

Einstein pointed out that his equation applied to *all* energy changes, not just nuclear processes. So, for example, it applies to chemical changes, too. If we burn some carbon, we start off with carbon and oxygen. At the end, we have carbon dioxide and energy. If we measure the mass of the carbon dioxide, we find that it is very slightly less than the mass of the carbon and oxygen at the start of the experiment. Some of the original mass is now 'seen' as energy. A better way to express this is to say that 'mass + energy' is conserved. In a chemical reaction such as this, the change in mass is very small, less than a microgram if we start with 1 kg of carbon and oxygen. Compare this with the change in mass that occurs during the fission of 1 kg of uranium, mentioned above. The change in mass in a chemical reaction is a much, much smaller proportion of the original mass, which is why we don't notice it.

Here is another surprising consequence of mass–energy conservation. If you take a ride upwards in a lift, your gravitational potential energy (GPE) increases. If you could measure your mass with sufficient precision, you would find that it is greater at the top of the building than at the bottom. Energy has been transferred to you to get you to the top of the building, and this appears as an increase in your mass. For a person of mass 60 kg who travels in a lift to the top of a 30 m high building:

increase in GPE, $\Delta E = mg\,\Delta h$
$$= 60\,\text{kg} \times 9.8\,\text{m s}^{-2} \times 30.0\,\text{m}$$
$$= 17\,640\,\text{J}$$
increase in mass, $\Delta m = \Delta E/c^2$
$$= 17\,640\,\text{J} / (3 \times 10^8\,\text{m s}^{-1})^2$$
$$= 2.0 \times 10^{-13}\,\text{kg}$$

This is a very tiny mass increase indeed, but it really does exist!

SAQ 13.9

For each of the following pairs, explain, using Einstein's equation $\Delta E = \Delta m c^2$, which has the greater mass.

a A person at the top of a mountain, or the same person at the foot of the mountain.

b A block of steel at $0\,°C$, or the same block at $500\,°C$.

c A mixture of hydrogen and oxygen at room temperature, or the water vapour formed after they have reacted together (also at room temperature).

d A stone lying on the ground, or the same stone rolling along the ground.

Energy units, mass units

Because the amounts of energy released during nuclear processes are so small, they are often quoted in electron-volts rather than joules. As we saw in *Physics 1*, an electron-volt is defined as the energy transferred when an electron moves through a potential difference of 1 V. So

$$1\,eV = 1.6 \times 10^{-19}\,J$$

■ To convert from J to eV: divide by 1.6×10^{-19}.
■ To convert from eV to J: multiply by 1.6×10^{-19}.

Similarly, masses on the nuclear scale are very small when given in kilograms. Masses are measured in terms of the unified atomic mass constant (u) (some examples are included in *tables 13.1* and *13.3*) where the mass of a carbon-12 nucleus is $12\,u$. (This is because carbon-12 is a readily available isotope against which other masses can be compared using instruments such as mass spectrographs.) So

$$1\,u = 1.6605 \times 10^{-27}\,kg$$

■ To convert from kg to u: divide by 1.6605×10^{-27}.
■ To convert from u to kg: multiply by 1.6605×10^{-27}.

It is useful to remember that:

mass of proton ~ mass of neutron ~ $1\,u$

(In fact, both the proton and the neutron have masses slightly greater than $1\,u$ – see *SAQ 13.11*.)

SAQ 13.10

An electron and a positron collide. They annihilate one another, so that all of their mass appears as energy.

a Use $\Delta E = \Delta m c^2$ to calculate the energy released, in joules.

b Calculate the energy released in MeV ($1\,MeV = 10^6\,eV$).
[Mass of electron = mass of positron $= 9.1 \times 10^{-31}\,kg$]

SAQ 13.11

a The mass of a proton is $1.6726 \times 10^{-27}\,kg$. Express this in terms of the unified atomic mass constant (u).

b The mass of a neutron is $1.008665u$. Express this in kg.

SAQ 13.12

Because mass and energy can be thought of as equivalent, the masses of atomic particles are sometimes given in energy units. For example, the mass of an electron is $0.51\,MeV$. Calculate the mass of an electron: a in kg, and b in terms of u.

SUMMARY

◆ Nuclear reactions can be represented by balanced nuclear equations. In any such reaction, the following quantities are conserved: proton number Z, nucleon number A, and 'mass + energy'.

◆ In nuclear fission, a heavy nucleus splits into lighter fragments. In nuclear fusion, light nuclei join to form a more massive one.

◆ In order to relate mass changes to energy changes, we use Einstein's equation $\Delta E = \Delta m c^2$.

◆ The binding energy of a nucleus tells us the energy required to break up the nucleus into separate nucleons.

◆ The binding energy per nucleon gives us an indication of the relative stability of the different nuclides.

◆ The variation of binding energy per nucleon shows that energy is released when light nuclei undergo fusion and when heavier nuclei undergo fission, because these processes increase the binding energy per nucleon and hence result in more stable nuclides.

Questions

1 In a nuclear reactor, a nucleus of uranium $^{238}_{92}U$ may capture a neutron $^{1}_{0}n$ and become a nucleus of plutonium $^{239}_{94}Pu$. Electrons are released. Write a balanced equation for this reaction, and deduce how many electrons are released. (The symbol for an electron is $^{0}_{-1}e$.)

2 The Sun releases vast amounts of energy. Its power output is 4×10^{26} W. By how much does its mass decrease each second as a result of this energy loss?

CHAPTER 14

Radioactivity

By the end of this chapter you should be able to:

1 describe the range, nature and penetration of α-particles, β-particles and γ-rays as different types of ionising radiation;

2 represent radioactive decay by nuclear equations;

3 show an awareness of the hazards of ionising radiation and the safety precautions that should be taken in the handling, storage and disposal of radioactive materials;

4 appreciate the spontaneous and random nature of radioactive decay;

5 illustrate the random nature of radioactive decay by observation of fluctuations in count rate;

6 define the terms activity and count rate;

7 recall and use $A = \lambda N$;

8 recognise, use and represent graphically solutions of the decay law based on $x = x_0\, e^{-\lambda t}$ for activity, number of undecayed nuclei and corrected count rate;

9 show an awareness of the possible limitations of the exponential decay law model in describing a random radioactive decay process;

10 define half-life as the mean time for the number of nuclei of a nuclide to halve;

11 use the relation $\lambda t_{1/2} = 0.693$.

Ionising radiation

The three types of radiation, α, β and γ, that are emitted by radioactive materials are invisible. Although they are around us all the time, they were not discovered until 1896. In this section we will look at the properties of these kinds of radiation.

Alpha (α), beta (β) and gamma (γ) radiations come from the nuclei of unstable atoms. Nuclei generally consist of protons and neutrons, and if the balance between these two types of particles is too far to one side, the nucleus may emit one or other kind of radiation as a way of achieving stability.

Table 14.1 shows the basic characteristics of the different types of radiation. *Table 14.2* is a reminder of the characteristics of protons, neutrons and electrons. (In these tables, masses are given relative to the mass of a proton; charge is measured in units of *e*, the electron charge.)

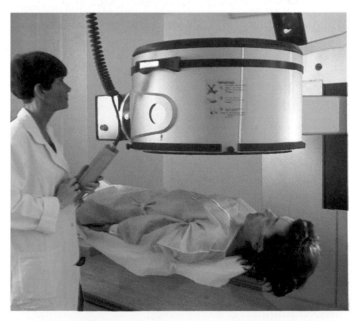

● **Figure 14.1** An example of γ-rays at work. Here a patient is being prepared for a scan to check for cancer.

Radiation	Symbol	Mass (relative to proton)	Charge (in terms of proton charge, +e)	Speed
alpha particles	α, $^4_2$He	4	$+2e$	'slow' ($10^6\,\text{ms}^{-1}$)
beta particles	β, β^-, e	1/1840	$-e$	'fast' ($10^8\,\text{ms}^{-1}$)
gamma rays	γ	0	0	speed of light ($3 \times 10^8\text{ms}^{-1}$)

● **Table 14.1** The nature of ionising radiation.

Particle	Symbol	Mass (relative to proton)	Charge (in terms of proton charge, +e)
proton	$^1_1$p	1	$+e$
neutron	$^1_0$n	1	0
electron	$^0_{-1}$e	1/1840	$-e$

● **Table 14.2** The nature of subatomic particles.

Note the following points:
- α and β are particles of matter, while a γ-ray is a photon of electromagnetic radiation, similar to an X-ray but with a higher frequency.
- An α-particle consists of two protons and two neutrons, as in the nucleus of a helium atom. A β-particle is simply an electron.
- The mass of an α-particle is nearly 10 000 times that of a β-particle; a β-particle travels roughly 100 times faster than an α-particle.

Balanced equations

In chapter 13, we saw how the nuclear processes of fission and fusion can be represented by balanced equations. The same is true for radioactive decay processes. Here are two worked examples.

Worked examples

1 *Alpha decay:* Radon is a radioactive gas that decays by alpha emission to become polonium. Here is the equation for the decay of one of its isotopes:

$$^{222}_{86}\text{Rn} \rightarrow ^{218}_{84}\text{Po} + ^4_2\text{He}$$

Note that, as for all equations representing nuclear processes, both mass (nucleon number) and charge (proton number) are conserved:

nucleon number A $222 = 218 + 4$
proton number Z $86 = 84 + 2$

2 *Beta decay:* We can represent a β-particle or electron as $^0_{-1}$e. Its mass is (almost) zero, and its charge is −1. Carbon-14 decays by beta emission to become an isotope of nitrogen. A gamma photon (γ) is also emitted. Here is the equation that represents this decay:

$$^{14}_{6}\text{C} \rightarrow ^{14}_{7}\text{N} + ^0_{-1}\text{e} + \gamma$$

As with alpha decay, both mass (nucleon number) and charge (proton number) are conserved:

nucleon number A $14 = 14 + 0$
proton number Z $6 = 7 - 1$

(Note that the gamma photon, since it has neither charge nor mass, does not contribute to these equations.)

SAQ 14.1
Study worked examples 1 and 2 of decay equations given above, and write balanced equations for the following:
a A nucleus of radon–220 ($^{220}_{86}$Rn) decays by alpha emission to form an isotope of polonium, Po.
b A nucleus of a sodium isotope ($^{25}_{11}$Na) decays by beta and gamma emission to form an isotope of magnesium, Mg.

Ionisation
Radiation affects the matter it passes through by causing ionisation. Both α- and β-particles are fast-moving charged particles, and if they collide with or pass close to atoms, they may knock or drag electrons away from the atoms (*figure 14.2*). The resulting atoms are said to be **ionised**, and the process is called ionisation. In the process, the radiation loses some of its energy. After many ionisations, the radiation loses all of its energy and no longer has any ionising effect.

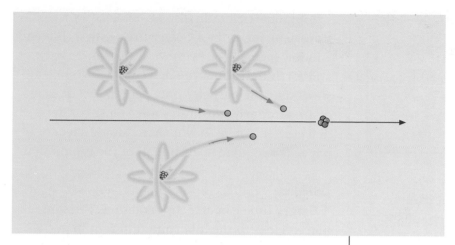

● **Figure 14.2** As an α-particle passes through a material, it causes ionisation of atoms.

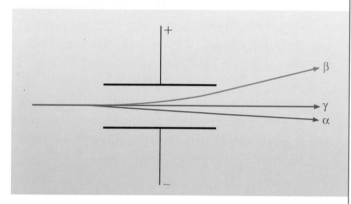

● **Figure 14.3** α-, β- and γ-radiations may be separated using an electric field.

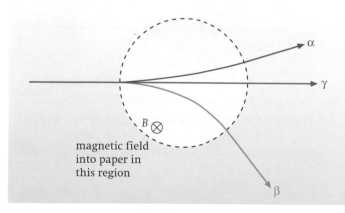

● **Figure 14.4** A magnetic field can also be used to separate α-, β- and γ-radiations.

Alpha radiation is the most strongly ionising, because the mass and charge of an α-particle are greater than those of a β-particle, and it usually travels more slowly. This means that an α-particle interacts more strongly with any atom that it passes, and so it is more likely to cause ionisation. β-particles are much lighter and faster, and so

their effect is less. γ-radiation also causes ionisation, but not as strongly as α- and β-particles, as γ-rays are not charged.

SAQ 14.2
a Explain why you would expect β-particles to travel further through air than α-particles.
b Explain why you would expect β-particles to travel further through air than through metal.

Electric and magnetic fields

Because α, β and γ-radiations have different charges, or no charge, they behave differently in electric and magnetic fields. This can be used to distinguish one kind of radiation from another.

Figure 14.3 shows the effect of an electric field. A mixture of α-, β- and γ-radiations is passing through the gap between two parallel plates; the electric field in this space is uniform (chapter 6). Since α- and β-particles are charged, they are attracted to the plate that has the opposite charge to their own. β-particles are deflected more than α-particles, since their mass is so much less. γ-rays are undeflected since they are uncharged.

Figure 14.4 shows the effect of a magnetic field. In this case, the deflecting force on the particles is at right-angles to their motion. Fleming's left-hand rule (chapter 8) gives the direction of the force on the moving particles; remember that β-particles moving to the right constitute an electric current towards the left.

SAQ 14.3
a Some radioactive substances emit α-particles having two different speeds. Draw a diagram similar to *figure 14.3* to show how these particles would move in a uniform electric field. Label your diagram to show the tracks of the faster and slower α-particles.
b A β-emitting radioactive substance usually emits β-particles with a range of speeds. Add to the diagram you drew in **a** to show how these particles would behave in the uniform electric field.

Absorbing radiation

Safety note
When working with **radioactive sources**, it is essential to **follow the relevant safety regulations**, which your teacher will explain to you.

α-radiation

Because α-radiation is highly ionising, it cannot penetrate very far into matter. A cloud chamber can be used to show the tracks of α-particles in air (*figure 14.5*); the tracks are very dense, because of the dense concentration of ions produced, and they extend for only a few centimetres into the air. By the time the α-particles have travelled this far, they have lost virtually all of their kinetic energy.

● **Figure 14.5** α-particle tracks show up in this photograph of a cloud chamber. Notice that all the particles travel roughly the same distance through the air, indicating that they all have roughly the same energy.

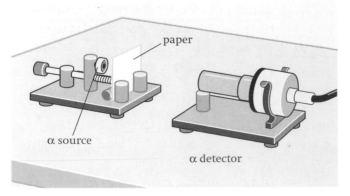

● **Figure 14.6** α-radiation can be absorbed by a single sheet of paper.

Alpha particles can also be detected by a solid-state detector, or by a Geiger tube with a thin end-window (*figure 14.6*). By moving the source back and forth in front of the detector, it is simple to show that the particles only penetrate 5 or 6 cm of air. Similarly, with the source close to the detector, it can be shown that a single sheet of paper is adequate to absorb all of the α-radiation.

β-radiation

A Geiger tube can detect β-radiation. The source is placed close to the tube, and different materials are positioned between source and tube (*figure 14.7*). Paper has little effect; a denser material such as aluminium or lead is a more effective absorber. A few millimetres of aluminium will completely absorb β-radiation.

γ-radiation

Since γ-radiation is the least strongly ionising, it is the most penetrating. Lead can be used to absorb γ-rays, as shown in *figure 14.8*. The intensity of the radiation decreases gradually as it passes through

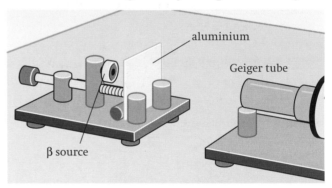

● **Figure 14.7** β-radiation passes readily through thin paper, but can be absorbed by a few millimetres of a light metal such as aluminium.

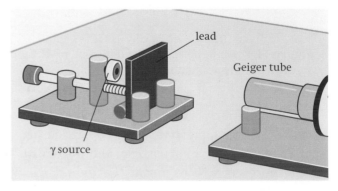

● **Figure 14.8** γ-rays are absorbed by lead, but a considerable thickness may be needed to reduce their intensity to background levels.

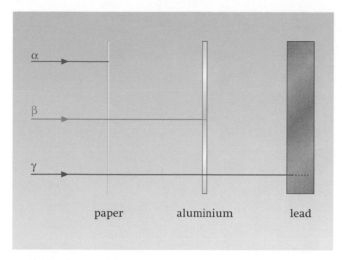

• **Figure 14.9** A summary of the penetrating powers of α-, β- and γ-radiations.

the lead; in principle, an infinite thickness of lead would be needed to absorb the radiation completely.

The different penetrating properties of α-, β- and γ-radiations are summarised in *figure 14.9*.

■ α-radiation is absorbed by a thin sheet of paper.

■ β-radiation is absorbed by a few millimetres of metal.

■ γ-radiation is absorbed by a few centimetres of lead, or several metres of concrete.

SAQ 14.4 _____

Explain why the most strongly ionising radiation (α-particles) are the least penetrating, while the least ionising (γ-rays) are the most penetrating.

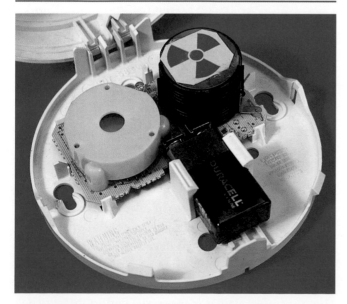

• **Figure 14.10** A smoke detector that uses the absorption of α-radiation as the principle of its operation.

SAQ 14.5 _____

A smoke detector (*figure 14.10*) uses a source of α-radiation to detect the presence of smoke in the air. Explain how the smoke detector works, and why an α source is more suitable for this than a β or γ source.

Hazards of ionising radiation

Because of their ionising effects, alpha (α), beta (β) and gamma (γ) radiations present a hazard to living organisms. When radiation enters a cell, it can damage it in one of three ways:

■ Intense radiation can kill cells so that whole tissues stop working.

■ A single ionisation can damage DNA so that it no longer functions correctly.

■ A single ionisation can break up a water molecule, which can then react with and damage DNA.

In the first case, the tissue damage is known as a radiation burn. In the same way, intense γ-radiation can be used to iradiate food to kill any microbes present and give it a longer shelf life; some medical equipment is also sterilised like this.

With the last two types of damage, the altered DNA may cause cells to divide in an uncontrolled way, leading to the development of a tumour. This is how radiation causes cancer.

If the damaged DNA is in a gamete cell (egg or sperm), the result may be a mutation which is passed on to future generations. It is thought that this is how many mutations arise. In the past (millions of years ago), levels of background radiation were higher than today, with correspondingly higher mutation rates.

Alpha radiation is the most strongly ionising, and thus the most likely to cause cell damage. Fortunately for us, our skin has a layer of dead cells which is sufficient to absorb α-particles. However, if an α- source enters our bodies, we are no longer protected. This is why radon gas is so damaging. We breathe the gas into our lungs where the radiation from radon (and its daughter products) can do most damage.

Since a single ionising event caused by one α- or β- particle or a γ- photon can trigger the development of cancer, there is no low level of radiation which can be described as 'safe'. Hence, we should always try to reduce exposure to radiation to a minimum by employing sensible safe-handling procedures.

Safe handling

Because of the hazards of the ionising radiations they produce, radioactive materials must be handled, stored and disposed of carefully. Here are some points to note:

- **Handling**

  Solid sources are most easily handled. They should be manipulated remotely, for example using tongs, or in a glove-box, or by means of robots. Care must be taken not to drink liquid sources, or to breathe in gaseous sources. No source should be allowed to come into contact with the skin.

- **Storage**

  The penetrating powers of the different types of radiation give a clue to safe practice. Pure α-sources present little hazard when enclosed in a container; however, most are also sources of γ-radiation, and hence lead-lined containers are needed. The same is true for β- sources.

- **Disposal**

  The aim must always be to ensure that the environment (and people in it) are not put at significant risk. Two approaches are adopted: dilution, in which a radioactive material is mixed with a lot of other material – for example, by pouring it into the sea; and containment, in which a radioactive material is placed in secure containers until the hazard has dropped to a low level.

Randomness and decay

Listen to a Geiger counter that is detecting the radiation from a weak source, so that the count rate is about one count per second. You will notice, of course, that the counts do not come regularly. The counter beeps or clicks in a random, irregular manner. If you try to predict when the next clicks will come, you are unlikely to be right.

You can see the same effect if you have a rate meter, which can measure faster rates (*figure 14.11*). The needle fluctuates up and down. Usually a

● **Figure 14.11** The time constant of this ratemeter can be adjusted to smooth out rapid fluctuations in the count rate.

ratemeter has a control for setting the 'time constant' – the time over which the meter averages out the fluctuations. Usually this can be set to 1 s or 5 s. The fluctuations are smoothed out more on the 5 s setting.

So it is apparent that radioactive decay is a random, irregular phenomenon. But is it completely unpredictable? Well, not really. We can measure the average rate of decay. We might measure the number of counts detected in 1000 s, and then calculate the average number per second. We cannot be sure about the average rate, either, because the number of counts in 1000 s will fluctuate, too. So all of our measurements of radioactive decay are inherently uncertain and imprecise.

Spontaneous decay

Radioactive decay occurs within the nucleus of an atom. A nucleus emits radiation, and the atom becomes an atom of a different substance. This is a spontaneous process, which means that we cannot predict, for a particular nucleus, when it will happen. If we sit and stare at an individual nucleus, we cannot see any change that will tell us that it is getting ready to decay. And if it doesn't decay in the first hour when we are watching it, we cannot say that it is any more likely to decay in the next hour. What is more, we cannot affect the probability of an individual nucleus decaying, for example by changing its temperature.

This is slightly odd, because it goes against our everyday experience of the way things around us change. We observe things changing. They gradually age, die, rot away. But this is not how things are on the scale of atoms and nuclei. Many of the atoms of which we are made have existed for billions of years, and will still exist long after we are gone. The nucleus of an atom does not age.

If we look at a large number of atoms of a radioactive substance, we will see the number of undecayed nuclei gradually decreases. However, we cannot predict when an *individual* nucleus will decay. Each nucleus 'makes up its own mind' when to decay, independently from its neighbours. This is because neighbouring nuclei do not interact with one another (unlike neighbouring atoms). The nucleus is a tiny fraction of the size of the atom, and the nuclear forces do not extend very far outside the nucleus. So one nucleus cannot affect a neighbouring nucleus by means of the nuclear force. Being inside a nucleus is a bit like living in a detached house in the middle of nowhere; you can just see out into the garden, but everything is darkness beyond, and the next house is 1000 km away.

The fact that individual nuclei decay spontaneously, and independently of their neighbours and of environmental factors, accounts for the random pattern of clicks that we hear from a Geiger counter and the fluctuations of the needle on the ratemeter dial.

Decay constant

Because we cannot say when individual nuclei will decay, we have to start thinking about large numbers of nuclei. Then we can talk about the average number of nuclei that we expect to decay in a particular time interval; in other words, we can find out the *average* decay rate. Although we cannot make predictions for individual nuclei, we can say that certain nuclei are more likely to decay than others. For example, a nucleus of carbon-12 is stable; carbon-14 decays gradually over thousands of years; carbon-15 nuclei last, on average, a few seconds.

So, because of the spontaneous nature of radioactive decay, we have to make measurements on large numbers of nuclei and then calculate averages. One quantity we can determine is the probability that an individual nucleus will decay in a particular time interval. For example, suppose we observe one million nuclei of a particular radio-isotope. After one hour, 200 000 have decayed. Then the probability that an individual nucleus will decay in 1 h is 0.2 or 20%, since 20% of the nuclei have decayed in this time. (Of course, this is only an approximate value, since we might repeat the experiment and find that only 199 000 decay. The more times we repeat the experiment, the more reliable our answer will be.)

The probability that an individual nucleus will decay per unit time interval is called the **decay constant**, symbol λ (lambda). For the example above, we have:

decay constant $\lambda = 0.2\,h^{-1}$

Note that, because we are measuring the probability of decay per unit time interval, λ has units of h^{-1} (or s^{-1}, day^{-1}, $year^{-1}$, etc.).

Activity

The **activity** A of a radioactive sample is the rate at which nuclei decay. Activity is measured in decays per second (or h^{-1}, day^{-1}, etc.). An activity of one decay per second is one becquerel (1 Bq):

1 Bq = 1 s^{-1}

Clearly, the activity of a sample depends on the decay constant λ of the radio-isotope under consideration. The greater the decay constant (the probability that an individual nucleus decays per unit time interval), the greater is the activity of the sample. It also depends on the size of the sample. For a sample of N undecayed nuclei, we have

$A = \lambda N$

We shall now look at a worked example.

Worked example

A sample consists of 1000 undecayed nuclei of a nuclide whose decay constant is 0.2 s^{-1}. What would the activity of this sample be? What would you expect its activity to be after 1 s?

Since activity $A = \lambda N$, we have

$A = 0.2\,s^{-1} \times 1000 = 200\,s^{-1}$, or 200 Bq

After 1 s, we might expect 800 nuclei to remain undecayed. The activity of the sample would then be

$$A = 0.2\,\text{s}^{-1} \times 800 = 160\,\text{s}^{-1}$$
$$= 160\,\text{Bq}$$

(In fact, it would be slightly higher than this. Since the rate of decay decreases with time all the time, less than 200 nuclei would decay during the first second.)

Count rate

Although we are often interested in finding the activity of a sample of radioactive material, we cannot usually measure this directly. This is because we cannot easily detect all of the radiation emitted. Some will escape past our detectors, and some may be absorbed within the sample itself. So our measurements give a received **count rate** R that is significantly lower than the activity A. If we know how efficient our detecting system is, we can deduce A from R. If the level of background radiation is significant, then it must be subtracted to give the *corrected* count rate.

SAQ 14.6

A sample of carbon–15 initially contains 500 000 undecayed nuclei. If the decay constant for this isotope of carbon is $0.30\,\text{s}^{-1}$, what is the initial activity of the sample?

SAQ 14.7

A piece of radium gives a received count rate of 20 counts per minute in a detector. It is known that the counter detects only 10%

of the decays from the sample. If the sample contains 1.5×10^9 atoms, what is the decay constant of this form of radium?

SAQ 14.8

A radioactive sample is known to emit α-, β- and γ-radiation. Suggest four reasons why the count rate measured by a Geiger counter placed next to this sample would be lower than the activity of the sample.

Decay graphs and equations

Radioactive substances gradually diminish as time goes by. The atomic nuclei emit radiation and become different substances. The pattern of radioactive decay is an example of a very important pattern found in many different situations, a pattern called exponential decay. *Figure 14.12* shows the decay graphs for three different radio-isotopes, each with a different rate of decay.

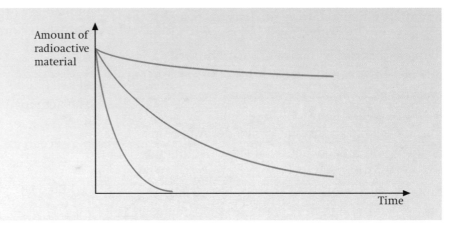

● **Figure 14.12** Some radioactive materials decay faster than others.

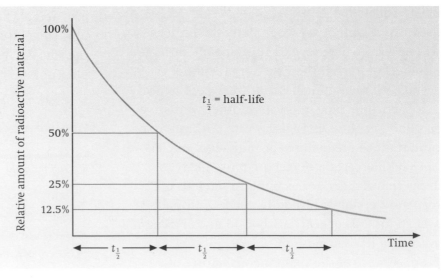

● **Figure 14.13** All radioactive decay graphs have the same characteristic shape.

Although the three graphs look different, they all have something in common – their shape. They are curved lines having a special property. If you know what is meant by the half-life of a radio-isotope, then you will understand what is special about the shape of these curves. The half-life $t_{1/2}$ of a radio-isotope is the average (or mean) time taken for half of the nuclei in a sample to decay (figure 14.13). It takes the same amount of time again for half of the remainder to decay, and a third half-life for half of the new remainder to decay.

In principle, the graph never reaches zero; it just gets closer and closer. (In practice, when only a few undecayed nuclei remain, it will cease to be a smooth curve and will eventually reach zero.) We use the idea of half-life, because we cannot say when a sample will have completely decayed.

Measuring half-life

If you are to measure the half-life of a radioactive substance in the laboratory, you need to choose something that will not decay too quickly or too slowly. In practice, the most suitable radio-isotope is protactinium-234, which decays by emitting β-radiation. This is produced in a bottle containing uranium (figure 14.14). By shaking the bottle, you can separate the protactinium into the top layer of solvent in the bottle. The Geiger counter allows you to measure the decay of the protactinium.

After recording the number of counts in consecutive 10-second intervals over a period of a few minutes, you can then draw a graph, and use it to find the half-life of protactinium-234.

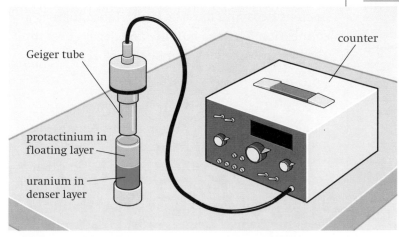

● **Figure 14.14** Practical arrangement for observing the decay of protactinium-234.

Mathematical decay

We can write an equation to represent this graph. If we start with N_0 undecayed nuclei, then the number N that remain undecayed after time t is given by

$$N = N_0\, e^{-\lambda t} \qquad \text{or} \qquad N = N_0 \exp(-\lambda t)$$

In this equation, λ is the decay constant as before. Note that you must take care with units. If λ is in s^{-1}, t must be in s. (You should recognise the form of this equation from our study of capacitor discharge in chapter 7.)

The symbol e represents the number e = 2.718 28..., a special number in the same way that π (pi) is a special number. You will need to be able to use the e^x key on your calculator to solve problems involving e.

Usually, we measure the corrected count rate R rather than the number of undecayed nuclei. This also decreases as the substance decays, and we can write

$$R = R_0\, e^{-\lambda t}$$

Similarly, the activity of the sample decreases exponentially:

$$A = A_0\, e^{-\lambda t}$$

We shall now go through two worked examples.

Worked examples

1 Suppose we start an experiment with 1000 undecayed nuclei of a radio-isotope for which $\lambda = 0.02\,\text{s}^{-1}$. How many will remain undecayed after 20 s?

In this case, we have $N_0 = 1000$, $\lambda = 0.02\,\text{s}^{-1}$ and $t = 20\,\text{s}$. Substituting in the equation gives

$$N = 1000\, e^{(-0.02 \times 20)}$$

Calculating the expression in brackets first gives

$$N = 1000\, e^{-0.4}$$

Using the e^x key and multiplying by 1000 gives

$$N = 670$$

(This answer has been rounded off to the nearest whole number, because we cannot

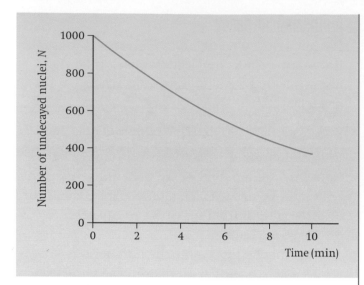

● **Figure 14.15** Radioactive decay graph for the second worked example.

have a fraction of a nucleus. In practice, we would expect the number of undecayed nuclei after 20 s to be close to this answer.)

> 2   A sample initially contains 1000 undecayed nuclei of an isotope whose decay constant $\lambda = 0.1$ min^{-1}. Draw a graph to show how the sample will decay over a period of 10 min.

The equation for this decay is

$$N = 1000\ e^{-0.1t}$$

Calculating values of N at intervals of 1 min gives the table below and the graph shown in *figure 14.15*.

t (min)	0	1	2	3	4	5
N	1000	905	819	741	670	607

t (min)	6	7	8	9	10
N	549	497	449	407	368

SAQ 14.9

The radio–isotope nitrogen–13 has a half-life of 10.0 min. A sample initially contains 1000 undecayed nuclei.

a   Write down an equation to show how the number undecayed, N, depends on time, t.

b   How many will remain after 10 min, and after 20 min?

c   How many will decay during the first 30 min?

SAQ 14.10

A sample of a radio-isotope, for which $\lambda = 0.1$ s^{-1}, contains 5000 undecayed nuclei at the start of an experiment.

a   How many will remain after 50 s?

b   What will its activity be after 50 s?

SAQ 14.11

The value of λ for protactinium–234 is 9.63×10^{-3} s^{-1}. The table shows the number of undecayed nuclei, N, in a sample.

Time (s)	0	20	40	60	80	100	120	140
N		400	330					

Copy and complete the table. Draw a graph, and use it to find the half-life of protactinium–234.

SAQ 14.12

Carbon–14 is the radio–isotope used by archaeologists for radiocarbon dating of dead organic matter. Its value of λ is 1.21×10^{-4} year^{-1}. In laboratory tests, a sample of fresh material gives a count rate of 200 min^{-1}. Calculate how this rate will decrease at 1000-year intervals over a period of 10 000 years. Draw a graph, and use it to determine the age of a sample that gives a count rate of 116 min^{-1}.

Decay constant and half-life

A radio-isotope that decays rapidly has a short half-life $t_{1/2}$. Its decay constant must be high, since the probability per unit time of an individual nucleus decaying must be high. Hence there is a connection between half-life and decay constant. They are inversely related by the expression

$$\lambda = \frac{0.693}{t_{1/2}}$$

(The constant 0.693 comes in to this because $e^{-0.693} = 1/2$, approximately.)

Thus if we know either $t_{1/2}$ or λ, we can calculate the other. For a nuclide with a very long half-life, we might not wish to sit around waiting to measure the half-life; it is easier to determine λ by measuring the activity (and using $A = \lambda N$), and then deduce $t_{1/2}$.

Note that the units of λ and $t_{1/2}$ must be compatible; for example, λ in s^{-1} and $t_{1/2}$ in s.

SAQ 14.13

Figure 14.16 shows the decay of a radio-isotope of caesium, $^{134}_{55}Cs$. Use the graph to determine the half-life of this nuclide, and hence find the decay constant.

SAQ 14.14

The decay constant of a particular radio-isotope is known to be $3 \times 10^{-4} s^{-1}$. After how long will the activity of a sample of this substance decrease to one-eighth of its initial value?

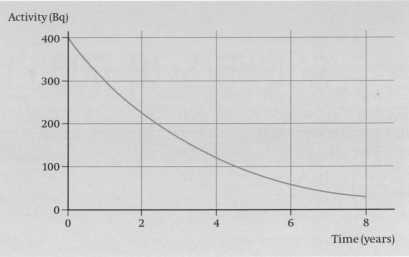

● **Figure 14.16** Decay graph for a radio-isotope of caesium.

SUMMARY

◆ There are three types of ionising radiation produced by radioactive substances, α-particles, β-particles and γ-rays.

◆ The most strongly ionising, and hence the least penetrating, is α. The least strongly ionising is γ.

◆ Their different charges, masses and speeds can be distinguished by the effect of an electric or magnetic field.

◆ Nuclear decay is a spontaneous and random process. This unpredictability means that count rates tend to fluctuate, and we have to measure average quantities.

◆ The half-life $t_{1/2}$ of a nuclide is the average time taken for half of the nuclei in a sample to decay.

◆ The decay constant λ is the probability that an individual nucleus will decay per unit time.

◆ These two quantities are related by $\lambda = 0.693/t_{1/2}$.

◆ We can represent the exponential decrease of a quantity by an equation of the form $x = x_0 e^{-\lambda t}$, where x can be activity A, corrected count rate R, or number of undecayed nuclei N.

Questions

1 Copy and complete the following equation, which represents the decay by β- and γ- emission of a nucleus of argon:

$^{41}_{18}Ar \rightarrow K + ? + ?$

2 The isotope $^{16}_{7}N$ decays with a half-life of 7.4 s.
  a What is the decay constant for this nuclide? (The decay constant and half-life are related by $\lambda t_{1/2} = 0.693$.)

  b A sample of $^{16}_{7}N$ initially contains 5000 nuclei. How many will remain after 14.8 s?
  c How many will remain after 20 s?

3 Explain how the ionising powers of the different types of ionising radiation (alpha, beta and gamma) are related to their ranges as they pass through materials.

Answers to questions

The answers are sometimes given to more figures than are allowed by the data, to allow for checking.

Chapter 1

1.1 Car: 450 kJ; truck: 18 MJ

1.2 **a** From you (your muscles)
b The force you exert on the ball

1.3 6.98 MJ

1.4 **a** $31.3 \, \text{m s}^{-1}$
b $31.3 \, \text{m s}^{-1}$ (use $v^2 = u^2 + 2as$)

1.5 **a, b** Work is done
c, d No work is done

1.6 **a** 1000 J   **b** $1 \, \text{m s}^{-1}$

1.7 500 kJ

1.8 **a** 0.92 (92%)
b Heat (because work is done against friction/air resistance)

End-of-chapter questions

1 **a** 0.7(70%)
b Electrical energy to GPE + heat energy

2 **a** 2940 J
b 5760 J = 66%; raising pulley, heat

3 **a** Fastest when closest; slowest when furthest.
b GPE decreases as it approaches the Sun, then increases again.
KE increases towards the Sun.

Chapter 2

2.1 **a** B   **b** A

2.2 **a** $10 \, \text{kg m s}^{-1}$ **b** $5 \times 10^5 \, \text{kg m s}^{-1}$
c $1.82 \times 10^{-23} \, \text{kg m s}^{-1}$

2.3 Momentum before = momentum after
= $0.5 \, \text{kg m s}^{-1}$

2.4 See *table*

Type of collision	Momentum	Kinetic energy
elastic	conserved	conserved
inelastic	conserved	not conserved

2.5 **a** $6 \, \text{kg m s}^{-1}$, $10 \, \text{kg m s}^{-1}$
b $10 \, \text{kg m s}^{-1}$, $6 \, \text{kg m s}^{-1}$
c Yes
d KE before = KE after = 4.5 J + 12.5 J = 17 J

2.6 **a** See *figure*
b $0.4 \, \text{m s}^{-1}$, in reverse direction

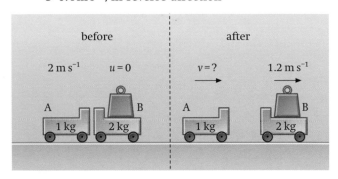

● **Answer for** SAQ 2.6a

2.7 See *figure*

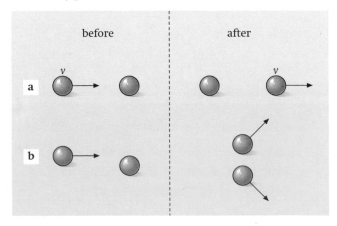

● **Answer for** SAQ 2.7

2.8 **a** He has given momentum to spanner, and so gains momentum in opposite direction.
b 200 s

2.9 **a** Matter starts to move in all directions, but total momentum is zero.

   b You give downward momentum to Earth; as you slow down, so does the Earth; as you start to fall back down, the Earth starts to 'fall' back up towards you.

2.10 $0.4\,\mathrm{m\,s^{-1}}$

2.11 $1.6\,\mathrm{m\,s^{-1}}$

2.12 1770 N

2.13 50 N (bouncing: greater force)

End-of-chapter questions

1 **a** $p = mv$
   b $\mathrm{kg\,m\,s^{-1}}$
   c Vector

2 $470\,\mathrm{kg\,m\,s^{-1}}$

3 **b** Inelastic

4 $1.855\,\mathrm{kg\,m\,s^{-1}}$

5 **a** $3.42 \times 10^5\,\mathrm{m\,s^{-1}}$
   b 0.98

6 **a** $10^7\,\mathrm{kg\,m\,s^{-1}}$
   b $10^6\,\mathrm{N}$

Chapter 3

3.1 **a** 30°   **b** 180°, 105°

3.2 **a** 0.52 rad, 1.57 rad, 1.83 rad
   b 28.6°, 43.0°, 180°, 90°
   c $\pi/3$ rad, $\pi/2$ rad, π rad, 2π rad

3.3 Speed does not change.

3.4 **a** $0\,\mathrm{m\,s^{-1}}$ **b** $0.4\,\mathrm{m\,s^{-1}}$

3.5 **a** Gravitational pull of Earth on Moon.
   b Frictional force of road on wheels.
   c Tension in string supporting the pendulum.

3.6 No frictional force between wheels and road. If driver turns steering wheel, car will carry straight on.

3.7 Speed and kinetic energy are scalar quantities; the others are all vectors. Speed is constant; velocity has constant magnitude but direction is changing (it is tangential to the circle); kinetic energy is constant; momentum has constant magnitude but direction is changing (tangential to the circle); centripetal force has constant magnitude but direction is changing (radial

force); centripetal acceleration behaves in the same way as centripetal force.

3.8 84.6 min

3.9 $3.5\,\mathrm{m\,s^{-1}}$

3.10 Tension in string must have a vertical componenet to balance the weight of the conker.

3.11 In level flight, lift balances the weight. During banking, the vertical component of lift is less than the weight, so the aeroplane loses height unless lift can be increased.

End-of-chapter questions

1 **a** 184 kN   **b** $7.71\,\mathrm{km\,s^{-1}}$
   c 5500 s   **d** 15.7 times

2 **a** $9.4\,\mathrm{m\,s^{-1}}$ **b** $177\,\mathrm{m\,s^{-2}}$
   c 88 N

3 **a** $24.3\,\mathrm{km\,s^{-1}}$ **b** $2.6 \times 10^{-3}\,\mathrm{m\,s^{-2}}$
   c $1.6 \times 10^{21}\,\mathrm{N}$

4 The normal reaction (contact force) of the wall of the slide has a horizontal component, which provides the centripetal force. If you are going fast, you need a bigger force, so the horizontal component must be greater. This happens when you move up the curve of the wall of the slide.

Chapter 4

4.1 *Free:* pendulum in clock; cymbal *after* being struck.
   Forced: wing beat of mosquito; shaking of building *during* earthquake.

4.2 Curved

4.3 10 cm, 120 ms, 8.3 Hz

4.4 **a** Half
   b Different frequencies means that the term *phase difference* is meaningless.

4.5 The mass is the weight on the end of the pendulum. The central position is where the mass is hanging vertically downwards. The restoring force is the force of gravity. (In fact, it is the component of the mass's weight at right angles to the string.)

4.6 **a** 2.0 cm   **b** 0.40 s
   c $31\,\mathrm{cm\,s^{-1}}$ **d** $0.50\,\mathrm{m\,s^{-2}}$

4.7 At the extreme left of the oscillation, the acceleration is positive (towards the right).

4.8 Gradient = 0, so $v = 0 \, \mathrm{cm\,s^{-1}}$

4.9 **a** $0 \, \mathrm{cm\,s^{-1}}$ **b** $47 \, \mathrm{cm\,s^{-1}}$ **c** $0 \, \mathrm{cm\,s^{-2}}$

4.10 **a** $0.5 \, \mathrm{s}$ **b** $2 \, \mathrm{Hz}$ **c** $4\pi \, \mathrm{rad\,s^{-1}}$

4.11 **a** $0.3 \, \mathrm{mm}$ **b** $120 \, \mathrm{Hz}$

4.12 $x = 20 \, \mathrm{cm} \times \cos(2\pi \times 0.5 \, \mathrm{Hz} \times t)$; see also *figure*

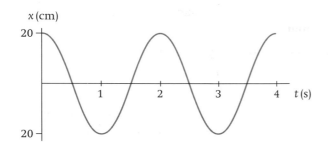

● **Answer for** SAQ 4.12

4.13 **a** $a = -(2.8\pi \, \mathrm{Hz})^2 x$ **b** $-3.9 \, \mathrm{m\,s^{-2}}$

4.14 $2.76 \, \mathrm{Hz}$

4.15 **a** Gravitational potential energy
b Gravitational potential energy has changed to kinetic energy by the midpoint of the oscillation; then kinetic energy changes back to gravitational potential energy again.

4.16 See *figure*

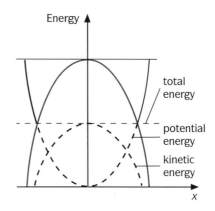

● **Answer for** SAQ 4.16

4.17 See *figure*

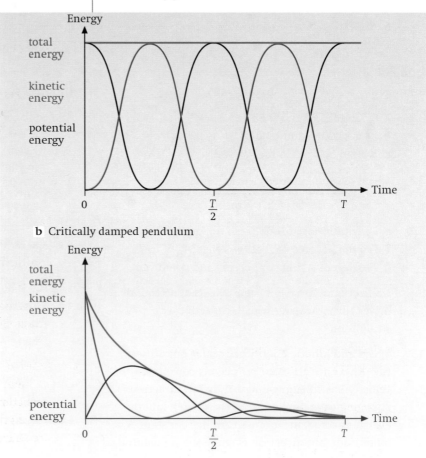

b Critically damped pendulum

● **Answer for** SAQ 4.17

4.18 Useful and problematic examples of resonance:

Example	Useful/problem?	What is resonating?
Buildings in earthquake	Problem	Mechanical structure forced by energy from waves of earthquake
Components in engines	Problem	At certain rates of rotation, parts of an engine may resonate mechanically; the resonance is driven by the energy output of the engine. This can lead to components cracking or disintegrating, with dangerous consequences
Positive feedback in amplification systems (gives high-pitched squealing sound)	Problem	Microphone held too close to loudspeaker that is emitting waves of the same frequency as the microphone is tuned to, so the waves from the loudspeaker force the amplifier to resonate
Tuned radio	Useful	Electric signal in circuit forced by incoming radio waves
Microwave cooker	Useful	Water molecules forced by microwaves
Magnetic resonance in atoms	Useful	Nuclei in atoms behave as magnets; they can be made to resonate by electromagnetic waves. Each nucleus resonates at a different frequency, so the structures of molecules can be determined

End-of-chapter questions

1　They are not in equilibrium at the midpoint of their 'oscillation'; the force on them does not vary uniformly. When they are in the air, the force (gravity) is constant.

2　**a** 20 cm　**b** 0.4 s　**c** 2.5 Hz
　d −11 cm　**e** 0 cm s^{-1}　**f** 310 cm s^{-1}

3　**a** See *figure*

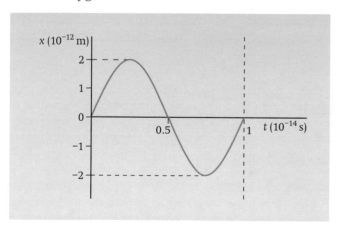

● **Answer for** question 3a

　b Use the gradient at the steepest point;
　　$v_{max} = 1.3 \times 10^3$ m s^{-1}

4　**a** 2 s　　**b** 0.5 Hz　**c** π rad s^{-1}
　d $a = -(2\pi \times 0.5)^2 x$
　　$a = -\pi^2 x$

5　**a** 0.37 m s^{-1}　**b** 0.137 J　**c** 0.137 J
　d 1.86 m s^{-2}　**e** 3.72 N

Chapter 5

5.1　6.67×10^{-9} N

5.2　10^{-6} N. Weight greater than this by factor of 10^9.

5.3　9.86 m s^{-2}

Box questions on measuring G

A　6.67×10^{-9} N

B　Lead is very dense, so for a manageable size of apparatus it will give the largest possible gravitational force.

C　1.69×10^{-6} N

D　6×10^{-8} degrees

E　In Cavendish's apparatus, the force between the masses is not balancing the weight of the sphere, so it can provide much more sensitive measurements than the 'pendulum' apparatus.

F　So that the gravitational force on one small sphere would arise from the attraction of the large sphere next to it, and there would be little attraction due to the other large sphere.

G　Cavendish's experiment can be used to determine a value for *G*. Then this can be used in Newton's equation for the gravitational force to estimate the mass of the Earth. So in effect it is 'weighing' the Earth.

End-of-chapter questions

1   3.1 N (or 0.3 kg on scales). Measurable with bathroom scales, though hard to achieve accuracy.

2   $1.6\,N\,kg^{-1}$, $272\,N\,kg^{-1}$. Only a very thin atmosphere on the Moon because the gases can escape the weak gravity.

3   $2.8 \times 10^{-3}\,N\,kg^{-1}$, $2.1 \times 10^{20}\,N$, $2.8 \times 10^{-3}\,m\,s^{-2}$

4   $25.0\,N\,kg^{-1}$

5   Field strength due to Sun at Earth
    $= 5.93\,m\,N\,kg^{-1}$
    Field strength due to Moon at Earth
    $= 0.0342\,m\,N\,kg^{-1}$
    So the Sun exerts a greater pull per kilogram on sea-water.

6   $1.7 \times 10^{-8}\,N$, $5.3 \times 10^{-8}\,N$

7   Closer to the Moon. The point will be $3.42 \times 10^{5}\,km$ from the centre of the Earth.

Chapter 6

6.1   **a** Positive charges repelling
      c Negative charges
      b Opposite charges

6.2   See *figure*

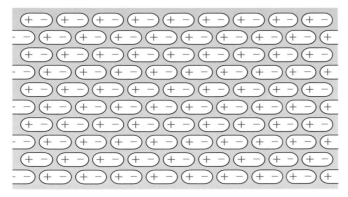

● **Answer for** SAQ 6.2

6.3   See *figure*

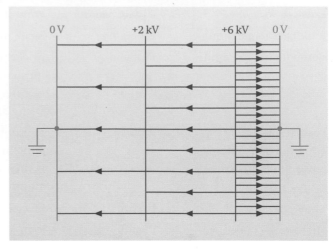

● **Answer for** SAQ 6.3

6.4   **a** 160 000 V   **b** 0.08 mm   **c** 400 MV

6.5 $50\,kV\,m^{-1}$ ($50\,kN\,C^{-1}$), 0.1 N

6.6 $8.8 \times 10^{17}\,m\,s^{-2}$

6.7   See *figure*

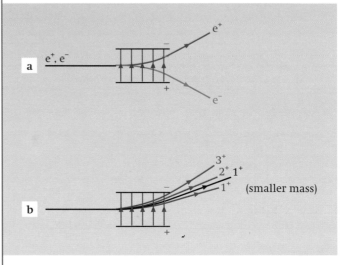

● **Answer for** SAQ 6.7

6.8   230 N, $1.9 \times 10^{-34}\,N$. This answer tells us that gravity is nowhere near enough to balance the electric repulsion. Therefore, some other force must hold the protons together (in fact, it is the *strong nuclear force*, but we do not need to cover it in this module).

6.9 $1.8 \times 10^{-5}\,C$

Box questions on measuring *e*

A   Charge on droplet must be negative.

B $180 \, \text{V cm}^{-1}$

C $5.78 \times 10^{-15} \, \text{N}$

D $5.78 \times 10^{-15} \, \text{N}$

E $-3.2 \times 10^{-19} \, \text{C}$

F   β-radiation must be adding negative charge to the droplet. (You could argue that it is somehow reducing the mass, but this is less plausible and is not the correct interpretation.)

G $120 \, \text{V}$

Box questions on comprehension

A   Field strongest near church spire (field lines closer together).

B   Lightning is more likely to strike the spire.

C   See *figure*

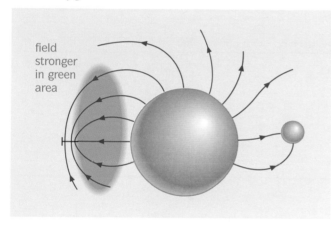

field stronger in green area

● **Answer for** box question C

End-of-chapter questions

1 $5000 \, \text{N C}^{-1}$

2   **a** See *figure*

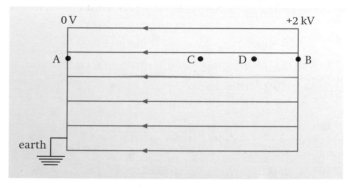

0 V   +2 kV

A●   C●   D●   ●B

earth

● **Answer for** question 2a

   b $2 \, \text{kV}$
   c $8 \, \text{kV m}^{-1}$ at both
   d $0.04 \, \text{N}$ to the left

3   **a** $2.9 \times 10^6 \, \text{V m}^{-1}$
   b $5.0 \, \text{N}$

Chapter 7

7.1 $3000 \, \mu\text{C}$, $0.003 \, \text{C}$

7.2 $2 \times 10^{-6} \, \text{F}$, $2 \, \mu\text{F}$, $2 \times 10^6 \, \text{pF}$

7.3 $0.05 \, \text{A}$ ($50 \, \text{mA}$)

7.4 $800 \, \mu\text{F}$

7.5   **a** $0.0625 \, \text{J}$ **b** $6.25 \times 10^{-8} \, \text{J}$ **c** $5.29 \, \text{J}$

7.6   Charge is the same for both capacitors ($2 \times 10^4 \, \text{C}$). Energy stored is greater in the $100 \, \mu\text{F}$ capacitor ($4 \times 10^6 \, \text{J}$ compared to $2 \times 10^6 \, \text{J}$).

7.7   **a** $0.72 \, \text{J}$ **b** $0.02 \, \text{s}$

7.8   Gradient $= V/Q = 1/C$

7.9   **a** See *table*.

Q (mC)	V (V)	Area of strip ΔW (mJ)	Sum of areas W (mJ)
1	1	0.5	0.5
2	2	1.5	2.0
3	3	2.5	4.5
4	4	3.5	8.0

   b The graph is a parabola.
   c $1 \, \text{mF}$

7.10 **a** 200 μF   **b** 4000 μC

7.11 2000 μC, 5000 μC, 7000 μC

7.12 Two 20 μF and one 10 μF connected in parallel; or two 100 μF connected in series.

7.13 100 μF

7.14 **a** C_{total} = one-half (or one-third) of C for two (or three) capacitors
b For n capacitors in parallel, $C_{total} = n \times C$

7.15 **a** $1/G_{total} = 1/G_1 + 1/G_2$
b $G_{total} = G_1 + G_2$

7.16 **a** 33.3 μF   **c** 66.7 μF
b 300 μF   **d** 150 μF

7.17 **a** Four in parallel
b Four in series
c Two in series with two in parallel

7.18 **a** 25 μF   **b** 4000 μC
c 160 V   **d** 80 mJ

7.19 See *figure*

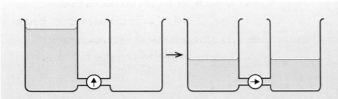

● **Answer for** SAQ 7.19

a Half original level
b Halving of energy stored when equal capacitors are connected together.

7.20 80 μA, 400 μC

7.21 **a** See *table*

Point	A	B	C	D	E
I (μA)	2.2	1.7	1.2	0.9	0.7
t (s)	10	20	30	40	50

b   See *figure*

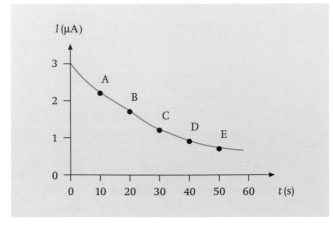

● **Answer for** SAQ 7.21b

7.22 2.7 mC

7.23 2.8 V

7.24 **a** 500 μA   **b** $I = 500\,μA \times e^{-t/200\,s}$
c See *table*   **d** See *figure*

Time t (s)	0	100	200	300	400	500
Current I (μA)	500	303	184	112	68	41

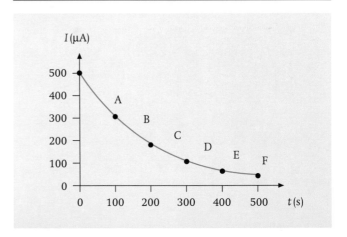

● **Answer for** SAQ 7.24d

7.25 22 ms

7.26 **a** 80 μA   **b** 29.6 μA
c 2.4 s   **d** 2400 μF
e 4.8 s
f A large uncertainty in R would give an equally large uncertainty in C.

End-of-chapter questions

1 Greatest: in parallel, 900 pF
   Least: in series, 60 pF

2 $4\,\mu F$

3 **a** $40\,\mu F$ **b** $0.4\,C$ **c** $2\,kJ$

4 **a** $1.8\,C$, $8.1\,J$ **b** $810\,W$
   c $180\,A$ **d** $0.025\,\Omega$

5 **a** $0.5\,mA$
   b $0.27\,mA$
   c $50\,s$

6 **a** $50\,s$
   b $Q = 600\,\mu C \times e^{-(0.02 \times t)\,s}$
      $I = 12\,\mu A \times e^{-(0.02 \times t)\,s}$
      $V = 6\,V \times e^{-(0.02 \times t)\,s}$
   c $3.6\,\mu A$

Chapter 8

8.1 **a** $0.375\,N$ **b** $0.265\,N$ **c** $0\,N$
     All downwards into page

8.2 See *figure*

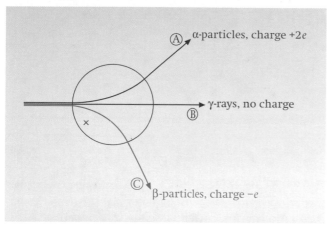

● **Answer for** SAQ 8.2

8.3 **a** $8 \times 10^{-14}\,N$ **b** $5.66 \times 10^{-14}\,N$

8.4 See *figure*

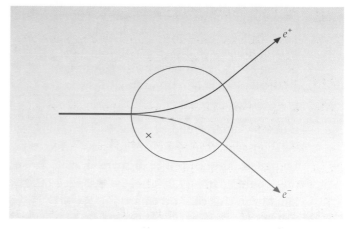

● **Answer for** SAQ 8.4

8.5 Back-to-front

8.6 All have same mass, charge and speed.

8.7 **a** Circular path will have smaller radius.
     b Electrons will circle in the opposite
        direction.
     c Circular path will have larger radius.
     d Electrons will spiral around field lines because
        they will have a constant component of
        velocity in the direction of the field lines.

End-of-chapter question

1 **a** $1.6 \times 10^{-16}\,J$, $1.87 \times 10^{7}\,m\,s^{-1}$
   b $10\,000\,V\,m^{-1}$, $1.6 \times 10^{-15}\,N$
   c No field in horizontal plane. $5.35 \times 10^{-9}\,s$
   d $1.76 \times 10^{15}\,m\,s^{-2}$, $9.4 \times 10^{6}\,m\,s^{-1}$
   e $26.7°$
   f $25.1\,cm$
   g Deflection decreased; deflection increased
   h $5.35 \times 10^{-4}\,T$, into page

Chapter 9

9.1 Wire or coil cuts magnetic flux, driven by the
     pedals via the chain. Cut flux means current gen-
     erated in wire to light the lamps.

9.2 Stronger magnet means more flux and more flux
     linkage, so larger e.m.f.
     Faster movement means more flux cut/linked per
     second and more current generated, so larger
     e.m.f.

9.3 A→B, C→D. So X is positive.

9.4 Left wingtip positive. It is negative in the Southern Hemisphere because the field direction is reversed.

9.5 Cutting much less flux. Only small components cut due to slight curvature at edges of field, rather than all the parallel flux in the space between the magnets.

9.6 Frequency determined by speed of rotation (so to keep constant, must be geared). E.m.f. affected by magnet strength, number of turns in coil, size of coil. Would normally be affected by speed of rotation, but in this case that has to be fixed.

9.7 2.25×10^{-5} Wb

9.8 1.45×10^{7} Wb

9.9 3.9×10^{-6} Wb

9.10 0.54 Wb

9.11 6 mV

9.12 0.6 V

9.13 0.4 T

9.14 a Stop pushing implies no flux is cut, so no current is generated. Therefore, no magnetic poles are formed and no work is done; there is no movement.
b Pull away implies that flux is cut, but near end to magnet becomes a S pole, so the poles attract each other, and work has to be done to pull magnet and coil apart.

9.15 See *figure*

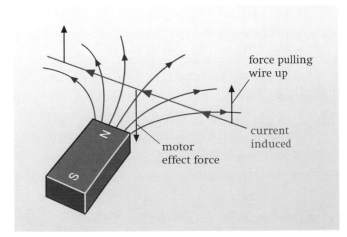

● **Answer for** SAQ 9.15

9.16 a Flux linkage, flux cut as magnet moves, so there is an induced e.m.f.
b No flux cut inside coil, the motion is parallel to the field.
c Magnet leaves coil, flux lines cut again, but e.m.f. is in reverse (negative) direction because current has to flow the other way (Lenz's law). Peak e.m.f. greater because magnet moving faster (acceleration due to gravity), the flux is cut at a faster rate and the e.m.f. is proportional to the rate at which the flux is cut. Also, faster movement means it takes less time to complete the section.

9.17 Have to do work against motor effect force from induced current when lights are on.

9.18 For direct current supply, flux lines constant means no e.m.f. induced.

9.19 See *figure*

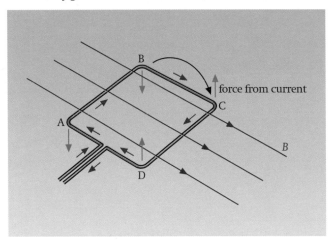

● **Answer for** SAQ 9.19

9.20 Alternating current. Usually, a bar magnet rotates inside a fixed coil. As the N pole passes one side of the coil, the current flows one way. Then the S pole passes, and the current reverses.

9.21 B greater means flux greater means $d\Phi/dt$ greater if same rate of movement.
A greater means flux greater means $d\Phi/dt$ greater if same rate of movement.
N greater means flux greater means $d\Phi/dt$ greater if same rate of movement.
ω greater means rate of cutting flux greater means $d\Phi/dt$ greater.

End-of-chapter questions

1   a In the opposite direction – the flux is being cut in the opposite direction.

  b Move wire or magnet faster; use stronger magnet; wind wire into a coil; etc.

2   a 5×10^{-3} Wb

  b 0.05 V

Chapter 10

10.1 *Solid:* well ordered, small spacing, no motion except lattice vibrations.
  Liquid: less well ordered, small spacing but some gaps, motion fairly slow.
  Gas: no order, large spacing, much fast and random motion.

10.2 a Takes energy (implying work and time) to separate all the molecules to form steam.

  b Much greater energy required to separate all the molecules (to form gas) than to create some disorder but not separate (to form liquid).

  c Speeds up evaporation from its tongue. Energy required for evaporation means that it cools down.

10.3 1.67 MJ

10.4 Copper (just)

10.5 $455\,\mathrm{J\,kg^{-1}\,K^{-1}}$

10.6 3340 J; 12 °C

10.7 At higher temperatures, energy escapes more quickly, so the temperature rises more slowly.

10.8 Systematic; can be removed (in principle) by insulation.

10.9 $5700\,\mathrm{J\,kg^{-1}\,K^{-1}}$; biggest source of error will be energy loss due to poor insulation.

10.10 10 min; energy escapes

10.11 a Temperature of kettle is not changing.

  b Value will be too high.

End-of-chapter questions

1   3.01 MJ

2   a AB: solid; BC: solid + liquid; CD: liquid

  b Increasing in all sections

  c Greater when a liquid: CD has steeper slope than AB, so it takes more energy to heat the liquid through 1 K than the solid.

Chapter 11

11.1 $\frac{1}{2}MV^2 = \frac{1}{2}mv^2$

  So

  $$\frac{M}{m} = \frac{v^2}{V^2} = \left(\frac{v}{V}\right)^2$$

  So $M \ll m$ implies that $v \gg V$.

11.2 a 273 K, 293 K, 393 K, 773 K, 250 K, 73 K

  b −273 °C, −253 °C, −173 °C, 27 °C, 100 °C, 227 °C

11.3 a With V fixed, if T increases, so does p (because pV/T is constant).

  b With p fixed, if T decreases, so does V.

11.4 See *figure*; the copper atoms are not moving so the electrons can travel freely through the metal.

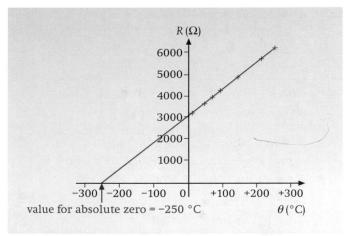

● **Answer for** SAQ 11.4

11.5 3.57 mol, 80 dm³

11.6 385 K (= 112 °C)

11.7 164 g, 2.63 kg

11.8 Temperature is proportional to (average speed)². So if average speed doubles, temperature increases by a factor $2^2 = 4$.

11.9 Mass smaller means that average speed must be greater to keep average kinetic energy and hence temperature the same. So nitrogen speed is greater than oxygen speed.

End-of-chapter questions

1   1200 K

2   a halved

  b stays the same

3   0.2 m³

Chapter 12

12.1 If there were air molecules in the container, the α-particles would scatter off them as well and distort the results.

12.2 The mass of the neutron is similar to that of the proton, so neutrons can affect the protons and neutrons in cells quite significantly, through the transfer of energy in collisions.

12.3 **a** 7   **b** 44
      c 60   **d** 118
      e 122

12.4 **a** $+e$ **b** No charge
      c $+Ze$, where Z is the proton number
      d No charge   **e** $+2e$

12.5 **a** Proton number 80 for all
        Neutron numbers 116, 118, 119, 120, 121, 122, 124
      b 200.5

12.6 They are grouped into isotopes as follows:
      A and E;   C;   D, F and G;   B and H
      $A = {}^{44}_{20}\text{Ca}$ isotope of calcium
      $B = {}^{50}_{23}\text{V}$ isotope of vanadium
      $C = {}^{46}_{21}\text{Sc}$ isotope of scandium
      $D = {}^{46}_{22}\text{Ti}$ isotope of titanium
      $E = {}^{46}_{20}\text{Ca}$ isotope of calcium
      $F = {}^{48}_{22}\text{Ti}$ isotope of titanium
      $G = {}^{50}_{22}\text{Ti}$ isotope of titanium
      $H = {}^{51}_{23}\text{V}$ isotope of vanadium

12.7 There are 38 protons and 52 neutrons in the nucleus.

12.8 **a** There are different numbers of neutrons in the nuclei.
      b There is the same number of protons in each nucleus.

End-of-chapter questions

1 **a** More back-scattered, because greater chance of close approach to gold nuleus.
      b Fewer back-scattered, because their inertia would tend to carry them forward.
      c Fewer back-scattered, because the repulsive force would be less. (Note: gold and silver atoms occupy roughly the same volume.)

2 Low-energy electrons have wavelength comparable to atomic spacing. High-energy electrons have a much shorter wavelength, comparable to nuclear diameter.

3 143 and 146 neutrons

Chapter 13

13.1 ${}^{235}_{92}\text{U} + {}^{1}_{0}\text{n} \rightarrow {}^{138}_{54}\text{Xe} + {}^{95}_{38}\text{Sr} + 3{}^{1}_{0}\text{n}$
      For A $235 + 1 = 138 + 95 + (3 \times 1)$ is correct
      For Z $92 + 0 = 54 + 38 + (3 \times 0)$ is correct

13.2 **a** $2{}^{1}_{0}\text{n}$ **b** ${}^{90}_{36}\text{Kr}$

13.3 ${}^{1}_{1}\text{H}$

13.4 $2{}^{1}_{1}\text{H}$

13.5 ${}^{15}_{7}\text{N} + {}^{1}_{1}\text{H} \rightarrow {}^{12}_{6}\text{C} + {}^{4}_{2}\text{He}$

13.6 **a** $4.5 \times 10^{-12}\,\text{J}$ **b** $1.1 \times 10^{-12}\,\text{J}$

13.7 Energy released $= -1.0 \times 10^{-4}$ relative mass units, so energy is required rather than given out.

13.8 Fission for $A<20$ unlikely since forming less stable nuclei; similarly for fusion with $A>40$.

13.9 **a** At top   **b** At $500\,^{\circ}\text{C}$
      c Before reaction   **d** Rolling

13.10 **a** $1.6 \times 10^{-13}\,\text{J}$ **b** $1.02\,\text{MeV}$

13.11 **a** $1.0073\,u$ **b** $1.67 \times 10^{-27}\,\text{kg}$

13.12 **a** $9.1 \times 10^{-31}\,\text{kg}$ **b** $5.46 \times 10^{-4}\,u$

End-of-chapter questions

1 ${}^{238}_{92}\text{U} + {}^{1}_{0}\text{n} \rightarrow {}^{239}_{94}\text{Pu} + 2{}^{0}_{-1}\text{e}$
    2 electrons are released

2 $4.4 \times 10^{9}\,\text{kg}$

Chapter 14

14.1 **a** ${}^{220}_{86}\text{Rn} \rightarrow {}^{216}_{84}\text{Po} + {}^{4}_{2}\text{He}$
      b ${}^{25}_{11}\text{Na} \rightarrow {}^{25}_{12}\text{Mg} + {}^{0}_{-1}\text{e} + \gamma$

14.2 **a** A β-particle is smaller and travels faster.
      b Air is much less dense; also metal may 'poach' β-particles (electrons) for conduction.

14.3 See *figure*.

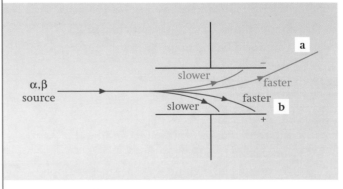

• **Answer for** SAQ 14.3

14.4 Most strongly ionising implies many more collisions occur, so there is greater loss of momentum
and therefore less penetration.

14.5 The α-particles are detected by an electronic
circuit. When smoke enters the device, the
α-particles are absorbed. The circuit then
switches on the alarm. Alpha radiation is most
suitable because it is the most strongly ionising
and so it is more likely to be absorbed by smoke.

14.6 $150\,000\,\text{s}^{-1}$, or $150\,000\,\text{Bq}$

14.7 $2.2 \times 10^{-9}\,\text{s}^{-1}$

14.8 Count rate less than activity because:
  (i) γ-rays not always detected (weakly ionising);
  (ii) counter inefficient;
  (iii) some radiation absorbed within sample
      before reaching detector;
  (iv) detector is directional, so some radiation will
      move away from detector rather than
      towards it.

14.9 **a** $N = N_0\,e^{-\lambda t}$ **b** 500, 250   **c** 875

14.10 **a** 34   **b** $3.4\,\text{s}^{-1}$; or 3.4 Bq

14.11 See *figure*. Half-life is 72 s.

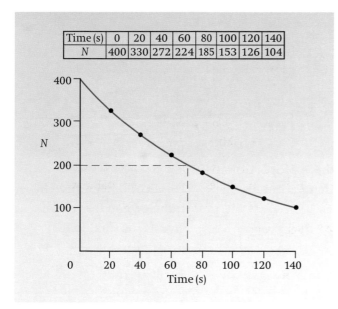

Time (s)	0	20	40	60	80	100	120	140
N	400	330	272	224	185	153	126	104

● **Answer for** SAQ 14.11

14.12 See *figure*. Rate becomes $60\,\text{min}^{-1}$. Age will be
4500 years.

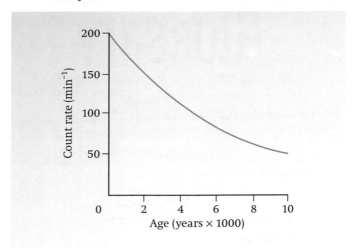

● **Answer for** SAQ 14.12

14.13 2.3 years, $0.30\,\text{year}^{-1}$

14.14 6900 s

End-of-chapter questions
1     $^{41}_{18}\text{Ar} \rightarrow\ ^{41}_{19}\text{K} +\ ^{0}_{-1}\text{e} + \gamma$

2   **a** $0.094\,\text{s}^{-1}$
      b 1250
      c 768 (approximately)

3   Alpha has greatest ionising power, so it is most
      easily absorbed.
      Gamma has least ionising power, so it is least
      easily absorbed.
      Beta is in between.

Glossary

Term	Definition	Amplification
activity	The rate at which nuclei decay in a sample of a radioactive material	Symbol: A Units: becquerel (Bq) $1\,\text{Bq} = 1\text{ decay s}^{-1}$
capacitance	The charge stored per unit p.d.	$C = Q/V$ Units: farad (F)
conservation of momentum	In a closed system, when bodies interact, the total momentum remains constant	
Coulomb's law	The electrostatic force between two point charges is proportional to the product of the charges, and inversely proportional to the square of their separation	$F = kQ_1Q_2/r^2$ $F = (1/4\pi\varepsilon°) \times Q_1Q_2/r^2$ $F = 9 \times 10^9 \times Q_1Q_2/r^2$
critical damping	The degree of damping required for the displacement of a system to reach a constant value in the minimum time without oscillation	Any less damping and it will oscillate; any more, and it will take longer to reach a constant value
decay constant	The probability that an individual nucleus will decay per unit time	Symbol: λ Units: s^{-1} $\lambda t_{1/2} = 0.693$
farad (F)	The SI unit of capacitance: one farad is one coulomb per volt	$1\,\text{F} = 1\,\text{C V}^{-1}$
Faraday's law	The e.m.f. induced in a conductor is proportional to the rate of change of magnetic flux linkage	$E \propto N\,d\Phi/dt$ For a coil: magnitude of induced e.m.f. = rate of change of flux linkage (in SI units)
force	The rate of change of momentum of the body in the direction in which the force acts	$F = d(mv)/dt$ $F = (mv - mu)/t$
half-life	The mean (average) time for the number of nuclei of a nuclide to halve	Symbol: $t_{1/2}$ Units: s $\lambda t_{1/2} = 0.693$
Lenz's law	The induced e.m.f. acts in such a direction as to produce effects to oppose the change producing it	

linear momentum	The product of an object's mass and velocity	$p = m \times v$ A vector quantity
magnetic flux	The magnetic flux passing through an area is the product of the area and the flux density perpendicular to the area	$\Phi = AB$ Units: weber (Wb)
magnetic flux linkage	The product of the magnetic flux passing through a coil and the number of turns on the coil	Flux linkage $= N\Phi = NAB$ Units: weber (Wb)
Newton's law of gravitation	The gravitational force of attraction between two point masses is proportional to the product of the masses and inversely proportional to the square of their separation	$F = Gm_1m_2/r_2$ G is the universal gravitational constant
nucleon number	The number of nucleons (protons and neutrons) in a nucleus	Symbol: A
proton number	The number of protons in a nucleus	Symbol: Z
simple harmonic motion	When the force on a body is always directed towards a fixed point, and is proportional to the body's displacement from the fixed point	$a = -(2\pi f)^2 x$
specific heat capacity	Numerically equal to the energy required to raise the temperature of unit mass of a substance by one degree	$1\,K = 1\,°C$ Units: $J\,kg^{-1}\,K^{-1}$
specific latent heat	Numerically equal to the energy required to change the state of unit mass of a substance, at constant temperature	Change of state = melting or boiling
time constant	The product of capacitance C and resistance R in an R–C circuit	$\tau = CR$ Units: s The time taken for charge stored to fall to 0.37 of its initial value
weber (Wb)	The SI unit of magnetic flux: one weber is one tesla metre squared	$1\,Wb = 1\,T\,m^2$ $1\,T = 1\,Wb\,m^{-2}$

Index

Terms shown in **bold** also appear in the glossary (see pages 162–3). Pages in *italics* refer to figures.

absolute zero, 114–6
absorption of radiation, 142, *142*
acceleration, 28
   centripetal, 29
acceleration-time graph, *39*
activity, 145
alpha (α) radiation, 139–43, *141*
alpha-particles, 121–2, *122*
amplitude, 35, *36*
angular displacement, 25
angular frequency, 40
atomic mass constant, unified, 137
atomic structure, 120–9, *123*
atom, 120

becquerel (Bq), 145
beta (β) radiation, 139–43, *141*, *143*
binding energy, nuclear, 134–6, *135*
boiling 102–4, *103*
Boyle's law, 113–14, *114*
Brown, Robert, 111
Brownian motion, 111–12, *111*, *112*
bubble chamber, *18*

cancer, ionising radiation and, 143
capacitance, 68–9
capacitors, 67–80, *67*
   electrolytic, 69
   energy stored, 69–71, *71*
   in parallel, 72, *72*
   in series, 72–3, *73*
   networks, 74–5, *74*
   discharge, 76–9, *76*, *79*
cathode-ray tube, 87
Cavendish, Henry, 54
Celsius scale, 115–16
centrifugal force, 28–31, *28*
centripetal acceleration, 29
centripetal force, 26–30, *28*, *30*, 85
Chadwick, James, 122–3

changes of state, 102–4, *102*, *103*, 106–9
Charles' law, 114, *114*
chemical potential energy, 19
circular motion, 3, 24–32, *24*, *26*, *27*
coils, transformer, 98, *98*
collisions, 11–16
collisions, elastic, 14–15, *14*, *15*
   inelastic, 15, *15*
conduction of electrons, 58
conservation of energy, 7–9
   principle of, 9
conservation of mass-energy, 136
conservation of momentum,
   principle of, 13, *13*
contact force, 6, *6*, 30, *30*
Coulomb's law, 63–4, *63*, *64*
Coulomb, Charles, 63
count rate, 146
critical damping, 44–5, *45*

damped oscillations, 43–5, *44*, *45*, *47*, *47*
damping, 43–7, *44*, *45*, *47*
   critical, 44–5, *45*
de Broglie equation, 128
decay constant, 145, 147–9,
decay equations, 146–9
decay graphs, 146–9, *146*, *148*, *149*
deflection tube, 86, *86*
deuterium, 125, *125*
diffraction, 127–8
   X-ray, 127, *127*
   of electrons, 128
   of neutrons, 128
discharge (capacitors), 76–9, *76*, *77*, *79*
   equations of, 77–9
   time constant, 78–9, *79*
displacement, angular, 25
displacement-time graph, 35–6, *36*, *39*, *39*
DNA, 143
driving frequency, 46–7, *47*

dynamo, 88, *88*, 91, *91*, 98, *98*
dynamo rule, 90–1, *90*

e.m.f., 91
   induced, 91–8
Einstein, Albert, 130, 133
elastic potential energy, 42–3, *42*
electric charge, 57–8, *58*
electric field strength, 60–2, *60*, 64–5
electric fields, 57–66, *59*, *60*, *61*, *64*, 141
   investigating, 58–9
   representing, 59, *59*
   uniform, 60, *60*
electric force, 61–4, *61*
electric generator, 88, *88*
electric motor, 88
electrical power, 1
electricity, static, 57–8, *58*
electromagnetic force, 81–7, *82*
electromagnetic induction, 88–99
   origin of, 95–7
electromagnetism, 81–99, *86*, *93*
electromotive force (e.m.f.), 91
electron beam tube, 82–3, *82*, *83*
electron diffraction, 128
electron scattering, high-energy, 128
electron-volt, 137
electrons, conduction, 58
electrostatic attraction, 27
electrostatic fields, 57–66, *59*, *60*, *61*
electrostatic force, 126
energy and s.h.m., 42–3, *43*
energy
   conservation of, 7–9
   chemical potential, 19
   elastic potential, 42–3, *42*
   gravitational potential (GPE), 3–5, *4*
   internal, 104–6, *105*
   kinetic, 2–3, *3*, 19
   molecular, 105, 118

principle of conservation of, 9
  rotational kinetic, 118, *118*
equation of state (ideal gas), 117
equations of s.h.m., 41–2
evaporation, 104, *104*
explosions, 11, 19–20

Fahrenheit scale, 116
farad (F), 68
Faraday's law, 93–5
field
  electric, 57–66, *59*, *60*, *61*, *64*, 141
  gravitational, 50–6, *52*
  magnetic, 81, 141
field strength, gravitational, 53–5,
  55
fission reactors, 132
Fleming's left-hand rule, 81, *81*, 83,
  96
Fleming's right-hand rule, 90–1, *90*
flux, magnetic, 89–90, *89*, 92–3
flux density, 92
  magnetic, 92
flux linkage, 93
  magnetic, 93, *93*, 163
force
  centrifugal, 28–31, *28*
  centripetal, 26–30, *28*, *30*, 85
  contact, 6, *6*, 30, *30*
  definition of, 22
  electromagnetic, 81–7, *82*
  electrostatic, 126
  gravitational, 50–6, *53*
  magnetic, 84, *84*
  motive, 5
  strong nuclear, 126
forced oscillations, 33–4
free oscillations, 33–4, *34*
free space, permittivity of, 63
frequency, 34, 36, 40
  angular, 40
friction, 6, 30, *30*

gamma (γ) radiation, 139–43, *141*, *143*
gas constant, 117
  universal, 117
gas laws, 113–5, *114*
gases, ideal, 111–19
generator, electric, 88, *88*
gravitation, Newton's law of, 52–3,
  63, 65, 163

gravitational constant, 53
gravitational field, 50–6, *52*
gravitational field strength, 53–5,
  55
gravitational force, 50–6, *53*
gravitational potential energy
  (GPE), 3–5, *4*
gravitational pull, 27, *27*, 29
gravity, 50–6, *53*

half-life, 147–9, *149*
hazards of ionising radiation,
  143–4
heat, 1
Helmholtz coils, 86, *86*
high-energy electron scattering,
  128

ideal gas equation, 117
ideal gases, 111–19
induced e.m.f., 91–8
induction, electromagnetic, 88–99
  origin of, 95–7
internal energy, 104–6, *105*
ionising radiation, 139–41
  hazards of, 143–4
isotopes, 124–5, *125*, *126*
  uses of, 127, *127*

joule (J), 2
Joule, James Prescott, 7, *7*
joulemeter, 70

Kelvin scale, 115–16, *115*
kinetic energy (KE), 2–3, *3*, 19
  rotational, 118, *118*
  translational, 118, *118*
kinetic model, 101–2, *101*

Lenz's law, 95–7, *95*
lift force, 30
linear momentum, 13
loudspeaker, 34

magnetic field, 81, 141
magnetic flux, 89–90, *89*, 92–3
  density, 92
magnetic flux linkage, 93, *93*
magnetic force, 84, *84*
magnetic resonance imaging (MRI),
  48

mass spectrograph, 85
mass-energy conservation, 136
mass-spring system, 34, *34*
melting, 102–4, *103*
microscope, scanning tunnelling,
  101
microwaves, 48
Millikan, Robert, 62
molecular energy, 105, 118
momentum, 11–23
  principle of conservation of, 13,
  13, 162
motion sensor, 38, *38*
motion, Newton's laws of, 11, 21–2,
  21
  first, 21, 27
  second, 21–2, 29
  third, 22
motor effect, 81–2, *81*
motor rule, 81, 83, 96
motor, electric, 88

natural frequency (of oscillation),
  45–48, *46*, *47*
neutron diffraction, 128
neutron number, 123–4, *124*
neutron, discovery of, 122–3, *123*
Newton, Isaac, 51–3
Newton's law of gravitation, 52–3,
  63, 65, 163
Newton's laws of motion, *see*
  motion, Newton's laws of
Newton's 'thought experiment',
  29
normal reaction, 6, 30, *30*
nuclear fission, 130–3, *131*
  and binding energy, 135–6, *135*
nuclear force, strong, 126
nuclear fusion, 131–3, *132*
  and binding energy, 135–6, *136*
nuclear physics, 130–8
nuclear stability, 134–6, *135*
nucleon number, 123, *124*
nucleons, 123–4
nucleus, 121–3, *122*
nuclide, 124

oscillations, 33–49
  forced, 33–4
  free, 33–4, *34*
oscilloscope, 83

particle model, 100
particles, sub-atomic, 18, *18*
pendulum, 35, *35*
period, 36
permittivity of free space, 63
Perrin, Jean, 112
phase, 36
phase difference, 36, *36*
plum pudding model, 120–1
potential difference (p.d.), 91
potential energy, gravitational, 3–5, *4*
pressure, 112–13
pressure law, 115, *115*
primary coil, 98, *98*
principle of conservation of energy, 9
principle of conservation of momentum, 13, *13*
protactinium, 147
protium, *125*
proton number, 123, *124*
proton, discovery of, 122, *122*

quantities,
  scalar, 3
  vector, 3

R-*C* circuits, 79, *79*
radian (rad), 25, *25*
radiation, absorption, 142, *142*
radiation,
  alpha (α), 139–43, *141*, *143*
  beta (β), 139–43, *143*
  gamma (γ), 139–43, *141*, *143*

hazards of, 143–4
  ionising, 139–41
radioactive materials, safe handling of, 144
radioactivity, 139–49
reaction, normal, 6, 30, *30*
reactors, fission, 132
recoil, 20
resonance, 45–8, *45*, *46*, *47*
rotational kinetic energy, 118, *118*
Rutherford scattering, 121–2, *122*
Rutherford, Ernest, 121–2, *121*

Sankey diagram, 8, *8*
scalar quantities, 3, 26
scanning tunnelling microscope, *101*
scattering, 127
secondary coil, 98, *98*
simple harmonic motion (s.h.m.), 37–48, *39*, *41*
  equations of, 41–2
sine curve, 35, 39
smoke cell, 111–12, *111*
specific heat capacity, 106–9
  measurement of, 108–9, *108*
specific latent heat, 106–9, 163
  measurement of, 109
speed, 26
spontaneous decay, *144–5*
stability, nuclear, 134–6
static electricity, 57–8, *58*
steam engines, 1
strong nuclear force, 126
structure, atomic, 120–9, *123*

television, 83
temperature scales, 115–16, *115*
tension, 5, 6
tesla (T), 93
thermal physics, 100–10
thermodynamic scale, 115–16, *115*
Thomson, J.J., *120*
time constant, 78–9
transformer, 98, *98*
translational kinetic energy, 118, *118*
triangle, vector, 18, *18*
tritium, 125, *125*

unified atomic mass constant, 137
universal gas constant, 117

van de Graaff generator, 61, *61*
vector
  diagram, 28, *28*
  quantities, 3, 26
  triangle, 18, *18*
velocity, 26
velocity-time graph, 39, *39*
vibrations, 33–49

water power, 1
wave model, 100
weber (Wb), 92, 163
weightlessness, 51
wind power, 1
work, 5–7, 105–6

X-ray diffraction, 127, *127*